COLORED GEMSTONES

3RD EDITION

D1302236

JUN 2010

Books by Antoinette Matlins

(all GemStone Press)

DIAMONDS: THE ANTOINETTE MATLINS BUYING GUIDE
*How to Select, Buy, Care for & Enjoy Diamonds
with Confidence and Knowledge*
2nd edition

ENGAGEMENT & WEDDING RINGS
The Definitive Buying Guide for People in Love
3rd edition

GEM IDENTIFICATION MADE EASY
A Hands-On Guide to More Confident Buying & Selling
4th edition

JEWELRY & GEMS: THE BUYING GUIDE
*How to Buy Diamonds, Pearls, Colored Gemstones, Gold & Jewelry
with Confidence and Knowledge*
7th edition

JEWELRY & GEMS AT AUCTION
*The Definitive Guide to Buying & Selling at the Auction House
& on Internet Auction Sites*

THE PEARL BOOK: THE DEFINITIVE BUYING GUIDE
How to Select, Buy, Care for & Enjoy Pearls
4th edition

COLORED GEMSTONES

3RD EDITION

The Antoinette Matlins Buying Guide

How to Select, Buy, Care for & Enjoy
Sapphires, Emeralds, Rubies
and Other Colored Gems
with Confidence and Knowledge

Antoinette Matlins, P.G.

GEMSTONE PRESS
Woodstock, Vermont

Colored Gemstones, 3rd Edition:
The Antoinette Matlins Buying Guide

2010 Third Edition, Quality Paperback, First Printing
© 2010 Third Edition by Antoinette Matlins

For information regarding permission to reprint material from this book, please mail or fax your request in writing to GemStone Press, Permissions Department, at the address / fax number listed below, or e-mail your request to permissions@ gemstonepress.com.

Library of Congress Cataloging-in-Publication Data
Matlins, Antoinette Leonard.
Colored gemstones : the Antoinette Matlins buying guide : how to select, buy, care for & enjoy sapphires, emeralds, rubies, and other colored gems with confidence and knowledge / Antoinette Matlins. — 3rd ed.
    p. cm.
Includes bibliographical references and index.
ISBN-13: 978-0-943763-72-9 (quality pbk.)
ISBN-10: 0-943763-72-X (quality pbk.)
1. Gems. 2. Gems—Purchasing. I. Title.
TS740.M38 2010
553.8'4—dc22
                                                                    2010005254

10 9 8 7 6 5 4 3 2 1
Manufactured in the United States of America
Cover Design: Stacey Hood   Cover Photographs: John Parrish and Helen Kim
Cover Art: Platinum "Orbit" ring featuring pink spinel, spessartite garnets, and diamonds by James Currens, J. W. Currens, Inc., New York, NY (photo/Helen Kim).
Interior Design: Chelsea Cloeter   Color Insert: Bridgett Taylor and Tim Holtz

GemStone Press
A Division of LongHill Partners, Inc.
Sunset Farm Offices, Route 4, P.O. Box 237
Woodstock, VT 05091
Tel: (802) 457-4000   Fax: (802) 457-4004
www.gemstonepress.com

Contents

PART ONE Getting to Know Gems

PART TWO Colored Gemstones

PART THREE
Important Advice Before & After You Buy

Appendix

Index 200

Price Guides

Special Charts and Tables

Color Photograph Sections

Colored Gemstones—The Rarest of Them All...

Red and Pink Gemstones to Warm Any Heart

Blue Gemstones Offer Heavenly Choices

Yellow and Orange Gems to Brighten the Day

Green Gems That Everyone Will Envy

Opals—A Fiery World of Color

Color-Change Gems—Keep the Mystery Alive

Classic Shapes and Cutting Styles

Gemstone Cutters and Carvers...Artists Creating a
New Style (two pages)

Gemstone Artists Create Objets d'Art...And Art to
Wear (two pages)

Ornamental Stones

Colored Gemstones and Great Design—
A Natural for Endless Possibilities

Timeless Ring Designs...And New Classics by Modern
Designers (two pages)

Bold New Looks in Colored-Stone Rings...A Natural
Fit (two pages)

Colorful Creations from Winning Designers...To Suit
Every Style (two pages)

More Winning Creations...And "Suite" Possibilities
(two pages)

Cabochons of Every Type...Simply Captivate Designers
(two pages)

Colored Gemstones...A Natural for Whimsical Jewels

Acknowledgments

There are many people who have helped me learn and understand the complexities of this exciting field—too many to try to mention all of them here. Nonetheless, there are a few people who have been especially influential and supportive of the work I have done, and I would like to take a moment to acknowledge them. In addition to my father, I would like to thank my brother Kenneth Bonanno, F.G.A., P.G., and my sisters Karen Bonanno DeHaas, F.G.A., P.G., and Kathryn Bonanno Patrizzi, F.G.A., P.G., from whom I continue to learn, and with whom I enjoy sharing and debating gemological issues. I would also like to thank, in particular, C. R. "Cap" Beesley, Founder and long-time Director of American Gemological Laboratories, New York; he has been a great teacher, and his research and leadership have benefited the entire gem and jewelry community.

I would also like to thank the late Robert Crowningshield, former Vice President of the Gemological Institute of America (GIA). A wonderful friend to my father, he was always generous in the time he gave me to address questions or issues I might have had. Mr. Crowningshield's work for the past half century in the field of colored gemstones, and his contributions to the gemological literature, have helped shape the world of gemology as we know it.

At GemStone Press I would like to thank Sandra Korinchak, Polly Short, Emily Wichland, and Danelle Sweeney, with whom it has been a pleasure to work, and who have made the project fun. I would also like to thank Richard Drucker from Gemworld International for providing valuable data on current gemstone prices from his trade publication *The Guide*.

And last, but not least, I want to thank my husband, Stuart Matlins, for his unfailing support and encouragement, and for his willingness to spend many lonely nights while I'm traveling around the world to pursue my work.

Dedication

This book is specially dedicated to my father, Antonio C. Bonanno, who died in 1996. He inspired me as a child and filled my world with awe and wonder. He was my teacher, my mentor, and my coauthor on three books. Although his name is not on this cover, his knowledge and wisdom—his words, his ideas, his values—fill its pages. My gratitude is eternal.

Colored gemstones were my father's first love, and so I felt his presence keenly as I worked on this volume. As one of the first gemologists to fully disclose gemstone treatments to his clients, and as Founding Father of the Accredited Gemologists Association—through which he and other gemologists worldwide have strongly advocated for full disclosure for almost twenty-five years—his influence is clearly present in this volume. This book could not be what it is without his indelible mark.

Preface

Whatever gem or jewel you are seeking, with each passing year there are more choices than ever. There are recently discovered "new" gemstones such as pezzottaite (see page 149) and Zultanite (see page 165), and gems in sensuous new colors; there are exciting new cutting styles that are creating greater brilliance and scintillation; and there are award-winning designers creating exquisite pieces in which to display them. For anyone who loves colorful gemstones, this is the most exciting time in history.

Having so many gemstone choices can be confusing, however, if you don't understand how one gem compares to another in terms of the unique characteristics of each and differences in wearability, rarity, and cost. More importantly, there are many more things to look *out* for, and more reasons *not* to base your choice on price alone. Now more than ever, understanding as much as possible about what you are buying is the key to getting what you really want, paying the right price, and enjoying your gem and jewelry purchases for years to come.

My first book, *Jewelry & Gems: The Buying Guide,* which I wrote with my father in the early 1980s, was the first book ever written to help consumers and laypeople understand what they were really buying. It provided step-by-step guidance to make the purchase of diamonds, colored gemstones, pearls, and gold jewelry safer, less confusing, and more pleasurable. Now, almost twenty-five years, seven editions, and over 400,000 copies later, in English, Arabic, Greek, Hungarian, Japanese, Russian, and Spanish, the information it provides remains indispensable. But with each updated edition of *Jewelry & Gems*, it became increasingly difficult to cover all that was happening in the world of colored gemstones. It became clear that there was just too much additional information on colored gemstones to try to incorporate it into a single volume inclusive of diamonds, pearls, and gold as well. Thus *Colored Gemstones: The Antoinette Matlins Buying Guide* was created. While some of the information here is also found in *Jewelry & Gems,* it has been edited to focus on colored gemstones, and it contains more extensive information about colored gemstones.

Today's colored gemstone market reflects the best of times and the worst of times: beautiful gemstones abound—in more colors, shapes, and designs than ever before—but today's jewelry counters are also filled with imitations, synthetics, and artificially enhanced gemstones. Where synthetics are concerned, almost *any* gem can now be created in a laboratory, some looking so much like the natural that they have been sold as such. And with each passing year there are creative new scams to fool even the most sophisticated. As with all my other books, this book gives you all the information you really need in order to make wiser choices and reduce the risk especially inherent when buying or selling colored gemstones.

One area of special focus deals with enhancement techniques used to alter the appearance of colored gemstones. While we discussed gemstone treatments candidly in the first edition of *Jewelry & Gems: The Buying Guide* back in 1984, they have only recently captured the public's attention and become the focus of numerous media stories. Today treatments are even more widespread, and are used for an increasing number of gemstones, so it is more important than ever before to understand the marketplace in order to be sure you get what you really want, and pay the right price for what you get. While covered in chapter 5, I would like to comment here on this situation.

Exceptionally fine *natural* gemstones are rarer and more costly than ever before. This scarcity has affected what is available in jewelry stores, and the choices available to consumers. *Natural* emeralds, rubies, and sapphires—that is, gems not subjected to any type of artificial enhancement— have never been rarer than they are today. While they can still be found, locating a natural gem in a particular size and quality can take months of intensive searching, and when one is found, the price is often prohibitive to all but the most wealthy collector or connoisseur.

As the beauty and overall quality of natural gemstones available in the marketplace began to decline over the past few decades, more and more treated gems—that is, gems on which some type of treatment is used to improve appearance—were introduced in an effort to meet an ever-increasing demand for beautiful ruby, emerald, sapphire, and other gemstone jewelry. Given a choice, most people seeking a lovely piece of jewelry would rather have a treated gem, at an affordable price, than spend the time and money necessary to find a natural gem and obtain proper documentation of its authenticity. As a result, this is what is now routinely sold in jewelry stores, including the most important salons worldwide.

Prices for exceptionally fine, untreated ruby from Burma (also called Myanmar) have increased by more than 75% since the first edition of this book, and today such a "rare gem" can easily cost $60,000 for a two-carat stone. By comparison, the cost of a two-carat Burmese ruby that may appear comparable after treatment by traditional heating (see chapter 5) would be about $20,000, while a ruby that has been treated by new diffusion techniques could cost as little as $500. You can also find attractive rubies from other locations that have been treated in a variety of ways for under $3,000. The differences in cost reflect differences in availability, the abundance of material that can be used for different treatment processes, and demand in the marketplace. In the case of natural, untreated gemstones, one thing seems clear: their rarity keeps increasing, and demand keeps rising, so costs will probably continue to rise.

There is nothing wrong with buying a treated *(also called* enhanced) *gem as long as you know the gem is treated, pay a fair price for it, and have been advised about the possibility of its appearance changing at some future time* (see chapter 5). In the case of ruby, however, one must be especially wary of a *very heavily* treated material now being described as *composition ruby* or *composite ruby*, which is extensively filled with glass—in some cases, the stone is more glass than ruby. They are very fragile and require extreme care (see chapter 6).

Anyone buying any colored gemstone sold in jewelry stores today should assume it has been treated in some way and should make sure it is priced appropriately for what it is. Keep in mind that, unfortunately, many salespeople do not know about treatments and, as a result, fail to disclose this information. In some cases, salespeople really believe that the stones they sell are "natural" and sell them as such, even when this is not the case.

The extensive use of treatments has led to greater reliance on reports from respected gem-testing laboratories, and I encourage anyone buying a fine, rare, natural colored gemstone to make sure it has accompanying documentation from a respected laboratory (see page 196). However, the presence of a laboratory report accompanying a gem is not a guarantee, and you must understand what should be included, and how to read a colored gemstone report (see chapter 7). It is also important to know that the increased use of lab reports has resulted in an increase in reports from laboratories that are not reliable, and in fraudulent reports attributed to respected laboratories. Therefore, one must also be sure to verify the laboratory and the report attributed to it, and make sure the report relates to the gem you are buying. (See chapter 12 on how to verify your purchase.)

For those who prefer only natural stones, some jewelers now offer sapphire, ruby, and emerald in a wider quality range to provide a natural alternative at a more affordable price, recognizing that some people prefer a natural stone—even if the color is not optimum or if it has visible internal characteristics—to a treated stone. Even more exciting, however, is the increasing interest in—and respect for—lesser-known gemstone varieties that are *not* routinely treated (see page 102). Some wonderful choices are now available in a wide range of colors, including ruby-red spinel, emerald-green tsavorite (a green variety of garnet discovered in the 1970s), blue spinel, and fiery orange "mandarin" garnet. A full list is provided in chapter 8. These gemstones offer beautiful, affordable, *natural* alternatives to treated gems and can usually be found at fine jewelry stores. If you have difficulty finding what you want, a gemologist or independent jeweler may be able to help you.

In short, today there are more alternatives—natural gems, treated gems, synthetic gems, and imitation gems—in more colors and more interesting designs than ever before. But the marketplace is also more complicated. This, combined with changes in the nature of retailing itself—and the increase in the number of jewelry salespeople who lack the knowledge necessary to provide reliable information and answer questions accurately—makes the situation for consumers more confusing than ever.

To help you deal with misleading or fraudulent practices, this book covers some of the most frequently encountered types of fraud and misrepresentation (see chapter 6). I want to stress, however, that the purpose is not to give you false confidence, nor is it to frighten or discourage you from buying gems and jewelry. My primary purpose in covering this material is to make you less vulnerable to the allure of fake bargains and to make you aware of the importance of buying only from knowledgeable, reputable jewelers (for advice on selecting a jeweler, see chapter 11).

Furthermore, while information provided here may give you greater confidence, no book can make you an expert. Be sure to follow the advice I offer regarding what questions to ask, what to get in writing, and how to check it out to be sure of your purchase. To further pursue the field of gem identification, treatment, and enhancement, see my book *Gem Identification Made Easy*, which is a nontechnical book for the layperson (GemStone Press, P.O. Box 237, Woodstock, VT 05091; 800-962-4544; www.gemstonepress.com; $36.99 plus $3.95 shipping/handling).

Whatever your interest in gems, I hope the gems you acquire will give you the pleasure and joy they have given me throughout the years. And I hope that *Colored Gemstones: The Antoinette Matlins Buying Guide* will bring greater clarity to the experience for you, and help make your gem and jewelry buying experience all that it should be: an experience filled with excitement, anticipation, romance, and pleasure.

Antoinette Matlins

Introduction

Throughout history, colored gemstones have been much sought after for their beauty, rarity, preciousness, and even "magical powers" sometimes attributed to them. They have symbolized power, wealth, and love. Every civilization, every society, grandly exhibits humankind's fascination with and desire to possess these beautiful natural creations.

We are no different from our ancestors. We too share the fascination, appreciation, and desire to possess and adorn ourselves with beautiful gemstones, and there are certainly no indicators to suggest that the allure of gems will not be as great in future generations.

Color is in vogue, even in engagement rings. Just look at London's royal family—the late Queen Mother, Queen Elizabeth, Princess Anne, and the late Princess Diana received *sapphire* engagement rings and Duchess Sarah Ferguson, a *ruby*. There has never been a more exciting time to search for a colored gem, and the experience can be a magical one. It can be filled with excitement, anticipation, and pleasure—and it is to that end that this book is dedicated.

The purpose of this book is to provide a basic but complete consumer's guide to buying a gem, whether it be for one's own personal pleasure, for a gift, or for investment in something beautiful to pass on as a treasured heirloom. It is designed and written for a wide market—husbands, wives, or parents buying gems as gifts for loved ones for some special occasion; young couples looking for an engagement ring; tourists, business travelers, and servicemen and servicewomen traveling throughout the world hoping to pick up gems at bargain prices while near the mines; investors looking for a hedge against inflation; and all those who are simply interested in gems as hobbyists and collectors. It will explain the variables that affect cost, provide information regarding fraudulent practices, and provide lists of relevant questions that should be asked of the seller. It will not make you a gemologist, but it will make you a more knowledgeable shopper and help transform a confusing—often frightening—experience into one that is truly interesting, exciting, and safe.

From the time I was a small child, I had the pleasure of being surrounded by beautiful gems and had a unique opportunity to learn the gem business. Having a father who was a well-known gemologist, appraiser, and collector—described as the "father of modern, practical gemology" prior to his death—I was able to spend hours marveling at stones, those in his own private collection as well as those brought to him to be professionally appraised.

Dinner conversation always centered on the day's events at my father's office. Sometimes he would thrill us with an account of a particularly fine or rare gem he had the pleasure of identifying or verifying. But too often the subject would turn to some poor, unknowing consumer who had been victimized. It might have been a soldier who thought he had purchased genuine sapphires while in Asia, who discovered sadly that they were glass or inexpensive synthetics. Or, it might have been a diplomat who had purchased jade in the Orient, only to learn it was not jade but serpentine, a common, inexpensive green stone often sold as jade. But occasionally, my father would have a wonderful story to share. One story in particular illustrates especially well how complex the gem business can be. One day an average-looking elderly woman came into my father's office with a green stone she wanted identified and appraised. She had already taken the stone to a well-known jeweler, who also had an excellent reputation as a gemologist-appraiser. The jeweler told her that the stone was a tourmaline worth only a few hundred dollars. She was very disappointed, since it was a family heirloom that she had believed for many years was a fine emerald. Her own mother had assured her of the fact. When she questioned the jeweler about its being an emerald, he laughed and told her that was impossible. He was the expert, so she accepted his appraisal, as most people would. Many months later, at the insistence of a friend who knew of my father's reputation from the curator of the Smithsonian's gem collection, she sought my father's opinion. In fact, her stone was a genuine emerald, one of the finest my father had ever seen. He could barely contain his excitement about the stone. It was worth about $60,000 even then, over forty years ago. Fortunately, the woman learned its true identity and value before it was too late.

My first response upon hearing the story was anger at the "dishonest" jeweler, but, as my father explained, he was not dishonest. Dad actually went to see this man, because he knew his reputation was good. The jeweler discussed the stone with my father, and it became clear that he genuinely believed it to have been a tourmaline. On the basis of the woman's "ordinary" appearance and the absence of any eye-visible characteristics so typical of an emerald, he drew the immediate conclusion that the stone could *only* be a green tourmaline. His experience with emeralds was limited to those of lesser quality, with their telltale inclusions. His limited experience, combined with his impression of the woman, led him to make an assumption regarding the identity of the stone without even performing any definitive test. He made an incorrect identification of this unusually fine stone, but certainly he was not acting dishonestly in the hope of picking up a steal.

This anecdote illustrates the danger consumers frequently face when they come to buy gems. They are vulnerable not only to intentional fraud but also to unintentional misrepresentation resulting from a jeweler's lack of experience and knowledge. The very person on whom one would naturally rely—the jeweler—sometimes lacks sufficient knowledge about the gems he is selling. Fortunately, educational institutions such as Gem-A (the Gemological Association of Great Britain) and GIA (Gemological Institute of America), and an increasing number of colleges, universities, and associations across the country and around the world that offer gemology courses, are helping to rectify this situation. More and more, reputable jewelers are concerned with increasing their own knowledge and that of their salespeople, not only to protect their valued customers but also to protect themselves!

Another incident proves how rewarding education can be. A former student of my father's was visiting in a midwestern city. She decided to go to some pawnshops to kill time, and in one shop she discovered a beautiful diamond-and-emerald ring. The pawnbroker told her that the diamonds were of an unusually fine quality, which her examination confirmed. The ring was also beautifully designed, with outstanding workmanship. Her question was whether the emerald was genuine or synthetic. As she examined the stone she began to suspect it was genuine. But she didn't have the right equipment with her to be sure. The $500 price was appropriate for the diamonds and the gold setting alone, indicating that the pawnbroker believed the emerald was synthetic. But since the visitor liked the ring, and the price was fair, she was willing to take a chance that it might in fact be genuine. Upon her return to Washington she brought the ring to my father's lab, where they proceeded immediately to examine the emerald. It was genuine. Its value was many times what she had paid; it could easily have sold for over $30,000 at a retail jewelry store. She sold it for a very handsome profit. The student profited because of her knowledge; the pawnbroker lost an opportunity because of his lack of it.

As the result of my father's long experience in the gem business, and my own professional experience, I felt that a book about gems—written just for the consumer—was desperately needed. The original edition of *Jewelry & Gems: The Buying Guide* was the first book ever written for the average gemstone consumer. This book is based upon the seventh edition of *Jewelry & Gems: The Buying Guide,* but it focuses exclusively on colored gemstones and provides more in-depth information. The cost of gems is greater than ever before, and projections indicate that prices will continue to rise. Thus, in a market where jewelers and gem dealers are often not as knowledgeable as they should be, where the price of gems continues to rise, and where consumers consider ever more frequently buying gems for investment, the gem buyer must become more informed. A consumer cannot learn to be an expert in gems through reading a single book; a gemologist is, after all, a highly trained, skilled professional. What I can provide here is some basic information that can make buying gems a more pleasurable, less vulnerable experience.

Colored Gemstones: The Antoinette Matlins Buying Guide covers everything you, the consumer, need to know before buying any of the most popular gems. I hope you will find as much pleasure as I have found in getting to know gems, and that your future purchases will be happy ones.

Antoinette Matlins

PART ONE

Getting to Know Gems

CHAPTER ONE

The Mystery & Magic of Colored Gems

The fascination with colored gemstones dates back to the very beginning of civilization. For our ancestors, the blue of sapphire produced visions of the heavens; the red of ruby was a reminder of the very essence of life. By Roman times, rings containing colored gems were prized symbols of power—and the most powerful wore rings on every joint of every finger!

Since ancient times, colored stones have been thought to possess innate magical powers and the ability to endow the wearer with certain attributes. According to legend, emeralds are good for the eyes; yellow stones cure jaundice; red stones stop the flow of blood. At one time it was believed that a ruby worn by a man indicated command, nobility, lordship, and vengeance; worn by a woman, however, it indicated pride, obstinacy, and haughtiness. A blue sapphire worn by a man indicated wisdom and high and magnanimous thoughts; on a woman, jealousy in love, politeness, and vigilance. The emerald signified for a man joyousness, transitory hope, and the decline of friendship; for a woman, unfounded ambition, childish delight, and change.

Colored gems, because of the magical powers associated with them, achieved extensive use as talismans and amulets, as predictors of the future, as therapeutic aids, and as essential elements to many religious practices: pagan, Jewish, and Christian.

Zodiac Stones

The following list of the zodiacal gems and their special powers has been passed on from an early Hindu legend.

3

Aquarius (Jan. 21–Feb. 21)	*Garnet*—believed to guarantee true friendship when worn by an Aquarian
Pisces (Feb. 22–Mar. 21)	*Amethyst*—believed to protect a Pisces wearer from extremes of passion
Aries (Mar. 22–Apr. 20)	*Bloodstone*—believed to endow an Aries wearer with wisdom
Taurus (Apr. 21–May 21)	*Sapphire*—believed to protect from and cure mental disorders if worn by a Taurus
Gemini (May 22–June 21)	*Agate*—long life, health, and wealth were guaranteed to a Gemini if an agate ring was worn
Cancer (June 22–July 22)	*Emerald*—eternal joy was guaranteed to a Cancer-born who took an emerald along his or her way
Leo (July 23–Aug. 22)	*Onyx*—would protect a Leo wearer from loneliness and unhappiness
Virgo (Aug. 23–Sept. 22)	*Carnelian*—believed to guarantee success in anything a Virgo tried if worn on the hand
Libra (Sept. 23–Oct. 23)	*Chrysolite* (peridot)—would free a Libra wearer from any evil spell
Scorpio (Oct. 24–Nov. 21)	*Beryl*—should be worn by every Scorpio to guarantee protection from "tears of sad repentance"
Sagittarius (Nov. 22–Dec. 21)	*Topaz*—protects Sagittarians, but only if they always show the stone
Capricorn (Dec. 22–Jan. 21)	*Ruby*—a Capricorn who has ever worn a ruby will never know trouble

An old Spanish list, probably representing an Arab tradition, ascribes the following stones to the various signs of the zodiac:

Aquarius—Amethyst	*Leo*—Topaz
Pisces—(indistinguishable)	*Virgo*—Magnet (lodestone)
Aries—Crystal (quartz)	*Libra*—Jasper
Taurus—Ruby and diamond	*Scorpio*—Garnet
Gemini—Sapphire	*Sagittarius*—Emerald
Cancer—Agate and beryl	*Capricorn*—Chalcedony

The Evolution of Birthstones

The origin of the belief that a special stone was dedicated to each month, and that the stone of the month possessed a special virtue or "cure" that it could transmit to those born in that month, goes back to at least the first century. There is speculation that the twelve stones in the great breastplate of the Jewish high priest may have had some bearing on this concept. In the eighth and ninth centuries, the interpreters of the Bible's book of Revelation began to ascribe attributes of the twelve apostles to each of those stones. The Hindus, on the other hand, had their own interpretation.

But whatever the reason, one fact is clear. As G. F. Kunz points out in *The Curious Lore of Precious Stones,* "There is no doubt that the owner of a ring or ornament set with a birthstone is impressed with the idea of possessing something more intimately associated with his or her personality than any other stone, however beautiful or costly. The idea that birthstones possess a certain indefinable, but none the less real significance has long been present, and still holds a spell over the minds of all who are gifted with a touch of imagination and romance."

The following is the current list of birthstones used by the jewelry trade. (It differs slightly from another list adopted by the trade in 1952 and causes some confusion among those who remember the earlier list!)

Present-Day Birthstones

Month	Birthstone	Alternative Stone
January	Garnet	
February	Amethyst	
March	Aquamarine	Bloodstone
April	Diamond	
May	Emerald	
June	Natural pearl, cultured pearl	Moonstone or alexandrite
July	Ruby	
August	Peridot	
September	Sapphire	
October	Opal	Tourmaline
November	Topaz	Citrine
December	Turquoise	Tanzanite or zircon

Besides the lists of birthstones and zodiacal or talismanic stones, there are lists of stones for days of the week, for hours of the day, for states of the union, for each of the seasons, and even for anniversaries!

Anniversary Stones

1	Gold jewelry	13	Citrine
2	Garnet	14	Opal
3	Pearl	15	Ruby
4	Blue topaz	20	Emerald
5	Sapphire	25	Silver jubilee
6	Amethyst	30	Pearl jubilee
7	Onyx	35	Emerald
8	Tourmaline	40	Ruby
9	Lapis lazuli	45	Sapphire
10	Diamond	50	Golden jubilee
11	Turquoise	55	Alexandrite
12	Jade	60	Diamond jubilee

The Importance of Color
and Its Mystical Symbolism in Gems

The wide spectrum of color available in the gemstone realm was not lost on our forebears. Not only did strong associations with specific stones evolve, but also associations of color with personal attributes. Over time, a fairly detailed symbolism came to join color with character. Those attributes, as they have come down to us, include the following:

Yellow	Worn by a man, denotes secrecy (appropriate for a silent lover); worn by a woman, indicates generosity.
White (colorless)	Signifies friendship, integrity, and religious commitment for men; purity, affability, and contemplation for women.
Red	On a man, indicates command, nobility, lordship, and vengeance; on a woman, pride, haughtiness, and obstinacy.
Blue	On a man, indicates wisdom and high, magnanimous thoughts; on a woman, jealousy in love, politeness, vigilance.
Green	For men, signifies joyousness, transitory hope, decline of friendship; for women, unfounded ambition, childish delight, and change.
Black	For men, means gravity, good sense, constancy, and strength; for young women, fickleness and foolishness; but for married women, constant love and perseverance.
Violet	For men, signifies sober judgment, industry, and gravity; for women, high thoughts and spiritual love.

The Exciting *New* World of Gemstones— New Colors, New Gems!

Today, gems are worn primarily for their intrinsic beauty and are chosen mainly for aesthetic reasons, not for mythical attributes. While we may own a birthstone that we enjoy wearing, our choice of stones is usually dictated by personal color preferences, personal style, and economics. The fashions of the day may also influence our choices. The world of colored gems today offers us an almost endless choice. New gems have been discovered, as well as "known" gems in colors previously "unknown," and they are now taking center stage in the most important jewelry salons. If you like red, there are rubies, garnets, red tourmalines, red spinels, and even red diamonds and red "emeralds" (gemologically, red "emerald" is known as red beryl—see *Emerald* in chapter 9). If you prefer blue, there are sapphires, iolite, blue spinel, blue topaz, blue tourmaline, tanzanite, and blue diamonds. For those who prefer green, there are emeralds, tsavorite (green garnet), green zircons, green tourmalines, green sapphires, peridots, and even green diamonds. And for those who love unusual shades of blue and green, and dazzling neon shades in sparkling, transparent stones, there are the remarkable, rare, newly discovered Paraiba or Hetorita tourmalines from Brazil, considered by many to be the most exciting gemological discovery, in terms of color, in this century. And there are even gemstones that *change* color depending upon the lighting in which they are seen!

The following chapters will look at colored stones in more detail and will suggest a variety of stones available in every hue. With colored gems available for almost everyone, in almost any color, at almost any price, you have a wide range of affordable options.

CHAPTER TWO

Getting What You Really Want
The First Steps

Fine gems should never be bought casually—there are too many risks and the uneducated consumer will always lose. This is a basic rule of thumb. The best way to take the risk out of buying a particular gem is to familiarize yourself with the gem. While the average consumer can't hope to make the same precise judgments as a qualified gemologist, whose scientific training and wealth of practical experience provide a far greater database from which to operate, the consumer can learn to judge a stone as a "total personality" and learn what the critical factors are—color, clarity (also referred to in the trade as "perfection"), cut, brilliance, and weight—and how to balance them in judging the gem's value. Learning about these factors and spending time in the marketplace looking, listening, and asking questions before making the purchase will prepare you to be a wise buyer more likely to get what you really want, at a fair price.

Try to learn as much as you can about the gem you want to buy. Examine stones owned by your family and friends, and compare stones at several different jewelry stores, noting differences in shades of color, brilliance, and cut. Go to a good, established jewelry store and ask to see fine stones. If the prices vary, ask why. Let the jeweler point out differences in color, cut, or brilliance, and if he can't, go to another jeweler with greater expertise. Begin to develop an eye for what constitutes a fine stone by looking, listening, and asking good questions.

Some good questions to ask yourself initially before you consider buying any stone are:

1. Is the color what *you* desire?
2. Is the shape what *you* want?
3. Is it lively, and does it have the character or personality that *you* like?

4. Do *you* feel excited by it?

5. Can you afford it?

Don't allow a salesperson to dictate your purchase; if you can honestly answer yes to all these questions, you are ready to examine the specific stone more carefully.

The Six Key Steps in Examining a Stone

1. *Whenever possible, examine stones unmounted.* They can be examined more thoroughly out of their settings, and defects cannot be hidden by the mounting or side stones.

2. *Make sure the gem is clean.* If you are buying a stone from a retail jeweler, ask that it be cleaned for you. If you are not in a place where it can be cleaned professionally, breathe on the stone in a huffing manner in order to steam it with your breath, and then wipe it with a clean handkerchief. This will at least remove any superficial greasy film.

3. *Hold the unmounted stone so that your fingers touch only the girdle* (the edge where top and bottom meet). Putting your fingers on the table (top) and/or pavilion (bottom) will leave traces of oil, which will affect color and brilliance.

   The *careful* use of tweezers instead of fingers is recommended only if you feel comfortable using them. Make sure you know how to use them, and get the permission of the owner before picking up the stone. It is easy for the stone to pop out of the tweezers and to become damaged or lost, and you could be held responsible.

4. *View the gem under proper lighting.* Many jewelers use numerous incandescent spotlights, usually recessed in dropped ceilings. Some use special spotlights that can make any gemstone—even glass imitations—look fantastic.

   Fluorescent lights are what professionals use for grading, but they may also adversely affect the appearance of some gems. Many red gemstones, such as rubies, look much better under incandescent light, while blue gems, such as sapphire, often look much better in daylight or fluorescent light. I recommend looking at stones in several types of light.

   The light source should come from above or behind you, shining down and through the stone, so that the light traveling through the stone is reflected back up to your eye.

5. *Rotate the stone in order to view it from different angles.*
6. *If you are using a loupe, focus it both on the surface and into the interior.* To focus into the interior, shift the stone slowly, raising or lowering it, until you focus clearly on all depths within it. This is important because if you focus on the top only, you won't see what is in the interior of the stone.

How to Use a Loupe

A loupe (pronounced *loop*) is a special type of magnifying glass. The loupe can be very helpful in many situations, even for the beginner. With a loupe you can check a stone for chips or scratches or examine certain types of noticeable inclusions more closely. Remember, however, that even with a loupe, you will not have the knowledge or skill to see or understand the many telltale indicators that an experienced jeweler or gemologist could spot. No book can provide you with that knowledge or skill. Do not allow yourself to be deluded, or let a little knowledge give you a false confidence. Nothing will more quickly alienate a reputable jeweler or mark you faster as easy prey for the disreputable dealer.

The loupe is a very practical tool to use once you master it, and with practice it will become more and more valuable. The correct type is a 10x, or ten-power, "triplet," which can be obtained from any optical supply house. The triplet type is recommended because it corrects two problems other types of magnifiers have: traces of color normally found at the outer edge of the lens, and visual distortion, also usually at the outer edge of the lens. In addition, the loupe must have a black housing around the lens, not chrome or gold, either of which might affect the color you see in the stone.

The loupe *must* be 10x because the United States Federal Trade Commission requires grading to be done under ten-power magnification. Any flaw that does not show up under 10x magnification is considered nonexistent for grading purposes.

With a few minutes' practice you can easily learn to use the loupe. Here's how:

1. Hold the loupe between the thumb and forefinger of either hand.
2. Hold the stone or jewelry similarly in the other hand.
3. Bring both hands together so that the fleshy parts just below the thumbs are pushed together and braced by the lower portion of

each hand just above the wrists (the wrist portion is actually a pivot point).

4. Now move both hands up to your nose or cheek, with the loupe as close to your eye as possible. If you wear eyeglasses, you do not have to remove them.

5. Get a steady hand. With gems it's very important to have steady hands for careful examination. With your hands still together and braced against your face, put your elbows on a table. (If a table isn't available, brace your arms against your chest or rib cage.) If you do this properly you will have a steady hand.

A 10x Triplet Loupe

How to hold a loupe
when examining a stone

Practice with the loupe, keeping it approximately one inch (more or less) from your eye, and about an inch from the object being examined. Learn to see through it clearly. A 10x loupe is difficult to focus initially, but with a little practice it will become easy. You can practice on any object that is difficult to see—the pores in your skin, a strand of hair, a pinhead, or your own jewelry.

Play with the item being examined. Rotate it slowly, tilt it back and forth while rotating it, and look at it from different angles and different directions. It won't take long before you are able to focus easily on anything you wish to examine. If you aren't sure about your technique, a knowledge-able jeweler will be happy to help you learn to use the loupe correctly.

What the Loupe Can Tell You

With practice and experience (and further education if you're really serious), a loupe can tell even the amateur a great deal. For a gemologist it can help determine whether the stone is natural, synthetic, glass, or a doublet (a composite stone, to be discussed later) and reveal characteristic flaws, blemishes, or cracks. In other words, the loupe can provide the necessary information to help you know whether the stone is in fact what it is supposed to be.

For the beginner, the loupe is useful in seeing these features:

1. *The workmanship that went into the cutting.* For example, is the symmetry of the stone balanced? Does it have the proper number of facets for its cut? Is the proportion good? Few cutters put the same time and care into cutting glass as they do into a stone.

2. *Chips, cracks, or scratches on the facet edges, planes, or table.* Some gemstones are softer or more brittle than others, and will scratch or chip easily. The scratches or chips will be seen fairly easily with a loupe. Be sure to check around prongs to make sure a careless setter hasn't inadvertently scratched or chipped the stone.

   In such stones as emeralds, the loupe can also help you determine whether or not any natural cracks are really serious, how close they are to the surface, how deep they run, or how many are readily visible.

3. *The sharpness of the facet edges.* Harder stones will have a sharp edge, or sharper boundaries between adjoining planes or facets, whereas many imitations are softer, so that under the loupe the edges between the facets are less sharp and have a more rounded appearance.

4. *Bubbles, inclusions, and flaws.* Many flaws and inclusions— microscopic crystals and characteristics *included* within the stone as it formed in nature—that cannot be seen with the naked eye are easily seen with the loupe. But remember, many are not easily seen unless you are very experienced. The presence of inclusions is not as serious in colored stones as in diamonds, and they don't usually significantly reduce the value of the stone. However, the *kind* of inclusions seen in colored stones can be important. They often provide the necessary key to positive identification and to determining whether a stone is natural or synthetic. Inclusions also provide the key to determining the country of origin of a stone, which may significantly affect the value. With minimal experience, the amateur can also learn to spot the characteristic bubbles and swirl lines associated with glass.

The loupe can tell you a great deal about the workmanship that went into cutting a gem. It can help a professional decide whether a gem is natural, synthetic, a doublet, or glass. It can provide the clues about the gem's authenticity, its durability, and its point of origin. But spotting these clues takes lots of practice and experience.

When you use a loupe, remember that you won't see what the experienced professional will see, but with a little practice, it can still be a valuable tool and might save you from a costly mistake.

CHAPTER THREE

Looking for a Gem That's a "Cut Above"

One of the most important things to learn is how to look at a gem, even if you won't see all that a gemologist will. Let's begin by making sure you understand the terms you will be hearing and using to describe what you want—especially terms pertaining to the stone's "cut" and the names for the parts of a cut stone.

It's important to be familiar with a few general terms that are commonly used in reference to faceted stones. The parts of a stone can vary in proportion and thus affect its brilliance, beauty, and desirability. This will be discussed later in greater detail.

- **Girdle.** The girdle is the edge or border of the stone that forms its perimeter; it is the edge formed where the top portion of the stone meets the bottom portion—its "dividing line." This is the part usually grasped by the prongs of a setting.
- **Crown.** The crown is also called the *top* of the stone. This is simply the upper portion of the stone: the part above the girdle.
- **Pavilion.** The pavilion is the bottom portion of the stone, the part from the girdle to the "point" at the bottom.
- **Culet.** The culet is the lowest part or point of the stone. It may be missing in some stones, which can indicate damage, or, particularly with colored stones, it may not be part of the original cut.
- **Table.** The table is the flat top of the stone and is the stone's largest facet, often called the

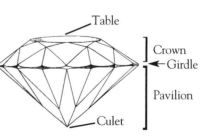

Parts of a faceted stone

15

face. The term *table spread* is used to describe the width of the table facet, often expressed as a percentage of the total width of the stone.

The Cut of the Stone

The most important—and least understood—factor that must be evaluated when one considers any gem is the *cutting*. When we talk about cut, we are not referring to the shape but to the care and precision used in creating a finished gem from the rough. There are many popular shapes for gemstones. Each shape affects the overall look of the stone, but if the stone is cut well its brilliance and value endure no matter what shape it is. For the average consumer, choosing a shape is simply a matter of personal taste. Some of the most popular shapes are pictured here (new shapes are discussed in chapter 4).

Classic Shapes

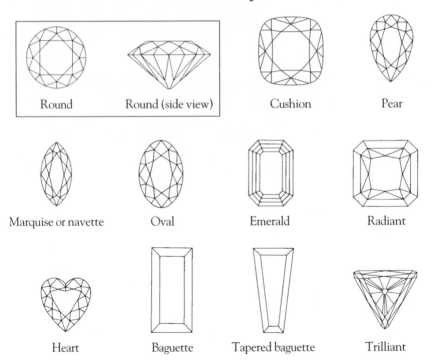

Round   Round (side view)   Cushion   Pear

Marquise or navette   Oval   Emerald   Radiant

Heart   Baguette   Tapered baguette   Trilliant

How to Know Whether a Stone Is Well Cut

The precision of the cutting dramatically affects the beauty and value of any stone. This is especially true in *faceted* stones, those on which a series of tiny flat planes (facets or faces) have been cut and polished. (Nonfaceted stones are called *cabochons;* these are discussed in part 2.) By following some general guidelines and tips for looking at faceted gemstones, you can better determine both the quality of the stone and the quality of the cut.

The first thing to keep in mind is that in any stone, if the basic material is of good quality, the way it is cut will make the difference between a dull, lifeless stone and a beautiful, brilliant one. In colored gems, the perfection of the cut is not as important as it is with diamonds, but proportioning remains critical because it will significantly affect the depth of color as well as the stone's brilliance and liveliness.

Look at the stone face-up, through the top (table). This is the most critical area to view, since this is the one most often noticed. Does the color look good from this direction? Is the table centered and symmetrical?

The stone's proportion—whether it is too thin or too thick—will have a marked effect on its overall beauty. With colored stones, the relative terms of thickness or thinness vary greatly because of the inherent optical properties of different gems. As a general guide when you are considering colored stones, keep in mind these three points:

1. If the stone appears lively and exhibits an appealing color when viewed through the table, no matter how the proportion appears (thick or thin), it is usually correct and acceptable proportioning for that particular stone.
2. The depth of color (tone) will become darker as the stone is cut thicker, particularly if the bottom portion (pavilion) is deep and broad.
3. A stone's depth of color will become lighter as the stone is cut thinner. This is especially important when you are considering a pastel-colored stone. A pastel stone should always have fairly deep proportioning.

Before Beginning

As you shop for any fine gem or piece of jewelry, keep in mind the importance of visiting fine jewelry stores to look at stones and compare them. Many of the factors discussed in the following chapters will become clearer when you have actual stones before you to examine, and you will gain a deeper understanding and appreciation for the gem you are considering. Knowledgeable jewelers will also be happy to take time to help you understand differences in quality and cost.

Also keep in mind the importance of buying only from a well-trained, reputable jeweler. Remember, you are not an expert. The information provided here should help you begin your search more confidently and gain insights that will make the experience more fun, more challenging, and more fulfilling. But perhaps just as important, I hope it will help you make a wiser decision about the jeweler with whom you decide to do business, and about his or her knowledge, professionalism, and integrity. If so, this book will have provided a valuable service and perhaps saved you from a costly mistake.

Colored Gemstones

CHAPTER FOUR

Determining Value in Colored Gems

What Makes a Gem a Gem?

The mention of the word *gemstone* instantly conjures up exotic images of dazzling gemstones in overflowing treasure chests or fabulous crown jewels or important museum collections. It conjures up images of dazzling color and shimmering brilliance. But the term *gemstone* or *gem* is often used carelessly to describe almost any stone. In fact, most stones are not "gems." Even among that rare group often described as "the *precious* three"—ruby, sapphire, and emerald—we find stones that are not "gems." So what is the definition of a gem?

No one has come up with a universally accepted definition, but most agree that a gemstone is a mineral (or in some cases, an organic material) that possesses unusual *beauty, durability*, and *rarity*. And I would add one more factor: it must have *cachet*. That is, it must possess mystery, mystique, and glamour—those things that bring it into the world of our dreams and make us yearn to possess it.

While somewhat subjective, and not without some exceptions, the first three criteria are always at the heart of how we classify stones and determine whether or not they are gems. The first, and perhaps the most important, is beauty. If it isn't beautiful, why would anyone want to possess it? But beauty alone is not enough. A gem must also be sufficiently durable to withstand the normal wear and tear of use, to stand the test of time. This is at the heart of why gemstones figure so prominently as heirlooms: they are durable. It is their durability that is the key to a gem's ability to retain its beauty and allure, to be passed on from generation to generation. And finally, we must consider the rarity factor, the most important in terms of valuation. Generally speaking, the rarer the gem, the more costly, and vice versa.

Let me provide an example that might put these factors into a more relevant scenario. Several years ago I came across a number of "gemstones"—emeralds, rubies, and sapphires—that had been consigned to an auction house for sale to the highest bidder. Each stone was encased in a small folder, accompanied by a "laboratory certificate" that basically identified the stone as genuine. I watched in disbelief as each stone was sold for anywhere from $50 to $300, because not one of them was worth more than $5 (including the cost of the packaging)!

I couldn't believe anyone would be interested in bidding anything at all for these stones, because they were, above all, terribly unattractive. The bidders, however, assumed that since they were "precious gems" they were valuable. One man said that he bought them for resale because, as he explained to me, "how could I go wrong buying a three-carat emerald for $100?" He expected to sell it for several thousand dollars. He, and others like him, quickly found out how wrong they were. What they bought were not "gems" but worthless stones with no value. I suggested they might want to add them to their driveway gravel.

Let's look at why these emeralds, rubies, and sapphires were not "gems." While all of the stones were genuine, they were not "*gem*stones," because they failed to meet any of the three criteria above. First, they were not beautiful: they did not possess lovely colors, had no sparkle or liveliness, and lacked any allure whatsoever. They were plain ugly. In terms of durability, these stones had so many flaws and cracks that they probably would have broken if anyone tried to set them into a piece of jewelry (and if they did survive being placed in a piece of jewelry, they would not have survived the first week of wear). And finally, in terms of rarity, stones of such poor quality are not rare at all; they are carried away from mine sites by the ton in dump trucks. Such low-quality emeralds, rubies, and sapphires are common; they can be found all over the world in inexhaustible quantities. There is no demand for such material, and it has no value.

Beauty, durability, and rarity are directly related to *quality* differences. Had the quality been much finer, the stones would have been more beautiful and more durable. In addition, as quality improves, rarity increases. Rarer stones are more valuable, so the cost would have been greater. Rarity and cost are directly related, especially in cases where gemstones have immediate recognition. But today, with newly discovered gemstones, we cannot understand the impact of rarity as it relates to value without understanding the "fourth" factor: *cachet*.

Let's look at one of the newest gemstones to enter the market: tsavorite. Tsavorite is a rare member of the garnet family. A fine tsavorite is one of the most beautiful gems available, occurring in a rich, deep emerald-green color. It was discovered in Tsavo National Park in Kenya and introduced to the jewelry trade in the 1970s. Let's compare it to another green gem, emerald. In terms of beauty, tsavorite is more brilliant and equally beautiful (some think it even surpasses the beauty of emerald). It is also more durable, and fine-quality stones over two carats are even rarer than emerald. In terms of value, however, its cost is about one-tenth that of emerald! If beauty, durability, and rarity are the only factors to consider, why isn't tsavorite more valuable than emerald? The answer is found in the fourth factor: it lacks cachet. In other words, people don't dream about owning one. At least, not yet. A gem's cachet is what will ultimately affect *demand,* and demand combined with rarity is what will ultimately determine its value.

Tsavorite has a very brief history to date, less than thirty years. Other newcomers, such as red beryl (better known as *Red Emerald*™) and fiery-orange mandarin garnet, have even briefer histories. Many people have not yet even heard of them, and fewer still have seen them. All of this affects supply and demand. Currently the supply of these gems is able to meet demand. But as we move into the twenty-first century and awareness and appreciation for these wonderful—and rare—beauties increases, so will demand. And who knows, as people become more knowledgeable about the wide range of gemstone choices available, supply and demand ratios may go topsy-turvy, along with the prevailing hierarchy. Tsavorite may become the "emerald" of the twenty-first century, red spinel the "ruby" of the twenty-first century, and Paraiba tourmaline the "sapphire" of the twenty-first century. But whatever choices *you* make, the key to selecting a *gemstone,* one that will give you lasting beauty and value, lies in an understanding and appreciation of quality differences.

The Four Cs of Colored Gems

Most people are familiar with the four Cs in the context of evaluating diamond quality, but colored gemstones have four Cs of their own: color, color, color, and color! This statement may sound like an exaggeration, but not so much as you might think.

Generally speaking, the finer and rarer the color, the less impact cutting, clarity, and carat weight have on the value of the gem. On the other hand, the more common the color, the more impact these other factors have.

When we discuss color, we are not talking simply about hue. Color science and the evaluation of color constitute a very complex area. But if you understand the various elements that must be factored into the evaluation of color, you can begin to look at colored gems in a totally different light.

Color is affected by many variables that make it difficult to evaluate precisely. Perhaps the most significant factor is light; the type of light and its intensity can affect color dramatically. In addition, color can be very subjective in terms of what is considered pleasing and desirable. Nonetheless, there has been extensive research and development in the field of color science, and experts are working to develop a viable color-grading system. Several systems have been developed, and many gem-pricing guides use at least one to describe the color of the stones they are pricing. These include the Gemological Institute of America's *Color Master* (a reliable but complicated system rarely used today), American Gemological Laboratories' *ColorScan* (one of the most comprehensive and reliable color-grading systems, but its use is limited almost exclusively to American Gemological Laboratories' colored-stone quality-grading reports), and *Gem Dialogue* (a practical, portable system for describing color). One of the most recent to be introduced is *Gem^{e}wizard™*, a new color-communication system that provides a very comprehensive computerized system using digital imaging to match and describe the color of a particular stone. In addition to matching color, it also incorporates clarity, size, and cutting factors into a pricing matrix. This system provides the capability to more closely and accurately match and describe color in many stones for which other systems have failed, and it may well succeed in finding international acceptance.

Until that time, no matter what system is used, given the numerous variables that affect color, nothing replaces the need to actually see any stone you are considering prior to purchase. Until there is a universally accepted grading system for colored gemstones, subjectivity still reigns. No system has yet replaced the age-old eye-and-brain, coupled with years of experience in the colored-stone field.

The Key Elements in Describing Color

The color we see in gems is always some *combination* of the pure spectral colors—which range from pure red to pure violet—coupled with varying degrees of brown, white, black, and gray. It is these latter colors, in combination with the spectral colors, that affect the *tone* of the color seen and that make the classification of color so difficult. For example, if white is present with red, you will have a lighter tone or shade of red; if black is present, a darker tone or shade. Depending on the degree of gray, white, black, or brown, an almost infinite number of color combinations can result.

As a general rule, the closer a stone's color is to the pure spectral hue, the better the color is considered to be; the closer it comes to a pure hue, the rarer and more valuable. For example, if we are considering a green stone, the purer the green, the better the color. In other words, the closer it comes to being a pure spectral green, having no undertone (tint) of any other color such as blue or yellow, the better the color. There is no such thing in nature, however, as a perfectly pure color; color is always modified by an undertone of another hue. But these undertones can create very beautiful, unusual, distinctive colors that are often very desirable.

In describing color we will often refer to these factors:

- *Hue*—the precise spectral color (red, orange, yellow, green, blue, indigo, violet)
- *Intensity* (or saturation)—the brightness or vividness (or dullness or drabness) of the color
- *Tone*—how much black, white, gray, or brown is present (how light or dark the stone is)
- *Distribution*—the even (or uneven) distribution of the color

Both the intensity and the tone of color can be significantly affected by the proportioning of the cut. In other words, a good lapidary (stone cutter) working with a fine stone will be able to bring out its inherent, potential beauty to the fullest, increasing the gem's desirability. A poor cutter may take the same rough material and create a stone that is not really pleasing, because the cut can significantly reduce the vividness and alter the depth of color, usually producing a stone that is much too dark to be attractive, or one in which the color seems washed-out or watery.

In general, stones that are either very light (pale) or very dark sell for less per carat. There seems to be a common belief that the darker the stone, the better. This is true only to a point. A rich, deep color is desirable, but not a color so deep that it appears black. The average consumer must shop around and train the eye to distinguish between a nice depth of color and a stone that is too dark.

As a general rule, it is even more important to shop around when considering colored stones than it is when buying diamonds. You must develop an eye for all of the variables of color: hue, intensity, tone, and distribution. Some stones simply exhibit a more intense, vivid color than other stones (all else being equal), but only by extensive visual comparison can you develop your eye to perceive differences and make reliable judgments.

For example, let's discuss the variations among rubies for a moment. The finest red rubies from Burma (also called Myanmar) exhibit a color that, while not truly "pure red" (there may be a slight bluish undertone), comes closest to being a pure red. The tone may vary, however, from very light to very dark. As with most stones, the very light stones and the very dark sell for less per carat. Burmese rubies are the most highly prized and the most expensive because of the desirability of their color and their scarcity. They also exhibit a beautiful red in all light, while rubies from most other locations may exhibit a lovely red only in incandescent light (such as you find in candlelight, lamplight, chandeliers, and most evening light) and become pinkish or purplish when seen in fluorescent light or outdoor daylight.

Thai rubies can vary tremendously in hue and tone, going from a light to a dark red with varying degrees of a bluish undertone, giving them a purplish cast and making them look like the much cheaper reddish-purple gemstone, the garnet. While some Thai rubies can have very fine color, rivaling the Burmese (these are very expensive), most Thai stones are much less expensive than the Burmese, primarily because the color can't compare.

African rubies from Tanzania usually have a tint or undertone of brown or orange, which makes them also less expensive than the Burmese reds, but depending on the precise shade, often more valuable than the Thai ruby, depending on the latter's color. Rubies from newly discovered deposits in Kenya, Cambodia, Vietnam, Kashmir (Pakistan), Madagascar, and parts of China may also be close in hue and tone to Burmese rubies, and may also retain their color in all light. These stones can command very high prices if other quality factors are fine.

Ceylon (Sri Lankan) rubies are also encountered with relative frequency. However, these are usually paler in tone. In the United States they are called pink sapphire, not ruby, when the tone is too light. The saturation of color is too weak to be technically described as ruby, since ruby should be red, not pink. You should be aware that in the United States, the color must be deep enough to be considered red to be called ruby, while in other parts of the world, the name *ruby* may be applied if the stone falls anywhere in the pink-to-red range. (It should be noted that sapphire and ruby are the same stone, physically and chemically. The red variety is called ruby, and the equally popular blue is called sapphire. Both belong to the corundum family.)

Next, let's look at the spectrum of emerald colors. Some of the finest emeralds today come from Colombia and are the color of fresh, young green grass—an almost pure spectral green with a faint tint of either yellow or blue. Colombian emeralds owe their color to trace elements of chromium, and the color in the finest of these emeralds is unrivaled; emeralds that contain chromium are more vivid than emeralds from other locations that derive their color also from trace elements of vanadium and often have much more iron content. Emeralds from other countries can also be very fine, with exceptional color, but few can match the color of the finest Colombian. Unfortunately, very fine Colombian emeralds with exceptional color are extremely rare now, and thus very costly.

Zambian emeralds can also exhibit a lovely shade of green but usually with a bluer undertone, due to higher vanadium content, and a slightly dark tone, probably caused by traces of iron. This color difference may make the stone less desirable and thus less valuable than a fine emerald from Colombia. However, the Zambian stones usually have fewer inclusions (flaws) than the Colombian, and may cut a more vivid stone. Therefore, some of the Zambian stones, depending on depth of color, compare very favorably to the Colombian aesthetically, while costing less per carat.

Light and Environment
Affect the Color You See

The color of a stone can be drastically affected by the kind of light and the environment in which the examination is being conducted; that is, variables as disparate as the color of the wallpaper or the tint of a shirt can alter a stone's appearance. If examined under a fluorescent light, a ruby may not show its fullest red because most fluorescent lights are weak in red rays; this causes the red in the ruby to be diminished and to appear more as a purple-red. The same ruby examined in sunlight or incandescent light (an ordinary electric lightbulb), neither of which is weak in red rays, will appear a truer, fuller red. Because the color of a ruby is dependent upon the "color temperature," or type of light used, it will always look best in warm light. A ruby looks even redder if examined against a piece of yellow-orange paper. For this reason, loose rubies are often shown in little envelopes, called parcel papers, that have a yellow-orange inner paper liner to show the red color to the fullest.

Blue sapphire, another intensely colored gem, comes in numerous tones of blue—from light to very dark, some so dark that they look black in incandescent (warm) light. Most sapphires, however, look bluest in fluorescent light, or daylight. Many contain some degree of green. The more green, the lower the price. Some even exhibit a color change— we've seen blue sapphires that were a magnificent blue in daylight turn to an amethyst purple in incandescent light. Some, like the stones from the Umba Valley in Tanzania, turn slightly lavender over time. The lighter blues are generally referred to as Ceylon-colored sapphire; the finest and most expensive blue sapphires generally come from Burma (Myanmar) and Kashmir and exhibit a rich, true blue in all kinds of light. Those from Kashmir exhibit a more subdued, soft, velvety look by comparison with Burmese or Ceylon-type sapphires, and are highly prized by connoisseurs.

An environment that is beneficial to your stone can also be created by the setting in which the stone is mounted. For example, an emerald-cut emerald mounted in a normal four-prong setting will not appear to have as deep a color as it will if mounted in a special box-type setting that encloses the sides of the stone. The "shadowing" effect created by this type of enclosure deepens the color of the stone. This technique, and other types of special mounting, can be used to improve the color of any colored gemstone where it is desirable to intensify the color.

Another example is found in the way imperial jade is set. A fine jade cabochon (a smooth, rounded cut that has no facets) is often *bezel set*, or mounted with a solid rim around the girdle, with the back of the ring constructed much deeper than the actual bottom of the stone, and the back side of the ring nearly completely closed except for a small opening at the bottom center. This can improve its body color (and can also hide a stone's defects).

Opal, too, is often set in ways that enhance color. The environment in this case is a closed, flat backing, which has been blackened on the inside. By contrast against the black background, the play of color (fire) seen in the stone is intensified.

A Word about Color Distribution, or Zoning

Even though zoning doesn't really describe color, and is sometimes evaluated as part of the clarity grade, I think it should be discussed as part of color evaluation.

In some stones, the color isn't always evenly distributed but exists in *zones;* in some stones, the pattern created by alternating zones of color and colorlessness resembles stripes. Zoning is frequently observed in amethyst, ruby, and sapphire. These zones are most easily seen if you look through the side of the stone and move it slowly, while tilting and rotating it.

Zones of color
in a stone

Sometimes a stone in the rough is colorless, or nearly so, but has a spot or layer of color. If the cutter cuts the stone so that the culet is in the color spot, the whole stone will appear that color. If there is a layer and the cutter cuts the stone so that the layer lies in a plane nearly parallel to the table, the whole stone will look completely colored. Evenness of color and complete saturation of color are very important in determining the value of colored gems. Even though you may not notice the zones themselves when looking at the stone from the top, a heavily zoned stone will lack the color vibrancy of another stone without such zoning. Normally, if the zoning isn't noticeable from the top, value is not dramatically reduced, but a stone with even color will appear more vivid from the top—the face-up position, as seen when mounted—and will cost more. And, depending upon the hue and tone, possibly much more.

A Word about Color-Change Stones

Some stones exhibit a very strange phenomenon when viewed in different types of light: they change color completely. These stones are called color-change gems. There are color-change spinels, color-change sapphires, color-change garnets, and even color-change tourmalines! In these gem families, however, the color change phenomenon is rare. The gem alexandrite, on the other hand, *always* exhibits a color change, and its value is based largely on the degree of change. There are even color-change synthetics, such as the inexpensive synthetic color-change sapphire that is often misrepresented and sold as genuine alexandrite. Alexandrite is a bluish-green gem in daylight or under daylight-type fluorescent light, and a deep red or purple-red under incandescent light. And one of the newest gems to enter the market is a color-change diaspore, sold as Zultanite (see page 165).

What Is Fluorescence?

If you have ever visited gem and mineral exhibits at museums such as the American Museum of Natural History in New York City, the Smithsonian in Washington, D.C., or the Houston Museum of Natural Science, you will probably remember seeing a display of common-looking rocks in various shades of white, gray, and black, which suddenly—and magically—changed into intense, psychedelic hues of red, orange, yellow, green, blue, and violet ... with just the touch of a switch!

The colorful reaction you saw in the museum is the result of *fluorescence*. Fluorescence is one of nature's most interesting phenomena to observe. To understand it, you simply need to know that there is visible and invisible light all around us. Light travels in waves, and the length of those waves determines whether they are *visible* or *invisible*, as well as what color we actually see. Some light waves are too short to be visible to humans; some are too long. The colors we are able to see—ranging from red to violet—occur between these two extremes. Beyond red are *infrared* wavelengths, and beyond violet are *ultraviolet* wavelengths: both are invisible to humans. But ultraviolet radiation can have very interesting effects on both rocks and gemstones.

We call rocks that are affected by ultraviolet wavelengths *fluorescent* rocks, and the reaction you saw in the museum is the result of switching the lighting from normal light to "black light," a type of light that produces ultraviolet radiation. The rays produced by this light are too short for us to see, but when they strike certain rocks, properties within those rocks *change the length of the invisible wavelengths into longer wavelengths so that they become visible to us.* When this happens, colors appear that were not visible before. But fluorescent colors are seen *only* when exposed to ultraviolet radiation—hence the incredible "magical" colors that appear under this special light! When you turn off the black light, the rocks go back to their stable state, and you see their normal colors again. In some rare cases, a stone may continue to glow for a short time; we call this continued glow *phosphorescence* (some watches have phosphorescent dials, which glow in the dark for a brief time when you go from light into dark).

When a gemstone produces colors that can be seen only under ultraviolet radiation, we say it *fluoresces* or it has *fluorescence*. Like fluorescent minerals, some colored gemstones also fluoresce. Whether or not a stone fluoresces, the color it fluoresces when it does, and the strength of its fluorescence (faint, weak, moderate, strong, very strong) can be quickly determined by viewing the stone with a special lamp known as an *ultraviolet lamp* (UV lamp) that emits only ultraviolet radiation. The ideal type of UV lamp for gemological purposes produces *two* ultraviolet wavelengths—longwave and shortwave; the "black light" used by museums to show the fluorescent colors of the rocks in their mineral collections is a *longwave* UV lamp. A UV lamp is a standard piece of equipment used in gem-testing laboratories and by gemstone dealers and knowledgeable jewelers, because a gem's fluorescent properties under both wavelengths can be an important indicator of a gemstone's true identity, and they may also indicate whether or not a gemstone has been treated.

Some stones fluoresce only under longwave ultraviolet radiation, some only under shortwave, and some fluoresce under both wavelengths but show a stronger reaction under one wavelength than the other. Whether or not a stone fluoresces, the particular colors in which it fluoresces, and the wavelength under which it fluoresces—longwave or shortwave—is important to note and will be indicated on any colored gemstone report.

Fluorescence Can Affect the Color Seen in Different Lighting Environments

As mentioned earlier, fluorescence is an important key to the identification of many gemstones and can also be indicative of certain types of treatment. But even more important, it can affect the color we see in daylight—in which ultraviolet radiation is present—and, as a result, a stone's color *trueness* (that is, showing essentially the same color) in all types of lighting.

Burmese ruby provides an excellent example of this. One of the characteristics that makes rubies from Burma more desirable than rubies from many other localities is the way they fluoresce. For example, let's compare Burmese ruby to Thai ruby. A Burmese ruby fluoresces a strong red under both longwave and shortwave ultraviolet wavelengths, which are both present in outdoor daylight. Thai ruby, on the other hand, has little or no fluorescent reaction. Both Burmese and Thai ruby will show a nice red color *indoors*, where the light source is usually an incandescent light (a "warm" light such as those in household lamps or chandeliers); *any* red stone looks great in this type of lighting due to the strong red component in the wavelengths of incandescent light. When viewed outdoors in daylight, however, the red color of Thai ruby is weakened because it does not have a strong red fluorescent reaction to ultraviolet radiation. Instead, Thai ruby becomes purplish because of exposure to the blue/violet rays present in daylight. The color of a Burmese ruby, however, will not be adversely affected by the presence of more blue/violet rays *because of its strong red fluorescent reaction stimulated by the ultraviolet radiation present in outdoor daylight.*

In Burmese ruby—and in rubies from some other localities as well—fluorescent behavior results in a rich red color both outdoors and indoors; hence, these rubies are very desirable and command prices higher than those of rubies that do *not* have a strong red fluorescent reaction. However, if you plan to wear your ruby mainly in the evening, or indoors where there is incandescent light, a Thai ruby, or other ruby that lacks the color-trueness of Burmese ruby, offers an attractive—and more affordable—alternative!

Clarity

As with diamonds, *clarity* refers to the absence of internal characteristics (inclusions) or external blemishes. Flawless colored stones are perhaps even rarer than flawless diamonds. However, while clarity is important, and the cleaner the stone the better, the absence of inclusions or blemishes in colored stones does not usually carry the premium that it does with diamonds. Light, pastel-colored stones will require better clarity because the inclusions are more readily visible in these stones; in darker-toned stones, the inclusions may not be as important a variable because they are masked by the depth of color.

The *type* and *placement* of inclusions and blemishes is a more important consideration in colored stones than the presence of these characteristics in and of themselves. For example, a large crack (also called a *fracture* or *feather)* that is very close to the surface of a stone—especially on the top—might be dangerous because it weakens the stone's durability. It may also break the light continuity, and may show an iridescent effect as well (iridescence usually means that a fracture or feather breaks through the surface somewhere on the stone). Such a large crack would detract from the stone's beauty and certainly reduce its value. But if the fracture is small and positioned in an unobtrusive part of the stone, it will have minimal effect on durability, beauty, or value.

Some inclusions actually help a gemologist or jeweler to identify a stone, since certain types are characteristic of specific gems and specific localities. In some cases, a particular inclusion may provide positive identification of the exact variety or origin and actually cause an increase in the per-carat value. For more information on the types of inclusions found in colored gems, I recommend the book *Gem Identification Made Easy.* I should note, however, that a very fine colored gem that really is free of inclusions will probably bring a disproportionately *much* higher price per carat because it is so rare. Because they are so rare, rubies, sapphires, and emeralds with *no* visible inclusions should always be viewed with suspicion; have their genuineness verified by a gem-testing lab. The newer synthetic gems are often flawless and are easy to confuse with genuine, natural gems.

If the inclusions weaken the stone's durability, affect color, are easily noticeable, or are too numerous, they will significantly reduce price. Otherwise, they may not adversely affect price, and in some cases, if they provide positive identification and proof of origin, they may actually increase the cost rather than reduce it. Such is the case with Burmese rubies and Colombian emeralds.

Again, it is important to shop around, become familiar with the stone you wish to purchase, and train your eye to discern what is "normal" so you can decide what is acceptable or objectionable.

Clarity Classifications for Colored Gemstones

Where clarity is concerned, colored gemstones are divided into several classifications reflecting differences in the geological conditions under which they formed and how those conditions affect the physical appearance of the stone, especially with regard to what you typically see within the stone, with and without magnification.

The Gemological Institute of America (GIA) divides colored gemstones into three classifications: Type I, Type II, and Type III. Gemstones classified as "Type I" form under geological conditions in which inclusions are not very noticeable, and such stones are often "eye clean" (that is, you see nothing with your eye alone). "Type II" gemstones form under more severe geological conditions, resulting in the presence of inclusions that are typically more noticeable. "Type III" gemstones form under the most violent geological conditions, resulting in stones that typically show inclusions, often to the unaided eye, and are rarely "eye clean." Aquamarine is classified "Type I" and is usually "eye clean." Emerald, on the other hand, which is "Type III," usually has characteristics that are readily visible, so much so that one *expects* to see something with the eye, and the absence of visible inclusions often arouses suspicion.

It is important to know whether or not a gemstone is classified as Type I, Type II, or Type III in order to understand what the clarity description means in terms of visible inclusions and their impact on value. This will give you a better understanding of what is typical—or exceptional—for any gemstone you are considering, and help you judge clarity more accurately.

Let's further compare aquamarine and emerald in terms of what their respective clarity grades would signify.

Using GIA terminology, the aquamarine (Type I) would be described as follows:

- "Eye Clean" if there are *no inclusions visible to the unaided eye*
- "Slightly Included" if there are *minute* inclusions, *difficult to see with the unaided eye*
- "Moderately Included" if *minor* inclusions are *somewhat easy to see with the unaided eye*
- "Heavily Included" if *inclusions are very noticeable* and *adversely affect beauty or durability*
- "Severely Included" if *inclusions are very noticeable* and have a *severe negative impact on beauty, durability, or both.*

By contrast, using GIA terminology, an emerald (Type III) would be described as follows:

- "Eye Clean" if there are *no inclusions visible to the unaided eye* (very rare in Type III stones)
- "Slightly Included" if there are *noticeable* inclusions a*pparent to the unaided eye*
- "Moderately Included" if there are *noticeable* inclusions that are *very apparent to the unaided eye*
- "Heavily Included" if *prominent inclusions negatively affect the stone's beauty or durability*
- "Severely Included" if *prominent inclusions* have a *very severe effect on appearance, durability, or both.*

A complete list of gemstones, by clarity classification, is provided below. To understand subtle differences, however, and their effect on value, it is very important to spend time looking at numerous stones to develop your own eye and to gain a clearer understanding of what is normal and what is exceptional for the particular stone you may be considering.

Gemstone Clarity Classifications Used by the Gemological Institute of America (GIA)

Gemstone	Type I	Type II	Type III
Andalusite		X	
Apatite	X		
Beryl			
Aquamarine	X		
Emerald			X
Deep blue		X	
Red			X
All other colors (pink, yellow, green)	X		
Chrysoberyl			
Alexandrite		X	
All other colors	X		
Corundum*		X	
Diopside		X	
Feldspar (Moonstone/sunstone)		X	
Garnet		X	
Iolite		X	
Opal (Fire)		X	
Peridot		X	
Quartz		X	
Spinel		X	
Topaz			
Blue	X		
All other colors		X	
Tourmaline			
Green	X		
Watermelon			X
All other colors		X	
Zircon			
Colorless and blue	X		
All other colors		X	
Zoisite (tanzanite)	X		

* While most ruby is classified as Type II, ruby of exceptional color from Burma (Myanmar) and certain other locations are more typically graded similarly to Type III gemstones.

Terms Used to Describe Optical Effects in Faceted and Nonfaceted Gems

The physical characteristics of colored stones are sometimes described in terms of the way light travels through them, or in terms of unusual visual effects (often referred to as *optical phenomena*). Such characteristics are related to the number, type, and placement of inclusions, combined with the way in which the stone is cut.

Asterism, a *star* effect, will only be present if there are numerous inclusions oriented in a particular way. But the presence of inclusions alone will not produce asterism. To see asterism, the stone must also be cut in the cabochon style rather than faceted (see page 38). A star ruby, for example, has numerous needle-like crystal inclusions of the mineral rutile. If the rutile inclusions are oriented properly along each crystal axis, the cabochon cut will allow the light to enter the stone in such a way that it will be reflected back from the inclusions, resulting in a lovely star. In the case of ruby, the star is typically a 6-ray star because the crystal form for ruby is hexagonal. A garnet may also have rutile inclusions, and similarly, when cut into a cabochon, may exhibit a lovely star as well, but star garnet typically exhibits a 4-ray star because its crystal form is cubic.

In order to understand the variety of optical effects seen in colored gemstones, here are some terms you need to know:

- *Transparent.* Light travels through the stone easily, with minimal distortion, enabling one to see through it easily.
- *Translucent.* The stone transmits light but diffuses it, creating an effect like frosted glass. If you try to read through such a stone, the print will be darkened and obscured.
- *Opaque.* The stone transmits no light; you cannot see through it even at a thin edge.

Special Optical Effects

- *Adularescence.* A billowy, movable cloud effect seen in some stones, such as moonstone; an internal, movable sheen.
- *Asterism.* Used to describe the display of a star effect (four- or six-rayed) seen when a stone is cut in a nonfaceted style (star ruby, garnet, and sapphire.)

- *Chatoyancy.* The effect produced in some stones (when cut in a cabochon style) of a thin, bright line across the stone that usually moves as the stone is moved from side to side; sometimes called a *cat's-eye* effect.
- *Iridescence.* A rainbow-color effect produced by a thin film of air or liquid within the stone. Most iridescence seen in stones is the result of a crack breaking the surface. This detracts from the value, even if it looks pretty.
- *Luster.* Usually refers to the surface of a stone and the degree to which it reflects light; seen as the shine on the stone. Diamond, for example, has much greater luster than amethyst. Pearls are also evaluated for their luster, but pearls have a softer, silkier-looking reflection than other gems. The luster in pearls is often called *orient*.
- *Play of color.* Used frequently to describe the fire seen in opal, or the multiple flashes or pattern of color.

Cut

Colored gems can be either *faceted* or cut in a *nonfaceted* style called *cabochon.* Generally speaking, the preference in the United States until

Cabochon cut
Note the smooth top of this *sugarloaf* cabochon.

recently was for faceted gems, so the finest material was usually faceted. However, this was not always the case in other eras and other countries. In Roman times, for example, it was considered vulgar to wear a faceted stone. Preference also varies with different cultures and religions, and the world's finest gems are cut in both styles. Don't draw any conclusions about quality based solely on style of cut.

Cabochon. A facetless style of cutting that produces a smooth surface. These cuts can be almost any shape. Some are round with high domes; others look like squarish domes (the popular "sugarloaf" cabochon); others are "buff-topped," showing a somewhat flattened top.

Many people around the world prefer the quieter, often more mysterious personality of the cabochon. Some connoisseurs believe that cabochons produce a richer color. Whatever the case, today we are seeing much more interest in and appreciation for cabochons around the world, and more beautiful cabochons than have been seen in the market in many years.

Faceted. A style of cutting that consists of giving to the stone many small faces at varying angles to one another, as in various diamond cuts. The placement, angle, and shape of the faces, or facets, is carefully planned and executed to show the stone's inherent beauty—fire, color, brilliance—to fullest advantage. Today there are many "new" faceted styles, including "fantasy" cuts, which combine rounded surfaces with sculpted backs.

The Importance of Cut

As stated earlier, cutting and proportioning in colored stones are important for two main reasons: they affect the *depth* of color seen in the stone; and they affect the *liveliness* projected by the stone.

Color and cutting are the most important criteria in determining the beauty of a colored stone. After that, carat weight must be factored in; a higher carat weight will usually increase the price per carat, generally in a nonlinear proportion. If a colored stone is of a good-quality material to begin with, a good cut will enhance its natural beauty to the fullest and allow it to exhibit its finest color and liveliness. If the same material is cut poorly, its natural beauty will be lessened, causing it to look dark, too light, or even "dead."

Therefore, when you examine a colored stone that looks lively to your eye and has good color—not too dark and not too pale—you can assume the cut is reasonably good. If the stone's color is poor, or if it lacks liveliness, you must examine it for proper cut. If it has been cut properly, you can assume the basic material was poor. If the cut is poor, however, the material may be very good and can perhaps be recut into a beautiful gem. In this case you may want to confer with a knowledgeable cutter to see if it is worthwhile to recut, considering cutting costs and loss in weight. If you don't know any cutters, a reputable jeweler, gemologist-appraiser, or local lapidary club may be able to recommend one.

Evaluating the Cut of a Colored Gem

When you are examining the stone for proper cut, a few considerations should guide you:

Is the shade pleasing, and does the stone have life and brilliance? If the answer is yes to both questions, then the basic material is probably good, and you must make a decision based on your own personal preferences and budget.

Is the color too light or too dark? If so, and if the cut looks good, the basic uncut material was probably too light or too dark to begin with. Consider purchase only if you find the stone pleasing, and only if the price is right, i.e., significantly lower than stones of better color.

Is the stone's brilliance even, or are there dead spots or flat areas? Often the brilliance in a colored gemstone is not uniform. If the color is exceptional, subdued brilliance may not have a dramatic effect on its allure, desirability, or value. However, the less fine the color, the more important brilliance becomes.

When the cut is not properly proportioned, a stone can either look too dark or too light. In other cases, a cut can mask the fact that a stone has little color. When evaluating the cut of a stone, here are some additional considerations:

When the color is too dark. While the inherent color of the material may be overly dark, in a deep stone, the original color tone may have been fine, and the undesirable darkness is simply the result of poor cutting in which the proportioning is too thick or too deep. The cost of such a stone should be less than that of one less dark, and it may, therefore, be feasible to purchase it (if the price is sufficiently low) and invest in recutting the stone to better proportions to enhance its natural color. While the size or weight would be reduced, the price per carat would be increased. At worst, there would be a trade-off: reduced size for increased beauty and increased price per carat. In some cases the price per carat may increase so substantially that the overall value of the stone also increases substantially, even though it weighs less.

This is often the case with "native cut" stones, a term used in the trade to describe stones cut by less skilled workers who are cutting with only one goal in mind: to get the heaviest stone possible. These stones are usually too deep and therefore look thick, heavy, very dark, and often lifeless. While many of these stones are undesirable in their "native cuts," they can often be recut into lively stones with a much more pleasing color and greater beauty and desirability. In such cases, the price per carat increases, resulting in a stone that may be more valuable than the larger stone before recutting.

When the color is too light. The basic color of the gemstone may simply be light in tone, but it may also be the result of poor proportioning from having been cut too shallow. Shallow stones usually lack liveliness, but it is usually not feasible to recut them.

A stone that is cut too shallow may also be more vulnerable to breakage. Some stones are so shallow that they really should not be worn at all, or only in a piece of jewelry that will be protected and less exposed to the normal knocks and blows of everyday wear.

In shallow-cut pastel or light-colored stones, such as aquamarine, amethyst, or topaz, any accumulation of dirt or grease on the back of the stone will quickly and dramatically diminish color and brilliance. This often happens with a ring worn daily and subjected to dishwashing, cosmetic application, bath oils, etc. To remain attractive, pastel or light-colored stones should be frequently cleaned (see chapter 14), especially when cut shallow.

You must also keep in mind that a gemstone is often cut in a particular way because of *where the color occurs within the stone.* As mentioned earlier, nature doesn't often create gemstones with the color evenly and uniformly distributed. Color often occurs in zones and the cutter must be sure that he or she doesn't cut the stone in a way that removes the color zone. This often affects the depth of the cut.

While gemstones are usually cut deep in an effort to get the heaviest stone possible, or to darken the tone if too light, there is another situation that you may encounter in colored gemstones—one that can cause a costly mistake. *A virtually colorless stone can appear to have color throughout if the cutter is able to capture a zone of color in the right part of the stone.* I've seen sapphires, for example, that were actually colorless, except for a tiny spot of color at the culet. One of the best bluff stones I've ever seen was a three-carat round blue sapphire that was cut very deep. For its weight it was small, so I looked more carefully from the side and back, only to discover that the stone had no blue at all except for a very tiny zone just above the culet. The entire stone looked blue because of the way the light traveled through it. The reflected light created the impression that the color was evenly distributed throughout the stone. It looked like a decent blue sapphire when viewed face-up in the mounting, but on closer examination it became immediately clear that it was not as fine as it appeared, and worth much less than the asking price.

Tip: Always turn the stone onto its table, against a white or light background, and view it carefully through the sides, while gently tilting and rotating the stone to see where the color is actually located. This can be done even with mounted stones.

Gemstones are usually cut deeper to improve the tone, but sometimes the tone or overall appearance is improved by cutting the stone shallow. Sometimes a stone will be cut on the shallow side because the basic color is very deep, perhaps overly deep, and it will appear too dark if cut to a more standard depth. In other cases, a stone might have to be cut shallow to eliminate unsightly inclusions, and the cutter must hope that the finished stone won't be too pale. If the inherent color is not very rich to start with, shallow cutting will result in a stone that will be too pale; if the inherent color is very rich, the color may still appear very fine regardless of its shallow cut. If it is not cut overly shallow, it may still be very desirable and still exhibit a good liveliness. I recall a lovely ruby that had belonged to an important family in India. The stone weighed just over eleven carats, but it appeared much larger. Its measurements were actually larger than an eighteen-carat ruby in another jewel. The cut was shallow, but the color was nonetheless very rich. The stone had a very mysterious personality, and the overall effect was one of great allure. It is also worth noting that the inherent color of the rough gem had to have been exceptional to have retained such color in a shallow stone.

When evaluating the cut of a colored gemstone, always pay special attention to its depth and the impact of the depth on the basic body color and overall liveliness and brilliance. Keep in mind, however, that there are exciting new cutting techniques (see below) that can create intense color and liveliness within stones that once would have been considered too shallow. Remember that the most important thing about the cutting and proportioning of any colored gemstone is the end result—its beauty. For this, the best test is simply your own eye.

Artists in Stone—The Art of Lapidary

Lapidary is the term used for gem cutting and gem cutters. The art of lapidary—fashioning a piece of "rough" stone or crystal into a sparkling gem that will dazzle the eye—is thousands of years old. For colored gemstones, one of the most famous lapidary centers is Idar-Oberstein, Germany, which has been a leading lapidary center for centuries. Famous in Roman times, it has continued into the present as a major cutting center, virtually without interruption. It continues to produce some of the finest cutters, carvers, and cutting innovations, such as the first "fantasy" cut created by Bernd Munsteiner, a well-known cutter in Idar.

Lapidary has evolved as an art form over the centuries, but it is really only within the past few decades that it has moved to center stage. Today, science and technology have provided cutters and carvers with the means to experiment with new approaches and techniques that have enabled them to reach new heights in their art. There is greater knowledge about how light moves within each gemstone and, perhaps even more important, how various cutting and carving techniques can affect the *behavior* of the light. As a result, lapidary artists are now creating visual effects never imagined—new dimensions that truly represent "art" in every sense.

Lapidary artists use gemstones as the medium in which they work, often studying the material for weeks or months before deciding how to proceed. Their work is distinctive and recognizable, and the skill and artistry they bring to the fashioning of the gemstone material not only enhances its beauty and desirability but also its value. Just as a painting is valued at more than the cost of the paint and canvas, so it is with gemstones; a magnificently cut gemstone is valued not just for its weight, color, and clarity, but for the beauty added by the cutter. The value of an exquisitely cut gem is much greater than one that is cut in a more common manner.

We now see the work of lapidary artists in breathtaking jewels, magnificent sculptures, objets d'art, and, in some cases, works that combine all three in a single creation. In recent years the work of some of the most important contemporary lapidary artists has been on exhibition at such revered institutions as the Smithsonian Institution in Washington, D.C., the Carnegie Museum of Natural History in Pittsburgh, and the Field Museum in Chicago. (See first color insert.)

The lapidary artist faces challenges unknown to artists working in other media. If they are to achieve the desired result, lapidary artists must constantly assess and reassess numerous elements—color, and where it occurs within the gemstone; light refraction; light reflection; the presence and placement of inclusions; and the shape of the rough. For some lapidary artists, this is doubly demanding because their work incorporates more than one gemstone material within the same piece. But even more challenging, the lapidary artist cannot ignore the intrinsic value of the gemstone material with which he or she is working. Mistakes can be very costly; the cost of canvas and oil is one thing, but the cost of a gemstone is quite another!

In addition to the risk of breaking or damaging a gem, creating maximum beauty usually means sacrificing the size of the finished gem and committing much more time to its creation. Many cutters cut the rough with one aim only: getting the largest possible size, and doing it as quickly as possible. But the goal of the lapidary artist is very different; the goal is to create the most beautiful gem possible, one that is unique, distinctive, and memorable.

Innovative Cutting Techniques
Change the World of Colored Gemstones

In traditional faceting, the primary goal of the cutter is to maximize the *brilliance* of a gemstone, the amount of light coming back *out* of the stone, back to the eye. The cutter must take into consideration the gemstone's *refractive index* (RI)—a number that indicates how light travels within the gemstone and provides a key to its relative brilliance. The higher the RI, the higher the brilliance can be; the lower the RI, the lower the brilliance. Every gem has a unique refractive index. Ruby, for example, has an RI of approximately 1.76–1.77, which is high; amethyst has an RI of approximately 1.54, which is much lower. This means that ruby has a much higher inherent brilliance factor than amethyst. So, if both stones were cut in the same manner, with the same proportions, angles, and so on, the ruby would be much more brilliant than the amethyst. Some of the earliest faceting innovations dealt with ways to get greater brilliance out of gemstones with lower RIs, that is, to get more light reflecting back out of the stone. Thus began experimentation with the shape, number, and placement of flat faces on the surface of the gemstone material, resulting in many exquisitely brilliant gemstones. Until recently, however, the techniques used involved conventional *flat* faceting, and the focus always remained on increasing the amount of light being reflected back and creating more intense brilliance.

Today's lapidary artists have introduced a whole new style of cutting with a totally different focus. The focus is no longer confined to how much light is coming *out* of the gemstone but on what is happening to the light *within* the gemstone. We are now seeing sculpturing techniques applied to this end, and some carvers have developed a unique style that involves the delicate carving of narrow "passageways" into the interior of a stone to alter the path of the light. But perhaps the most important development is in the faceting arena. Focusing on internal performance has led to a much more difficult and complex form of faceting: *curved* faceting. Using a combination of *concave* and *convex* facets, sometimes in conjunction with flat faceting and sculpturing techniques, the cutter's goal is now on using the stone's unique RI—the unique way in which light will behave when traveling through it—to capture the inner dimension and personality of the gem. Today the lapidary artist seeks to use the gemstone's own unique optical properties to create a unique interaction of color, brightness, and luminosity to reveal the inner world of the gem. These innovative techniques have resulted in some of the most beautiful gemstones ever imagined, gemstones that are truly as nature intended— one-of-a-kind.

We are now seeing incredible works by very gifted cutters and carvers, encouraged by international cutting competitions such as the Cutting Edge Awards sponsored by the American Gem Trade Association and, in Idar-Oberstein, Germany, the German Award for Jewelry and Precious Stones sponsored by the Federal Association of the Precious Stones and Diamond Industry and Industrial Association for Jewelry and Metalware. Some of the best-known award winners include Susan Allen, Stephen Avery, David Brackna, Michael Christie, Bart Curren, Michael Dyber, John Dyer, Mark Gronlund, Richard Homer, Martin Key, Dieter Lorenz, Thomas McPhee, Nicolai Medvedev, Bernd Munsteiner, Thomas Trozzo, Steve Walters, Larry Winn, and Phil Youngman. Each has played a significant role in creating new ways to reveal the maximum beauty of gemstones (see the color inserts for examples of work from some of these artists).

Weight

As with diamonds, weight in colored stones is measured in carats. All gems are weighed in carats, except pearls and coral, which are sold by the grain, momme, and millimeter. A grain is ¼ of a carat; a momme is 18¾ carats. Since 1913, most countries have agreed that a carat weighs 200 milligrams, or ⅕ of a gram. This carat is sometimes referred to as the *metric carat*.

Before 1913, the weight of a carat varied depending on the country of origin—the Indian carat didn't weigh the same as the English carat; the French carat was different from the Indian or the English. This is important if you have, or are thinking of buying, a very old piece that still has the original bill of sale indicating carat weight; the old carat weighed *more* than the post-1913 metric carat. Therefore, an old three-carat stone will weigh more than three carats by modern standards.

The carat is a unit of weight, *not size*. I wish to stress this point, since most people think that a one-carat stone is a particular size. Most people, therefore, would expect a one-carat diamond and a one-carat emerald, for example, to look the same size or to have the same apparent dimensions. This is not the case.

Comparing a one-carat diamond with a one-carat emerald and a one-carat ruby easily illustrates this point. First, emerald weighs less than diamond, and ruby weighs more than diamond. This means that a one-carat emerald will look larger than a one-carat diamond, while the ruby will look smaller than a diamond of the same weight. Emerald, with a mineral composition that is lighter, will yield greater mass per carat; ruby, with its heavier composition, will yield less mass per carat.

Let's look at the principle another way. If you compare a one-inch cube of pine wood, a one-inch cube of aluminum, and a one-inch cube of iron, you would easily choose the cube of iron as heaviest, even though it has the same *volume* as the other materials. The iron is like the ruby, while the wood is like the emerald and the aluminum like the diamond. Equal *volumes* of different materials can have very different weights depending on their *density*, also called *mass* or *specific gravity* (SG).

Each gemstone has its own unique specific gravity, a number that shows the ratio of the weight of the particular gem to the weight of an equal volume of water. The higher a gem's specific gravity, the heavier the gem; the lower the specific gravity, the lighter the gem (see chapter 9).

Equal volumes of materials with the same density should have approximately the same weight, so that in diamond, the carat weight has come to represent particular sizes. But these sizes are based on diamonds always being cut to more or less the same proportions. Consequently, diamonds of a particular weight will always be more or less the same size; a one-carat round diamond is always approximately 6.5 millimeters in diameter; a two-carat round diamond is always approximately 8.2 millimeters in diameter, and so on. *But these sizes do not apply to other gems.*

As a result of the close association between diamond weights and sizes, when most people describe the size gemstone they want in terms of carat weight, they are visualizing a size that is related to diamonds. For example, when someone says that they want a one-carat round sapphire, what they usually mean is that they want a sapphire that looks the *size* of a one-carat diamond—something about 6.5 millimeters in diameter.

In addition to the density of a particular gemstone affecting its size, the size of colored gemstones can be dramatically affected by the cutting. As mentioned earlier, sometimes the cutter just wants the heaviest carat weight possible and cuts a stone overly deep; it may weigh a lot, but if all the weight is in the bottom of the stone, it can look smaller than another stone that weighs half as much. Sometimes a stone is cut overly shallow in an attempt to lighten the color tone, which can create a larger-looking stone than one of the same weight with a deeper cut. Whatever the case, the proportions will affect the finished "size" of the stone.

With colored gemstones, rather than asking for a specific carat weight, it is better to show the jeweler the approximate *size* you want, perhaps using a diamond as a reference. Just remember that if you use a diamond as a reference size-wise, ask the jeweler to give you that stone's *millimeter dimensions* (the diameter or length and width), not the carat weight, so that you know what size you are seeking.

Normally, the greater the weight, the greater the value per carat, unless the stones reach unusually large sizes, for example, in excess of 50 carats. At that point, size may become prohibitive for use in some types of jewelry (rings or earrings), selling such large stones can be difficult, and price per carat may drop. There are genuine cut topazes weighing from 2,500 to 12,000 carats that could be used as paperweights.

Some stones are readily available in large sizes; tourmaline, for example, often occurs in stones over 10 carats. For other stones, sizes over 5 carats may be very rare and therefore considered large, and will also command a proportionately higher price. Examples include precious topaz, alexandrite, demantoid and tsavorite garnets, ruby, and red beryl. With gems that are rare in large sizes, a 10-carat stone can command any price—a king's ransom. A 30-carat blue diamond was sold in 1982 for $9 million. Today, $9 million would be considered a bargain for that stone!

Scarcity of certain sizes among the different colored stones affects the definition of *large* in the colored-gem market. A fine 5-carat alexandrite or ruby is a very large stone; an 18-carat tourmaline is a "nice size."

As with diamonds, stones under 1 carat sell for less per carat than stones over 1 carat. But here it becomes more complicated. The definition of large or rare sizes differs tremendously, as does price, depending on the type of stone. For example, an 8-carat tourmaline is an average-size stone, fairly common, and will be priced accordingly. A 5-carat tsavorite is extremely rare, and will command a price proportionately much greater than a 1-carat stone. Precious topaz used to be readily available in 20-carat sizes and larger, but today even 10-carat stones of very fine color are practically nonexistent, and their price has jumped tremendously.

The chart of colored gemstones in chapter 8 indicates the availability of stones in large sizes; and it shows where scarcity may exist, and at what size.

CHAPTER FIVE

Colored Gemstone Synthesis & Treatment

In addition to the wide variety of natural gemstone alternatives from which to choose today, numerous synthetic and treated materials are available. They make attractive jewelry, but you must understand what you have, and pay the appropriate price for it.

All Synthetics Are Not the Same

Scientific advances and new technology have resulted in a whole world of *synthetic* gemstone materials, but it's important to understand that a synthetic is *not* an imitation. Technically, the term *synthetic* indicates that the material is artificially made by *using the same chemical ingredients found in natural products*—in other words, using Mother Nature's recipe. This means that a synthetic gemstone will have essentially the same physical, chemical, and optical properties observed in natural gemstones. From a practical standpoint, this also means that they will respond to various gem-identification tests in the same way as do natural stones. This can make them difficult to distinguish from the natural gem.

An *imitation* is also artificially made but not by using "nature's recipe," so it is very different physically and chemically from the gem it is imitating, and it is very easy to distinguish it from the natural gem with standard gem-identification techniques. For example, a glass "gem" is an imitation. Red glass could imitate ruby. But it resembles ruby only in *color*; a quick examination with a simple jeweler's loupe would reveal telltale signs that it is glass, and any gemological test would clearly corroborate this conclusion.

Today there are numerous synthetic gems, but they are not all produced the same way. Some are produced inexpensively, and although they are made with nature's recipe, they don't really look like the natural gem. Some are made quickly by a process very different from nature's. These are often confused with imitations because of their unnatural appearance and low cost. This type of synthetic is widely available today and has been made for over a hundred years.

In recent years, technological advances have enabled scientists to create environments that come much closer to duplicating what is found in nature. As a result, crystals can actually be "grown" in laboratories, creating a product that very closely resembles the natural gem. These are often called *flux-grown*, *created*, or *laboratory-grown* synthetics. These laboratory-grown synthetics are expensive to produce and cost much more than other synthetics; in fact, the cost can be so high that consumers sometimes mistakenly conclude they are natural gemstones. Next to the natural, there is nothing that can compare to a fine lab-grown synthetic, and even though the stone may be expensive, the cost is only a fraction of that of a rare, natural gem with a comparable appearance.

Synthetics can make excellent alternatives for buyers unable to afford natural gems in the quality they desire. Be sure, however, not to confuse terms such as *created* or *grown* with *naturally created* or *naturally grown*. All synthetic products are made by humankind. Also, remember that inexpensive synthetics are abundant, so if you are paying a premium for the stone, be sure you have a lab-grown synthetic and not an inexpensive type. As you shop around and compare various synthetic products, you will find that there are significant visual differences among them. Develop an eye for the type you want.

Gemstone Treatment—From Routine to Not-So-Routine in Today's Jewelry Scene

The use of various treatments to improve the appearance of gemstones is not new. We find evidence of treatment in antique jewels, and ancient writings from Roman times and before attest to a long-standing knowledge of ways to improve the appearance of many gemstones. What is new, however, is the *routine* use of treatments, which began in the 1960s, necessitated by an ever-declining supply of natural, fine-quality gemstones. Fine-quality *natural* emeralds, rubies, and sapphires—that is, gems not subjected to any type of artificial treatment or enhancement—

have never been rarer than they are today. It is fair to say that if it were not for the use of various treatments, the supply of beautiful gemstones would be virtually depleted by now, and only the wealthiest and most powerful would be enjoying them!

While they can still be found, locating a natural gem in a particular size and quality can take months of intensive searching. When one is found, it can command a price prohibitive to all but the most wealthy collector or connoisseur. I was recently retained to help a couple acquire an exceptionally fine Colombian emerald. After discussing the options with me, and learning about different fillers and degrees of treatment used on emerald, they were willing to accept a stone with "minor traces of oil." They did not want a stone treated with other types of filler, however, or a stone with more than minimal treatment. It took several months to find the 3.64-carat emerald they selected, and the cost—at wholesale— was almost $100,000! Helping another couple search for an exceptionally fine 5-carat natural sapphire of Kashmir origin took almost as long, and the wholesale cost was over $50,000. And an 8.60-carat natural Burmese ruby of exceptional quality sold at auction for $465,000 *per carat*, a world record. This is not what people usually want, and most retail jewelers don't keep such gems in their regular inventory.

Many treatments simply continue the process that Mother Nature started; all gems are exposed to heat, and many to radiation, as they are forming in nature. Today, most rubies, sapphires, and many other gem-stones are routinely treated with heat or exposed to some type of radia-tion to change or enhance their color and improve clarity, and pricing is based on the assumption that enhancement has occurred. On the other hand, if the color of a gem is very fine, and if it can be documented that the color is natural and that there is no clarity enhancement, the stone will command a much higher price. Since such gems are very rare today, some of the best sources of fine, natural-color gems are major estate pieces that sometimes reenter the market when well-known auction houses hold their "magnificent" or "important" jewelry sales.

Whether from an auction house or another source, fine rare gems with natural color and clarity normally will be accompanied by a gem-testing report verifying those facts. Without a report, or any representa-tions to the contrary, assume that the color of any gemstone sold today has been enhanced in some manner and that the clarity may also have been improved in the process. When you are buying any expensive rare gem represented to be natural, be sure it is accompanied by a report from a respected gem-testing lab that verifies this fact (see chapter 7 and appendix), or make the purchase contingent on getting a report.

Some of the most common types of treatment include the following.

Heating

Subjecting certain gems to sophisticated heating procedures is a practice that is accepted within the jewelry industry as long as the change induced is *permanent*. Most sapphires and rubies are heated. The treatment may lighten, darken, or completely change the color and improve the clarity by melting some of the fine "silk" inclusions often present. A skilled gemologist or gem-testing laboratory can often determine whether or not the color of these gems has been altered by heating by examining the stone's inclusions under the microscope. Sapphire and ruby, for example, can withstand high temperatures, but often the heat causes small crystal inclusions present inside the stone to melt or explode. These altered inclusions then provide the evidence of heating.

It may be easy to determine that a stone *has* been heated, but it is often impossible to know for certain that it has *not* been—that is, that its color is natural. Making this determination can require a high degree of skill and sophisticated equipment, often only available at a major laboratory, and even then, it may not be possible to ascertain definitively. Gemologists must carefully examine the internal characteristics of the particular stone. Sometimes they see an unaltered inclusion that would lead to a conclusion that the color is natural; other times they see an altered inclusion that indicates treatment; and sometimes the inclusions, or changes and abnormalities in them, that one seeks to make a positive determination simply are not present. When there is nothing inside the gem to indicate whether it has or has not been heated, we cannot be sure.

Most rubies and sapphires sold since the 1960s have been heated to enhance their color and clarity. Other gemstones that are routinely heated today include amber, amethyst, aquamarine, pink beryl (morganite), carnelian, citrine, kunzite, tanzanite, pink topaz, several varieties of tourmaline, and zircon.

More sophisticated types of heating, however, are causing concern. Recently we have been seeing "heated" gems that are exposed to such high heat—often with glass or various gases or chemicals—that they are in a different category and lack the durability, and value, of others that have been exposed to more traditional heating techniques.

Diffusion Treatment

Diffusion is a recent addition to the world of gemstone treatments. There are several different processes being used—you will hear terms such as *surface* diffusion, *deep* diffusion, *bulk* diffusion, *lattice* diffusion, *beryllium* diffusion, or *elemental* diffusion—but the basic process is similar. It involves exposing the surface of the material to chemicals and heating it over a prolonged period, sometimes altering the atmosphere in which it is being heated. By so doing, the color of the treated material can be transformed into much "rarer" and more desirable colors. At present, diffusion is being used extensively to produce various colors of topaz, including green and pink, and much more desirable colors in sapphire—including various shades of blue, yellow, orange, and the rare pinkish-orange "padparadscha" color. Even "ruby" is being created from very common, inexpensive corundum. Diffusion is also used to create very natural-looking "star" rubies and sapphires. Diffusion treated gemstones should sell for *much less* than those treated by traditional heating techniques—about one-tenth the price of material treated by routine heating.

Usually the material being treated by diffusion techniques is colorless, pale, or heavily zoned, but extremely dark, almost black, material can also be improved by diffusion techniques. Early techniques produced stones in which color was confined to the surface (if you cut the stone in half you would see a very shallow rim of color around the perimeter of the stone, and a colorless interior) and a competent gemologist could easily identify them as diffusion treated. New processes are being used today that result in much deeper color penetration. These stones are much more difficult to detect and often require more sophisticated gemological testing and, in some cases, the services of a major gem-testing laboratory.

It is important to know whether or not the stone's color results from diffusion treatment so that you know you are paying an appropriate price. Furthermore, stones treated by some diffusion techniques require special care to prevent damage such as chipping, which might require recutting or polishing; if the color is confined to the surface, recutting or polishing could remove the color altogether. Should this happen, the stone can be retreated to restore the original color.

Unfortunately, diffused sapphires and rubies have been mixed in with parcels of nondiffused stones and some may have been inadvertently set in jewelry and sold without disclosure. So it is especially important to buy fine sapphires and rubies only from a reputable source, and to take what you purchase to a competent gemologist who can either verify your purchase, or determine that the services of a major gem-testing laboratory are required to know for sure.

Diffusion-treated stones offer affordable choices. Just take care to know whether or not the stone has been treated by diffusion techniques. If it has, pay the right price and exercise some care in wearing and handling it.

While diffusion treatment is being used routinely today on sapphire, ruby, and topaz, this treatment could have applications to other gemstone materials in the future. The increasingly popular gemstone called *andesine* has been found in many cases to have been diffusion-treated (see page 136). Andesine from Idaho is the only source at this time where natural color can be documented by lab reports. It should also be noted that sapphire produced in some parts of the world, such as Montana, is not subjected to diffusion treatments and is accompanied by a *guarantee* that no diffusion treatment is being used, only routine heating.

Radiation

Radiation techniques are relatively new. Frequently used on a wide range of gemstones, radiation is sometimes combined with heating. The effect is permanent on some stones, and when it is, it is accepted in the trade; it is not acceptable on other stones because the color fades or changes back to its original color over a relatively short time. There are still some questions regarding radiation levels and the long-term effects on health. The Nuclear Regulatory Agency has been working to establish standards, and the GIA Gem Trade Laboratory now has a facility with the capability to test gemstones for "acceptable" and six "unacceptable" radiation levels.

Until recently, virtually all blue topaz sold in jewelry stores was irradiated to obtain the various blue shades that have become so popular. Today these colors are also being created by using surface-coating and surface-diffusion techniques, but the color from surface treatments may not be permanent. Other gemstones that may have been irradiated to obtain color include deep-blue beryl (called maxixe; this color will always fade); yellow beryl; diamond; kunzite; yellow or orange sapphire (not stable; will fade quickly); yellow and green topaz; and red, pink, and purple tourmaline.

Fracture Filling

Fractures can interrupt light as it travels through a colored gemstone, creating a whitishness in the area of the fracture or, in some cases, reflecting back and making the fracture more noticeable. If a surface-reaching fracture is filled with the proper substance, the light will continue to pass through without blockage or reflection, so the color is not diminished and reflective fractures are much less noticeable because the reflectivity is greatly reduced. Certain gemstones, such as emerald, have more fractures than other gemstones because they form under extremely violent geological conditions. For this reason, emeralds are usually treated with fillers to reduce the visibility of fractures. The jewelry trade has always considered the oiling of emerald an acceptable practice, and it has been used routinely for many centuries. We don't know when the oiling of emerald began, but the practice was known during the Roman period, and we find many antique emerald pieces that still show traces of oil when examined with a microscope.

Today, gemstone treaters use various substances to fill fractures, including oil, wax, paraffin, glass, and various formulations of epoxy resin. Gemstones that may be treated with one of these substances include emerald, aquamarine, peridot, jade, turquoise, ruby, sapphire, and, in rare cases, alexandrite and garnet. Be especially alert to the possibility of fillers in ruby and sapphire; many rubies and sapphires from several new deposits contain reflective inclusions, so the use of oil and wax to improve the appearance of ruby and sapphire is increasing. A new ruby product is also being widely misrepresented as "treated" ruby when it is actually a new type of imitation, a composition of ruby and glass (see page 77).

Affordable Beauty

Treated gemstones can be a way for consumers to own lovely pieces at affordable prices. The most important consideration, here as in all purchases of gemstones, is to know exactly what you are buying. While some fraudulent practices involving treated stones certainly exist (see chapter 6), selling them is perfectly legitimate so long as all the facts are disclosed, the type of treatment used for enhancement is acceptable in the trade, and all important representations are stated on the bill of sale. With these safeguards you can be reasonably secure about the purchase you are contemplating and can enjoy the fine color and beauty of a treated stone for many years to come.

A Guide to Gemstone Treatments*

Name of Gemstone	Type of Treatment Used†	Frequency	Stability	Care Required	Comments
Alexandrite	O: to reduce visibility of fractures	Rarely	Very good/fair	Normal	Usually natural
Amber	H: to add spangles and improve color	Usually	Good to very good	Special	Avoid chemicals, ultrasonic cleaners
	D: surface treated	Rarely	Variable	Special	Avoid chemicals, ultrasonic cleaners
Amethyst (*see* quartz)					
Ametrine (*see* quartz)					
Ammolite	I: to increase stability	Usually	Good to fair	Special	Avoid heat, ultrasonic cleaners, chemicals
Beryl					
Aquamarine	H: to produce purer blue	Usually	Excellent	Normal	
Blue (maxixe— deep sapphire blue)	R: to create blue from colorless or pale pink	Always	Poor	Extra special	Color fades; avoid light, heat
Emerald	O: to reduce visibility of fractures	Usually	Very good to fair	Special	Avoid sudden temperature changes, steaming, chemicals, ultrasonic cleaners
	D: dye injected into fractures	Occasionally	Variable	Special	Same as above
Pink	H: to create purer pink	Commonly	Excellent	Normal	
Red	O	Commonly	Very good to fair	Special	Avoid ultrasonic cleaners, high heat/steam, chemicals
Yellow	R: to intensify color	Usually	Variable	Normal to special	Avoid prolonged exposure to light and heat
Yellow-green	**None**	NA	NA	Normal	

Chrysoberyl					
Cat's-eye	R: to change color	Occasionally	Excellent	Normal	Treatment by neutron radiation can create radioactive gemstones that may be dangerous to health: test at lab
Transparent varieties					
Alexandrite (*see* Alexandrite)					
Brown	None	NA	NA	Normal	
Green	None	NA	NA	Normal	
Yellow	None	NA	NA	Normal	
Citrine (*see* quartz)					
Coral					
Black	None	NA	NA	Normal	
White	B	Commonly	Good	Special	Avoid chemicals, cosmetics, ultrasonic cleaners
Pink	W	Commonly	Good	Special	"
Orange	I: stabilized with plastic	Commonly	Good	Special	"
Red	D	Occasionally	Variable	Special to extra special depending on dye used	"
Corundum					
Ruby	H: to improve color and clarity	Usually	Excellent	Normal	Avoid chemicals, ultrasonic cleaners
	D: with colored oil	Occasionally	Poor	Special	
	F: with several substances including glass and lead-glass	Commonly	Very good to very poor	Special	Fracture-filled rubies may be fragile, and filler may come out under extreme pressure: avoid heat, ultrasonic cleaners, chemicals (even lemon juice)

Chart continues on next page.

*Based on information developed by the American Gem Trade Association (AGTA).
†See page 62 for explanation of treatment codes used.

Name of Gemstone	Type of Treatment Used[†]	Frequency	Stability	Care Required	Comments
Corundum (*cont.*)					
Ruby (*cont.*)	R: to change color	Rarely	Unpredictable	Normal	Avoid repolishing, recutting since color is only on surface
	U: for "star" effect or to create color in pale, zoned, and colorless stones	Occasionally	Good	Special	
Sapphire	H: to improve color, clarity	Usually	Excellent	Normal	
	F: to reduce visibility or reflectivity of fractures	Occasionally	Very poor	Special	Avoid ultrasonic cleaners, chemicals
	U: for "star" effect or to create color in pale, zoned, and colorless stones	Occasionally	Good	Special	Avoid repolishing, recutting since color is only on surface
	R: to change color	Occasionally	Very poor	Extra special	Fades quickly in heat and light
Emerald (*see beryl*)					
Garnet[‡]					
Almandine	None	NA	NA	Normal	
Demantoid	O: to reduce visibility of fractures	Rarely	Fair	Special	Avoid harsh chemicals, ultrasonic cleaners
Pyrope	"	"	"	"	"
Rhodolite	"	"	"	"	"
Spessartite	"	"	"	"	"
Tsavorite	"	"	"	"	"
Hematite	None	NA	NA	Normal	
Iolite	None	NA	NA	Normal	
Jade					
Jadeite	W: with colorless wax	Commonly	Fair	Normal to special	Avoid ultrasonic cleaners
	B followed by W	Rarely	Poor	Special	Avoid heat, chemicals, ultrasonic cleaners
Green/white, purple	B followed by I	Commonly	Very good to good	Special	"

Nephrite	D				Avoid strong light, ultrasonic cleaners, chemicals
Kunzite (see spodumene)					
Lapis lazuli	W	Commonly	Fair	Normal to special	Avoid chemicals, ultrasonic cleaners
	D	Commonly	Variable	Special	"
Malachite	W	Occasionally	Fair	Special	"
	I	Rarely	Good	Special	"
Moonstone	None	NA	NA	Normal	
Opal					
White, black, semi-black	O: with oil, wax, resins	Rarely	Fair	Special	Avoid ultrasonic cleaners, heat, solvents
	I: with colorless plastic to improve durability	Rarely	Good	Special	Avoid heat, solvents
Matrix	D: by sugar-acid chemical reaction	Commonly	Good	Special	Avoid solvents
Boulder	O	Occasionally	Fair	Special	Avoid heat, chemicals, ultrasonic cleaners, repolishing
Fire opal	None	NA	NA	Special	Avoid heat
Peridot	O	Rarely	Good to fair	Special	Avoid sudden temperature changes, harsh chemicals, ultrasonic cleaners
Quartz					
Amethyst	H: to lighten color or remove smokiness	Often	Excellent	Special	Avoid long exposure to sunlight or heat
Ametrine	H: to create yellow portion of stone	Occasionally	Excellent	None	

†See page 62 for explanation of treatment codes used.

‡The use of fillers in garnet to reduce visibility of fractures has been reported; typically garnet is not enhanced and requires no special care.

Chart continues on next page.

Name of Gemstone	Type of Treatment Used†	Frequency	Stability	Care Required	Comments
Quartz (cont.)					
Citrine	H: to get yellow from other quartz varieties	Usually	Excellent	Normal	
Chalcedony varieties					
Agate	D	Usually	Excellent to good	Normal	
Banded	D	Usually	Excellent to good	Normal	
Blue	D	Commonly	Good to fair	Special	Some fade in light, heat
Green	D	Usually	Good to fair	Special	Some fade in light, heat
Jasper	D: to imitate other gems	Occasionally	Excellent	Normal	
Black onyx	D	Always	Excellent to good	Normal	
Carnelian	H: to produce color	Usually	Excellent	Normal	
Chrysoprase	None	NA	NA	Normal	
Rhodonite	D: to even out color	Occasionally	Poor	Special	Avoid chemicals, ultrasonic cleaners
Ruby (see corundum)					
Sapphire (see corundum)					
Serpentine	D or W	Commonly	Good to fair	Special	Dye may fade; avoid ultrasonic cleaners
Sodalite	D	Rarely	Fair	Special	Dye may fade; avoid acetone
Spinel	None	NA	NA	Normal	
Spodumene					
Kunzite	H	Commonly	Fair	Special	For natural or heated, avoid strong light, ultrasonic cleaners
	R	Commonly	Fair	Special	

Green	**R**: to produce color	Rarely	Poor	Extra special	Color fades in light, heat
Yellow	**R**: to produce color	Rarely	Poor	Extra special	Color fades in light, heat
Sugilite	None	NA	NA	Normal	
Tanzanite	**H**: to produce blue/violet color	Usually	Excellent	Special	Avoid sudden temperature change; may be somewhat brittle so wear with care
Topaz					
Blue	**R, H, and U**: to produce blue	Usually	Excellent	Special	Some may be radioactive; test at lab
Yellow/orange	**R**: to intensify color	Occasionally	Variable	Special	Avoid heat, strong light
Pink/red	**H**: to produce pink/red from orange and pinkish-brown stones	Usually	Excellent	Normal	
Brown	None	NA	NA	Normal	
Green	**R**: to produce color	Occasionally	Poor	Extra special	Color fades in sunlight
	U: surface color only	Usually	Good	Special	Don't repolish or recut
Tourmaline					
Chrome green	None	NA	NA	Normal	Avoid sudden temperature changes, steaming, chemicals, ultrasonic cleaners
Yellow/orange	**H**: to improve color	Rarely	Good	Normal	
Green, blue	**H**: to improve color	Commonly	Good	Normal	
	O: to improve clarity	Occasionally	Good to fair	Special	
Pink, red, purple	**H**: to improve color	Occasionally	Excellent	Normal	
	R: to intensify color	Commonly	Good	Normal	
	O: to improve clarity	Occasionally	Good to fair	Special	"
	D: to improve color	Occasionally	Fair to poor	Special	"

Chart continues on next page.

†See page 62 for explanation of treatment codes used.

Name of Gemstone	Type of Treatment Used†	Frequency	Stability	Care Required	Comments
Turquoise	I: to improve color, durability	Commonly	Good	Special	Avoid hot water and household cleaners
	W: to create color	Commonly	Fair to poor	Special	"
	D: to improve color	Rarely	Poor	Extra special	"
Zircon					
Green, brown	None	NA	NA	Special	Avoid abrasives; may be brittle so wear with care
Yellow	H: to improve color	Rarely	Good	Special	"
Blue, colorless	H: to change brownish crystals to colorless and blue	Always	Fair to poor	Special	Avoid abrasives, strong light; may be brittle so wear with care
Red	H: to change brownish crystals to red	Commonly	Fair to poor	Special	"

† **Key to Table: Symbols for Specific Types of Enhancements Used**

B: bleaching—using heat, light, or chemical agents to lighten or take color out of a gemstone

D: dyeing—infusing a coloring agent into a gemstone to create color, change color, enrich color, or produce the appearance of more even color distribution

F: filling—filling surface-reaching fractures or cavities with *colorless* glass, plastic, solidified borax, or similar substances, which are visible to a trained gemologist using 10x magnification with proper lighting

H: heating—using heat to alter or improve color and clarity, and to create optical phenomena such as a cat's-eye or star effect

I: impregnation—using a *colorless* substance, usually plastic, to impregnate a porous gemstone to improve appearance and/or durability

O: oiling/resin infusion—using *colorless* oil, wax, resin, or other substances, except glass or plastic, to fill surface-reaching fractures to improve appearance

R: irradiation—using neutron, gamma and/or electron bombardment to alter a gemstone's color; irradiation treatment may be combined with heating

U: diffusion—coating the surface of a gemstone with chemicals and heating at high temperatures to produce color on the surface of a gemstone, or to produce a star effect

W: waxing/oiling—impregnating a porous opaque gemstone such as turquoise or a translucent gemstone such as jade with *colorless* wax, paraffin, or oil to improve appearance

Various types of treatments are now used to improve the appearance of colored gemstones. Most treatments are accepted within the jewelry industry, but the value of treated gems is significantly affected by the *type of treatment* used and *how extensively* it is used. For this reason, the international gemological community developed a system to provide this information on laboratory reports. A chart from the Asian Institute of Gemological Sciences (AIGS) Laboratory (see facing page) provides an example of the designations and language used today by most respected labs to cover the type and extent of treatment. As new treatments are introduced, these codes may be revised or expanded.

As this chart illustrates, treatment issues are complex. For this reason, we recommend that colored gemstones be purchased only from knowledgeable sources that can provide complete treatment information or explain the information provided on any report that might accompany a gemstone you are considering. If the gemstone is not accompanied by a laboratory report, we highly recommend getting verification of quality and treatment from a gemologist-appraiser, and in the event the gemologist lacks the equipment to confirm the type of treatment used, that it be submitted to a laboratory to obtain a treatment report.

AIGS Laboratory New Disclosure Comments for Heat Process:

(for Full report, Brief report and e-Report)

1 - AIGS Grading Code for Foreign Substances (Flux residues) in Fissures and / or Cavities.

Effect of Heat Process	No Residue found	Foreign substance in Fissures			Foreign substance in Cavities		
Amount of Foreign Substance		minor	moderate	significant	minor	moderate	significant
AIGS Foreign Substance Grading Code	no						
	HT	HT(a)	HT(b)	HT(c)	HT(1)	HT(2)	HT(3)

Example: **HT (a.2)** means: **Minor** amount of residues in **fissures** and **Moderate** amount of residues in **cavities**.

2- Other Codes:

HT (Pb)   This stone has been clarity enhanced by heat process - **Lead-rich* foreign substance found in fissures and/or cavities**.

HT (Ba)   This stone has been clarity enhanced by heat process - **Barium-rich* foreign substance found in fissures and/or cavities**.

HT (Bi)   This stone has been clarity enhanced by heat process - **Bismuth-rich* foreign substance found in fissures and/or cavities**.

HT (LE)   **This stone has been enhanced by heat process with light element(s) (including Be*).**

HT (SD)   **This stone has been enhanced by heat process using surface diffusion process** (Some or all of the color is artificially created and lies just at and below the surface in a thin layer - color is stable but may be removed by (re)cutting or (re)polishing).

*: "**Pb**" is the symbol for Lead element, "**Ba**" is the symbol for Barium element, "**Bi**" is the symbol for Bismuth element and "**Be**" is the symbol for Beryllium element.

Remark: The mention "**Not LIBS tested**" on a report means that the stone wasn't tested for Light Elements treatment.

Note: New codes are effective starting from 15ᵗʰ August, 2009.

CHAPTER SIX

Fraud & Misrepresentation in Colored Gems

I would like to begin by emphasizing here that the percentage of misrepresentation and fraud in jewelry transactions overall is quite low, and that most jewelers are reputable professionals in whom you can place your trust. In the colored-gem market, there is a greater occurrence of misrepresentation than in the diamond market, however, primarily because of the scientifically complex nature of colored stones. So it is even more important to be aware of the deceptive practices you might encounter when buying a colored gem, both to protect yourself from the more obvious scams and to better understand the importance of dealing with a reliable jeweler. I also stress the importance, to an even greater degree, of seeking verification from a qualified gemologist—one with extensive experience with colored gems—when buying any expensive colored gem to ensure that your gemstone is what it is represented to be.

Misrepresenting Synthetic as Natural

Today it is very important to verify the genuineness of any fine, valuable gemstone because the new generation of synthetic products is so similar to the natural that the two can easily be confused. As I discussed in chapter 5, many very fine synthetics are available, and they can make attractive jewelry choices when properly represented. Still, you should protect yourself from intentional and sometimes unintentional misrepresentation.

Synthetics have been on the market for many years. Good synthetic sapphires, rubies, and spinels have been manufactured commercially since the early 1900s, and very good synthetic emeralds since the 1940s. While these early synthetics were attractive and popular because of their very low price, they didn't really look like natural stones. Most looked "too good to be true," so that they were readily distinguished from the real thing by a competent jeweler.

Today, this is often not the case. While older techniques for producing synthetics are still used and their products are still easy to recognize, new, sophisticated methods result in products that no longer possess the signature characteristics with which gem dealers and jewelers have long been familiar. To further complicate matters of identification, synthetics now often contain characteristics very similar to their natural counterparts. As a result, some are being sold as natural, intentionally and unintentionally. A gemologist with extensive experience, or a gem-testing laboratory such as the Gemological Institute of America (GIA) Gem Trade Laboratory (GTL) or American Gemological Laboratories (AGL), can differentiate between them and verify genuineness.

A true experience dramatically illustrates why making the extra effort required to verify genuineness is so important. I know a jeweler with an excellent reputation for honesty, reliability, and professional expertise. He had been in the business for many years and had extensive gemological training. Nonetheless, he bought a new type of synthetic ruby as a natural stone, then sold it to a customer for just under $10,000.

His customer, who had purchased the stone at a reasonable price, proceeded to resell it to a third party for a quick profit. The third party took it to a very competent gemologist with a reputation for having the skill and equipment necessary to identify new synthetic materials. The truth about the stone quickly came to light. The second and third parties in this case lost nothing (one of the benefits of buying from a reputable jeweler). The jeweler, however, suffered both a heavy financial loss and considerable damage to his reputation.

You may ask how he made such a mistake. It was easy. He was knowledgeable, like many other jewelers, and thought he knew how to distinguish a natural from a synthetic stone. But he had not kept current on technological advances and new synthetic products entering the marketplace. So he made an over-the-counter purchase of this lovely stone from a private party who had procured it in Asia. Many of these new synthetics are produced in the United States and then find their way to Asia—the source of many natural stones—where they are more easily sold as the "real thing." The jeweler had no recourse because he had no way of locating the seller, who had simply walked in off the street.

As this story shows, it is essential to have a highly qualified gemologist verify authenticity, particularly for fine rubies, emeralds, and sapphires. Thousands of dollars may be at stake, because jewelers may innocently buy one of these stones, believing it to be natural, and pass their error on to the customer. Don't delude yourself into believing that if a piece is purchased from a well-respected firm it is always what it is represented to be; even the best-known firms have made mistakes in this area. It may be inconvenient to obtain an expert analysis, and it may require an additional expense, but I believe it is better to be safe now than sorry later.

With sophisticated modern equipment and a greater knowledge of crystals, humans can now "create" or "grow" almost any gemstone. As a general rule, remember that any gem—alexandrite, amethyst, emerald, opal, ruby, sapphire, or even turquoise—could be synthetic, that many synthetics are themselves expensive, and that most have become more difficult to distinguish from their natural counterparts, resulting in inadvertent misrepresentation. So make sure you take time to verify a stone's true identity.

Simulated Stones

As already discussed (see chapter 5), simulated or imitation stones should not be confused with synthetics, which possess essentially the same physical, chemical, and optical properties of the natural gem. A simulated stone is usually a very inexpensive artificial imitation that resembles the natural stone in color, but little else. Many imitations are glass, but they can also be plastic. Imitations, or simulants as they are also called, are very easily differentiated from the genuine by careful visual examination and simple gemological testing. There are glass simulations of all the colored stones, and glass and plastic simulated pearls, turquoise, and amber are also common.

Imitations are frequently found in estate jewelry, sometimes mixed with natural gems in the same piece.

Look-Alike Substitution

Another form of deception involves misrepresenting a more common, less expensive stone for a rarer, more expensive gem of similar color. Today, as more and more natural gemstones in a wide variety of colors enter the market, both deliberate and accidental misrepresentation can occur.

Color and Clarity Enhancement

As I discussed in chapter 5, color enhancement of gemstones is not new, and many techniques used routinely today have been used for generations and do not in themselves constitute fraud. Some treatments, however, should not be applied to certain gems, normally because the results are not permanent and the color may revert to the original. Such treatments are not accepted by the trade.

Because color enhancement is so common, it's important for you to understand exactly which procedures are acceptable in the industry and which represent deceptive or fraudulent practices aimed at passing off inferior stones as much more expensive ones.

Here I will discuss various treatments and explain which are routine and which may constitute fraud or misrepresentation.

Heat-Treated Stones

Subjecting stones to sophisticated heating procedures is the most commonly used method of changing or enhancing a gem's color and is used routinely on a variety of gems to lighten, darken, or completely change color. Heat treatment is not a fraudulent practice when used on certain gems, on which the results are *permanent*. ***This procedure is an accepted practice routinely applied to the following stones:***

- *Amber*—to deepen color and add "sun spangles"
- *Amethyst*—to lighten color; to change color of pale material to "yellow" stones sold as citrine
- *Aquamarine*—to deepen color and remove any greenish undertone to produce a "bluer" blue
- *Carnelian*—to produce color
- *Citrine*—often produced by heating other varieties of quartz
- *Kunzite*—to improve color
- *Morganite*—to change color from orange to pinkish
- *Sapphire*—to lighten or intensify color; to improve uniformity
- *Tanzanite*—to produce a more desirable blue shade
- *Topaz*—in combination with radiation, to produce shades of blue; to produce pink
- *Tourmaline*—to lighten the darker shades, usually of the green and blue varieties
- *Zircon*—to produce red, blue, or colorless stones

The color obtained by these heating procedures is usually permanent.

Diffusion-Treated Stones

Sapphire and ruby. As mentioned in chapter 5, diffusion treatment is a method used to transform a colorless, pale, or heavily zoned stone into a much more desirable—and valuable—color by introducing chemicals into its surface and heating it over a prolonged period of time. Initially, the chemicals used were the same chemicals used by nature and created color on the surface only. Today, other chemicals are also used and color penetration is often much deeper and more difficult to detect. Colors produced by diffusion include yellow, orange, blue, red, and the rare orangy-pink known as "padparadscha."

Diffused rubies and sapphires are now being produced in many colors and are being substituted for nondiffused stones by unscrupulous merchants and purchased by dealers and jewelers unknowingly in parcels of stones that are subsequently mounted in jewelry. They are also being set in antique and estate jewelry. When you are buying any fine sapphire today, it is important to purchase from a knowledgeable, reputable jeweler. Be especially wary of bargains. Diffusion-treated "ruby" is less common than treated sapphire, but when buying *any* fine ruby or sapphire, in *any* color, we recommend getting a report from a respected gem-testing lab (see appendix).

Topaz. Diffusion treatment creates a lovely green color not found in nature, and the iridescent "mystic" topaz results from coating the surface with chemicals and applying heat. "Pink" topaz that looks like the costly natural pink can also be created by diffusion treatment, but it should sell for a fraction of the price of natural pink topaz.

There is nothing wrong with buying diffused stones as long as you know they are diffused and pay the right price (approximately one-tenth the cost of a comparable stone that has been subjected to routine heating only). You must also be aware that extra care may be required when wearing diffusion-treated stones to reduce the risk of chipping.

Irradiated Stones

Radiation techniques are now in common use, produced by any of several methods, each of which has a specific application. Sometimes radiation is used in combination with heat treatment. As long as the technique produces stable results, color enhancement by radiation techniques is not considered fraudulent.

Radiation techniques are routinely used for the following stones and do not constitute fraud:

- *Diamond*—to change the color from an off-white color to a fancy color (green, yellow, etc.)
- *Kunzite*—to darken color
- *Pearl*—to produce blue and shades of gray ("black" pearls)
- *Topaz*—to change from colorless or nearly colorless to blue; to intensify yellow and orange shades and create green
- *Tourmaline*—to intensify pink, red, and purple shades
- *Yellow beryl*—to create yellow color

Some very deep-blue topazes have been found to be radioactive and may be harmful to the wearer. Most blue topaz sold in the United States since 1992 has been tested for radiation level by the GIA or other centers established for that purpose. Exercise caution when purchasing deep-blue topaz outside the United States in countries where radiation testing is not required.

As far as we know now, the color changes resulting from radiation treatment on the above stones are usually permanent. Some stones subjected to radiation, however, obtain a beautiful color that is temporary. Some irradiated "blue," "orange," and "yellow" sapphires will fade quickly. I have seen nice "yellow" sapphires treated by radiation quickly lose their color when exposed to the flame of a cigarette lighter. If you are considering a "yellow," it may be worthwhile to try this simple flame test if the jeweler will permit. If not, be sure to have it fade tested by a qualified gemologist or gem lab. Deep-blue beryl known as *maxixe* beryl is created by irradiating off-color or pale beryl, but the color is *not* permanent and it *fades quickly*. (There has been a recent discovery in Canada and Pakistan of naturally deep-blue beryl with a color that does not fade. While not yet commercially available, this may change as production increases.) Irradiation of sapphire and blue beryl is not accepted in the trade.

When diamonds are irradiated to produce fancy colors, labs can usually determine that they have been treated. However, for most other gems on which radiation is used, testing procedures for determining whether or not color is natural have not been developed as of this date.

Dyed Stones

Gemstones have been dyed since the earliest times. Numerous examples of dyed chalcedony (an inexpensive variety of quartz) can be found in antique jewelry, imitating other gems. Gems that are frequently dyed include jade, opal, coral, lapis, and to a lesser degree, poor-quality star rubies, star sapphires, and emeralds.

Dyed material may be very stable, but it can also be very temporary. We've seen dyed lapis in which the "blue" came off with a cotton ball moistened in fingernail polish remover. Dyed gems may be genuine stones that have been dyed to enhance their color (as in dyeing pale green jadeite to a deeper green), or they may be a different gem altogether.

Dyed gems should always cost less than gems with natural color. Fine lapis and jadeite should always be checked for dyeing. Here are some gemstones that are often *faked* using dyeing techniques:

- *Black onyx*—dyed chalcedony (onyx rarely occurs naturally)
- *Banded agate*—dyed chalcedony, with white bands alternating with strong-colored bands
- *Carnelian*—chalcedony dyed reddish brown
- *Chrysoprase*—chalcedony dyed green
- *Jade (jadeite)*—chalcedony dyed green to imitate fine jadeite
- *Swiss lapis*—jasper dyed blue and sold as "lapis" or "Swiss lapis"

Here are some gemstones that are often dyed to change or improve color:

- *Jade (jadeite)*—color frequently improved by dyeing to a beautiful emerald or young grass-green color, to look like "imperial" jade (while jade occurs naturally in almost every color, it may also be dyed other colors)
- *Coral and lapis*—dyed to deepen the color or create more uniform color

Blackening Techniques

These are used to alter color, not by dyeing but by introducing a sugar-acid chemical reaction that creates black carbon, which blackens the color. The following stones are commonly faked by using this treatment:

- *Black onyx*—blackened chalcedony (black onyx rarely occurs naturally; most is actually blackened chalcedony)
- *Black opal*—blackened white opal (black opal is more valuable and precious)

Waxing

This is a process consisting of rubbing the stone with a tinted wax-like substance to hide surface cracks and blemishes and to slightly improve the color. It is used often on cheaper Indian star rubies and sometimes on star sapphires.

Oiling

Emerald. This technique is commonly used on emeralds. The emerald is soaked in oil (which may or may not be tinted green) to fill fine cracks, which are fairly common in emerald. These cracks look whitish and therefore weaken the green body color of the emerald. The oil fills the cracks, making them "disappear," and thereby improves the color by eliminating the white. It can also reduce the reflectivity of cracks.

This is an accepted procedure and will normally last for many years. However, if the stone is put in a hot ultrasonic cleaner (which is dangerous to any emerald and is *never* recommended), or soaked in an organic solvent such as gasoline, xylene, or substances containing these, such as paint remover, the oil may be slowly dissolved out of the cracks and the whitish blemishes will then reappear, weakening the color. If this should happen, the stone can be re-oiled. Using green-tinted oil, however, is not an accepted trade practice.

Other Gems. Oiling, usually colorless, is now used on other gems including sapphire, ruby, and rare garnet varieties to reduce the visibility of cracks or fissures.

Painting

This technique is often used with cabochon (nonfaceted) transparent ("jelly") or semitransparent opals to create a stone that looks like precious black opal. This is done by putting the stone in a closed-back setting that has a high rim (bezel). A black cement or paint is spread on the inside of the setting so that when the opal is placed inside, the light entering it gets trapped and reflected back, giving the opal the appearance of a fine black opal. (See also the section below, describing composite stones and opal doublets.)

Foil-Backed Stones

This technique is not frequently encountered in modern jewelry but is relatively common in antique jewelry, and anyone interested in antique jewelry should be aware of it. It is seen with both nonfaceted and faceted stones, usually set in a closed-back mounting. This technique involves lining the inside of the setting with silver or gold foil to add brilliance and sparkle (as with foil-backed glass imitating diamond), or with colored foil to change or enhance color by projecting color into the stone. Always be apprehensive when considering a piece of jewelry that has a closed back.

I recently examined a heavy yellow-gold cross set with five fine, flawless emeralds, which appeared to have exceptionally fine green body color. The stones were set "in the gold" so that the backs of the stones couldn't be seen. My suspicion was aroused, since the emeralds were all flawless and the color was so uniformly fine. Upon closer examination it became clear that the green body color was projected into the stones by a fine emerald-green foil back. The stones were probably not even emerald, but near-colorless aquamarines. Since both aquamarine and emerald belong to the same mineral family, beryl (*emerald* is the name given to the rare green variety of beryl, while we call the more common blue variety aquamarine), an inexperienced jeweler or gemologist using standard, basic procedures to identify the stones could have erroneously identified them as fine emeralds.

Smoking

This is a technique used only on opals. It is used to give off-white to tan-colored opals from Mexico a more desirable, moderately dark coffee-brown color that greatly enhances the opal fire. It consists of taking a cut and polished opal, wrapping it tightly in brown paper, and putting it in a covered container over moderate heat until the paper is completely charred. When cooled and removed, the opal now has a much more intense brown body color and fire. But if this smoke-produced color coating were to be badly scratched, the underlying color would show through and the stone would have to be resmoked.

This treatment can be easily detected by wetting the stone (preferably with saliva). While it is wet, some of the fire disappears; then it reappears after the surface has dried.

Fracture Filling with Glass and Epoxy Resins

Fractures that break the surface of a colored gem can be filled with a liquid glass or glasslike substance, or with an epoxy resin–type filler. Fillers make cracks less visible and improve a stone's overall appearance. A coloring agent can also be added to the filler to simultaneously improve a stone's overall color. Selling a filled gem without disclosure is not an accepted trade practice. To do so knowingly constitutes fraud. Nonetheless, the number of glass-filled rubies encountered in the marketplace and sold without disclosure has increased dramatically. Emeralds filled with epoxy resin are now in wide circulation and often are sold without disclosure of the presence of epoxy.

There is also a new ruby product in the marketplace that is being represented as "treated" ruby (in some cases the sellers misrepresent them to be only "heated," and in some cases, as "glass-filled"), but these products are altered so dramatically that they are in a different category from treated ruby. The product being sold is actually not "treated" but an artificial composite product created by a new technique (see p. 77).

Composite Stones

Composite stones are exactly what the term implies: stones composed of more than one part. Historically, composites included two basic types: *doublets* and *triplets*. Doublets are composite stones consisting of two parts, sometimes held together by a colored bonding agent. Triplets are composite stones consisting of three parts, usually glued together to a colored middle part. Today, however, we are seeing a new type of "composite" that is being called "composite ruby" (see p. 77).

Doublets

Doublets are especially important to know about because, while they were widely used in antique jewelry before the development of synthetics, today they are making a comeback and reappearing throughout the jewelry market.

In antique pieces, the most commonly encountered doublet, often referred to as a *false doublet,* consists of a red garnet top fused to an appropriately colored glass bottom. With the right combination, any colored gem could be simulated by this method. Garnets were used for the top portion of these false doublets because they possessed nice luster and excellent durability and were readily available in great quantity, which made them very inexpensive.

Another form of the doublet is made from two parts of a colorless material, fused together with an appropriately colored bonding agent. An "emerald" (sometimes sold as *soudé* emerald) can be made, for example, using a colorless synthetic spinel top and bottom, held together in the middle (at the girdle) by green glue. Red glue or blue glue could be used to simulate ruby or sapphire.

True doublets are created by using two genuine stone parts and fusing them together with an appropriately colored glue to create a "larger" gem of better color than the original components. For example, we sometimes see emerald doublets composed of two parts of genuine pale green emerald, fused with deep green glue to create a large, deep green "gem" emerald.

A clever version of a true doublet that we sometimes still encounter is a "sapphire" doublet composed of two pieces of genuine sapphire, but pale yellow sapphire fused together with blue glue. This creates an especially convincing "fine blue sapphire." The same techniques are used to make ruby doublets, although they don't look as convincing. And the same basic procedures can produce emerald doublets, using beryl instead of sapphire.

Opal doublets also occur, usually consisting of a thin top layer of genuine opal cemented to a base that can be either a poorer grade of opal or some other substance altogether. The most commonly encountered opal doublets are those made to look like the precious black opal. These doublets are usually composed of a translucent or transparent top, cemented by black cement to a bottom portion of cheaper opal or other material that acts as a support. Please note that the tops of these "black opal" doublets are usually not genuine black opal, though they certainly look like it.

Opal doublets are also made by cementing a thin piece of fine opal to a larger piece of less fine opal to create a larger overall appearance. The doublets can be identified by observing the *join* of the two pieces at the girdle; you can see the dark line of the cement between the two pieces.

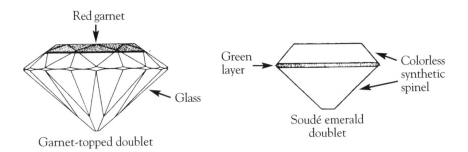

Red garnet

Glass

Garnet-topped doublet

Green layer

Colorless synthetic spinel

Soudé emerald doublet

When some composite stones are immersed in liquid (such as alcohol or methylene iodide), one can often see two or three distinct parts. With soudé emeralds, the top and bottom may seem to disappear, leaving only a green plane visible across the girdle area. (*Note*: Immersion will not reveal garnet-topped doublets.)

Because so many doublets are flooding the market, those who love sapphire, ruby, and emerald must be particularly careful and buy only from reputable jewelers. I know a woman who paid $16,000 recently for a pair of "genuine" emerald earrings from a jeweler on New York's 47th Street. They contained four soudé emerald doublets and were worth only a couple hundred dollars—and that for the gold and diamonds in the settings. Luckily, this woman had all the right information on the bill of sale, discovered the error in time, and was able to return the pieces and get her money back from the jeweler.

It is alarming to see the large number of ruby and sapphire doublets consisting of genuine tops—usually nearly colorless or a very inexpensive greenish brown color—and synthetic sapphire and ruby bottoms that are being sold as genuine. Avoid "bargains" from any merchant unless you can check them out. Be especially wary of street peddlers when you are traveling in Asia and South America. We've seen an incredible number of doublets in jewelry and unmounted stones brought back by unsuspecting travelers, especially those journeying to exotic spots known for gems.

Many of the doublets now appearing in jewelry sold by reputable firms were originally slipped in with genuine stones shipped to buyers around the world. Since doublets are difficult to spot and will even pass four gemological tests providing positive identification, it is easy for one to be passed on to a customer unknowingly, especially when it is set in a sleek, modern bezel setting.

There is nothing wrong with buying a doublet as long as you know what you are buying and pay a fair price. Just be careful not to buy a doublet unknowingly. Be sure to verify all the facts.

Triplets

Triplets are frequently encountered in the opal market and, because of opal's increasing rarity, have substantially replaced the doublet there. The triplet is like the opal doublet except that it uses a thinner opal layer that is then completely covered by a cabochon-shaped colorless quartz cap (the third part), providing the delicate doublet greater protection from breakage and greater luminescence (brightness). We are also seeing an increasing number of *mosaic* opal triplets, in which the opal layer is made of multiple small pieces of opal rather than a single piece. The quartz cap is then placed over this layer as in other triplets.

Colored Gemstones
The Rarest of Them All...

*Each a thing of beauty and preciousness,
unique and mysterious.*

Red and Pink Gemstones to Warm Any Heart

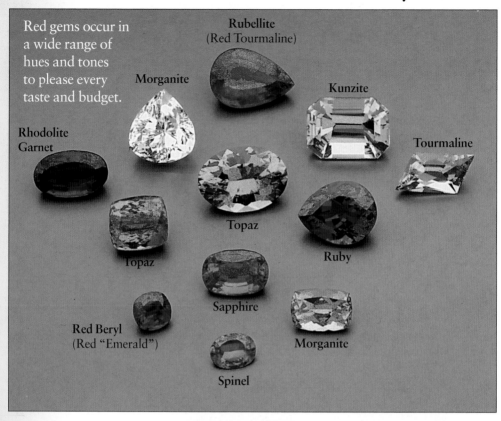

Red gems occur in a wide range of hues and tones to please every taste and budget.

Rubellite (Red Tourmaline)

Morganite

Kunzite

Rhodolite Garnet

Tourmaline

Topaz

Topaz

Ruby

Red Beryl (Red "Emerald")

Sapphire

Morganite

Spinel

Rare red beryl, also referred to as red "emerald"—

Left: The crystal as it occurs in nature.

Right: A brilliantly cut and polished gem waiting to be set.

A six-rayed **star ruby.**

Right: **Rhodochrosite,** an oval cabochon and a rare round faceted stone.

Blue Gemstones Offer Heavenly Choices

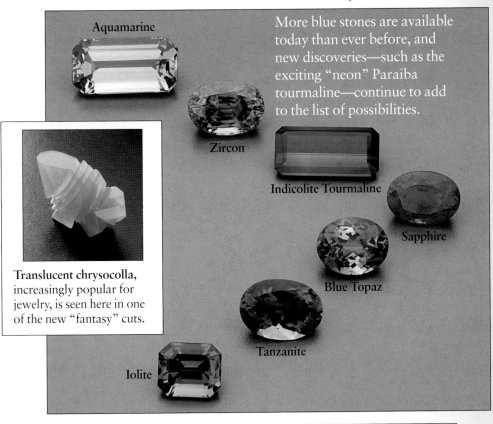

Aquamarine

Zircon

Indicolite Tourmaline

Sapphire

Blue Topaz

Tanzanite

Iolite

More blue stones are available today than ever before, and new discoveries—such as the exciting "neon" Paraiba tourmaline—continue to add to the list of possibilities.

Translucent chrysocolla, increasingly popular for jewelry, is seen here in one of the new "fantasy" cuts.

"Neon" tourmaline
from Paraiba, Brazil.

Exceptionally fine **star sapphire,** showing strong star, can be very costly today.

Moonstones, exhibiting their magical "adularescence"—a bright, billowing, milky sheen moving within the stone.

Yellow and Orange Gems to Brighten the Day

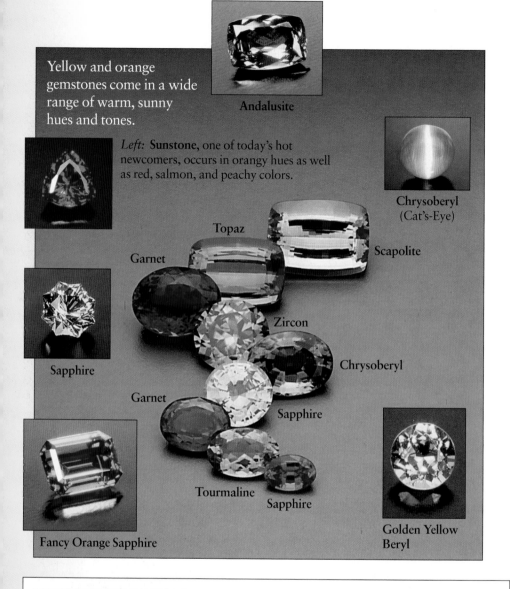

Yellow and orange gemstones come in a wide range of warm, sunny hues and tones.

Andalusite

Left: **Sunstone**, one of today's hot newcomers, occurs in orangy hues as well as red, salmon, and peachy colors.

Chrysoberyl (Cat's-Eye)

Topaz

Garnet

Scapolite

Zircon

Chrysoberyl

Sapphire

Garnet

Sapphire

Tourmaline

Sapphire

Sapphire

Fancy Orange Sapphire

Golden Yellow Beryl

Precious topaz, also known as "imperial" topaz.

Notice the similarity in color between some citrine and topaz. Citrine is often mistaken and misrepresented as topaz. Citrine is a lovely gem, but it is less brilliant, less rare, and less costly than topaz.

Citrine, a member of the quartz family, comes in shades from pale yellow to rich amber.

Green Gems That Everyone Will Envy

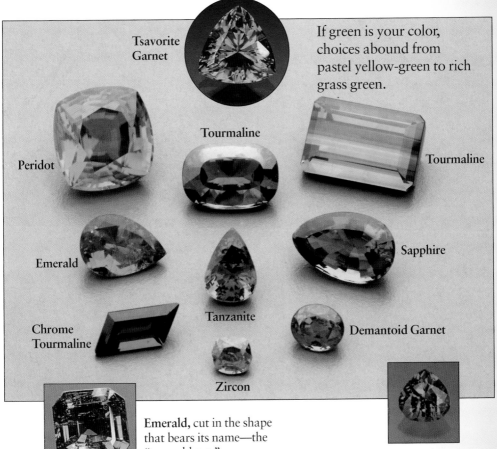

Tsavorite Garnet

If green is your color, choices abound from pastel yellow-green to rich grass green.

Tourmaline

Peridot

Tourmaline

Emerald

Sapphire

Chrome Tourmaline

Tanzanite

Demantoid Garnet

Zircon

Emerald, cut in the shape that bears its name—the "emerald cut."

Paraiba Tourmaline

Fine art deco period brooch with very fine green **jadeite** centerpiece.

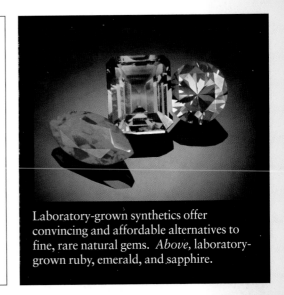

Laboratory-grown synthetics offer convincing and affordable alternatives to fine, rare natural gems. *Above,* laboratory-grown ruby, emerald, and sapphire.

Opals—A Fiery World of Color

In addition to the widely available white opal, very affordable "fire" opals and rare, costly black opals create excitement.

Above: Gaia Pelikan's boulder opal in 18-karat red gold and forged stainless steel. *Left:* Magnificent pendant by Kreg Scully, sculpted from white opal with semi-black opal inlay.

Australian **Andamooka crystal opal** and **Andamooka matrix opal** beads.

Mexican "fire" opals.

Below left: **Fine black opal**
Below right: **Boulder opal**

Color-Change Gems—Keep the Mystery Alive

Color-change gems have captivated collectors for generations, beginning with the nineteenth-century Russian discovery of rare and costly alexandrite. Today, other exotic color-change gems are being unearthed and adding distinctive choices. Note: in all color-change gems shown here, the left image is color seen in daylight, and right image is seen in incandescent light.

Zultanite (color-change diaspore).

Color-change garnet *(left)*, color-change spinel *(below)*.

Color-change alexandrite.

Classic Shapes and Cutting Styles

Briolette styles, an old cutting style enjoying a resurgence in popularity. Great for earrings, pendants, and necklaces.

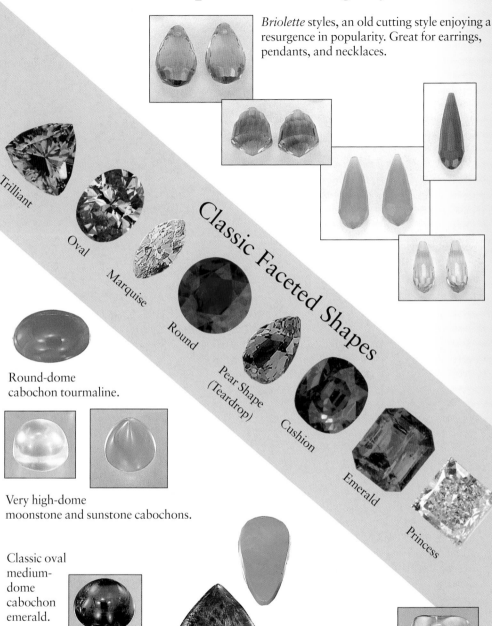

Classic Faceted Shapes

Trilliant

Oval

Marquise

Round

Pear Shape
(Teardrop)

Cushion

Emerald

Princess

Round-dome
cabochon tourmaline.

Very high-dome
moonstone and sunstone cabochons.

Classic oval
medium-
dome
cabochon
emerald.

Classic high-
dome oval
garnet
cabochon.

Classic *flat*
cabochons: pear-
shape turquoise and
multicolor
tourmaline.

Variations on the
"sugarloaf"
cabochon style.

Gemstone Cutters and Carvers...

Master cutters such as David Brackna, Michael Dyber, John Dyer, Mark Gronlund, Richard Homer, Glenn Lehrer, Steve Walters, and Clay Zava are changing the world of gemstone faceting. Their innovative *concave* faceting styles—often combined with other techniques—are winning prestigious international awards and producing dramatic new looks applauded by top designers seeking unique gemstones for their distinctive creations.

PHOTO: ROBERT WELDON

Faceting artist David Brackna's work *(above)* reflects great versatility, combining concave faceting, traditional faceting, carving, and inlay.

Triangular amethysts show effect of *concave* faceting by Mark Gronlund *(right)* compared to traditional faceting.

PHOTO: ROBERT WELDON

PHOTOS: LYDIA DYER

PHOTO: CLAY ZAVA

Innovative *pillow-cut* blue topaz by Clay Zava.

John Dyer has mastered *combination* faceting, as seen in these beautiful lime citrine, morganite, and golden beryl pieces.

David Brackna's Optical Inlay *(below)* achieves an amazing effect here; opal is inlaid above the culet of this concave-faceted green beryl.

Richard Homer's suite of concave-faceted gemstones attests to his skill as one of today's top award-winning artists in the world of faceting.

PHOTO: ROBERT WELDON

PHOTO: ROBERT WELDON

...Artists Creating a New Style

Artist Michael Dyber's signature Luminaire *(below)*, a 95-carat yellow citrine that is part of the permanent collection at the Carnegie Museum of Natural History, Pittsburgh, Pennsylvania, and his creation that took first place at the 40th German Award for Jewelry & Precious Stones in Idar-Oberstein, a 113.24-carat aquamarine *(left)* cut using his signature Dyber Optic Dish™ technique.

The TorusRing™ gem cut created by Glenn Lehrer *(above)* has the designer world in a whirl. Here in tanzanite, Paraiba tourmaline, and pink and orange garnet.

Cutting pioneer Bart Curren's rainbow-obsidian sculpture *(far right)* and his innovative enameled quartz *(right)* are boldly different.

Artist Mark Gronlund's concave-faceted gem adds drama to Gary Dulac's orange citrine pendant *(right)*. His 45-carat aquamarine *(above)* was an AGTA Cutting Edge Award winner.

Master carver Steve Walters combines shape, textured black onyx, rutilated quartz, and color for striking creations that can be used in a wide range of jewelry creations.

Gemstone Artists Create Objets d'Art...

From artistically executed sculptures to exquisite treasure chests to sensual "objets" to adorn the vanity, gemstone artists are moving from the jewelry salon to museums and art galleries.

One of Nicolai Medvedev's intricately executed *intarsia* boxes. Medvedev's work has been compared to that of Fabergé. His creations were on exhibition at the Smithsonian Institution in Washington, D.C.—the first one-man show ever produced for a living artist—and ran for an unprecedented 2½ years.

Michael Dyber's rich, sensual sculpture in very fine lapis.

Susan Allen's "Ocean Magic," carved in natural quartz crystals showing three dolphins, a smiling moray eel, and brain coral in this whimsical three-dimensional work.

Two exquisite carvings by Glenn Lehrer. The one above is carved from lavender drusy agate, topped with a lavender pearl and diamond. The masterpiece at right is constructed like a puzzle, without metal or glue. The yellow sapphire TorusRing™ is *friction-set* in black jade with blue chalcedony and stained-black drusy agate. It is all locked into place by a very thin, straw-like jade tube—fibrous and thin, flexible and durable. It is 3½" x 2¼".

One of David Brackna's Lightscape Optical Mosaics. The work was created from 32 pieces of amethyst, citrine, rock crystal, and ametrine and weighs 495 carats.

...and Art to Wear

Aromajewels®, designed and cut by Brian Cook, combine personalized aromatherapy in a line of sensual natural gemstone pendants, uniquely cut and balanced so that the oils remain within even if the pendant is inverted. Mandarin garnet heart *(top)*, sunstone *(center)*, and rutilated quartz *(below)*.

Award-winning gemstone artists Susan Allen and Michael Christie have combined their unique skills to create an unparalleled collection of *essence bottles* to adorn the vanity...or travel with you as the jewels you wear! Ms. Allen does the internal carvings for Mr. Christie's romantic creations. "Ambrosia," a three-dimensional work containing a "dipper" that converts to a pendant necklace, and accent stones that can be removed and worn as earrings: amethyst on a jadeite base, topped by pearl; lower base is charoite. The dipper is a natural emerald crystal, and is attached to the pearl for a stunning pendant *(left)*. All accent stones are emerald, and the rubellite earrings *(below)* are a surprise, hidden under the amethyst bottle. This work was on exhibition at the Carnegie Museum of Natural History, Pittsburgh, Pennsylvania.

Ornamental Stones

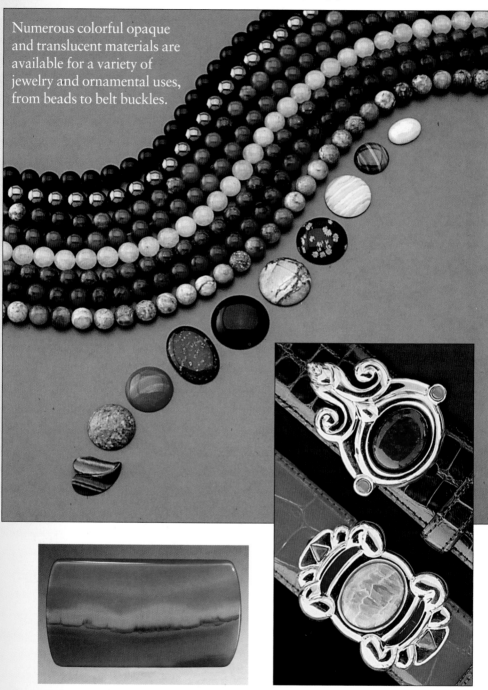

Numerous colorful opaque and translucent materials are available for a variety of jewelry and ornamental uses, from beads to belt buckles.

"Sedona Landscape" agate by Bill Heher combines natural landscape image in agate with dye pigments to create blue sky and reddish-brown earth tones.

Sterling belt buckles using rhodochrosite and small lapis triangles *(left)*, and lapis with small, round green chrysoprase accents *(right)*, by designer Elizabeth Rand.

With careful examination, a competent jeweler or gemologist should be able to easily differentiate a doublet or triplet from a natural. I should note, however, that detection of an opal doublet may be very difficult if it is set in a mounting with a rim (bezel set) covering the seam where the two pieces are cemented together. It might be necessary to remove the stone from its setting for positive identification. Because of opal's fragile nature, removal must be performed only by a very competent bench jeweler (a jeweler who actually makes or repairs jewelry), and the jeweler may agree to do so only at your risk, not wanting to assume responsibility for any breakage. In the case of a black opal worth several thousand dollars, it is well worth the additional cost and inconvenience to be sure it is not a doublet or triplet worth much less. Always be apprehensive when buying a "flat-topped opal" that is bezel-set.

Beyond Ruby Treatment ... to a New Type of Composite

A new type of "ruby" product has been entering the market for the past few years and is being sold without disclosure and at greatly inflated prices. Some of the first of these "rubies" seen in the United States were purchased abroad by military personnel who were led to believe they were buying sparkling "treasures" at bargain prices. Because they were so close to the mines, they never suspected that they were victims of a scam. Today these "rubies" are being sold by department store chains and mass merchandisers, on the Internet and television shopping channels, and at auctions across the country. In most cases, the prices seem to be "bargains" by comparison to the cost of seemingly comparable rubies seen in jewelry stores. In fact, nothing is further from the truth, because these new "rubies" are *not* what they appear to be.

Today an increasing number of people—in the United States and elsewhere—are finding that the "ruby" they bought is little more than a *composition of glass and low-quality corundum*. Currently these stones are being sold as "genuine ruby," but whether or not they can even be called "genuine" is now being debated. Many gemologists think they should be classified as a new type of composite, which would mean they should be classified as an "artificial" material, since composite stones are classified as "artificial."

Whatever it is called, this material is made using extremely low-quality corundum that has been strengthened by adding *tinted lead- or bismuth-glass*.

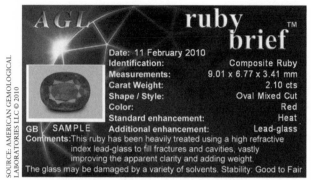

Identification report from American Gemological Laboratories (AGL) describing a
corundum-glass composition, which they call *composite ruby*.

Corundum is the mineral known as "ruby" only when it occurs in a red
color and in a durable form. The starting material used in creating these new
composites usually has a brownish or blackish appearance and is riddled
with other mineral components. A chemical process is now used to leech out
everything except the corundum, leaving a very porous, very fragile mass,
which cannot even be cut and polished in this form because it lacks a sufficiently cohesive structure. This porous material is then infused with tinted
glass to create a ruby-like material, following which it can be cut and polished
into what *looks like* a lovely ruby, but isn't. Some gemological researchers
have suggested that another process may also be used, starting with multiple small pieces of corundum that are bonded with tinted glass to create
larger and more beautiful stones (these would clearly be defined as composite stones), but this does not appear to be the technique used today.

Regardless of the technique used, *the glass content in these glass and
ruby compositions typically ranges from 15% to 50%*. As a result of the
percentage of glass, an increasing number of respected gem-testing laboratories today identify this material as a *"composite," "ruby composite,"* or *"glass composite"* (see also lab report on pages 94–95). Whatever
you call it, if you are buying a composition ruby it is important to know
that: (1) they are much less valuable than genuine rubies that have been
treated in other ways accepted in the jewelry trade; and (2) the extensive
amount of glass present makes them much less durable.

Unfortunately, the number of these composition rubies—and the incidence of misrepresentation regarding what they really are—has increased
dramatically, and consumers are rarely told that without special care these

Above, smooth surface of normal ruby in reflected light.
Below, composition ruby showing crazing from cracks related to glass bonding.

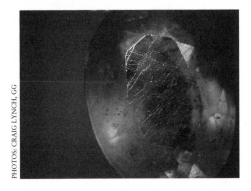

PHOTOS: CRAIG LYNCH, GG

"rubies" can be easily damaged. Many jewelers have learned the hard way when mounting or remounting one of these ruby-like products, or repairing a piece of jewelry containing one. Use of routine techniques by jewelers can quickly—and irreversibly—damage a composition ruby.

Whether classified as treated ruby or as an artificial stone, composition ruby should sell for very little. They are readily available for only a few dollars per carat, whereas treated rubies can sell for hundreds to thousands of dollars per carat, depending on size, type, and extent of treatment, and the appearance following treatment. If sold at the right price, with disclosure that special care is needed, they make lovely and affordable fashion jewelry, but all too often composition ruby is not accurately represented, and the prices at which it is sold are greatly inflated.

In the USA, because of the impact of this technique on the perceived value and durability of the stone, it is a violation of Federal Trade Commission guidelines to sell such products without disclosing how they have been treated and the need for special care. Nonetheless, these stones are being sold extensively without any disclosure. So when buying any ruby, be sure to ask whether or not it is a glass-composition ruby, and if you are assured it is not, make sure this is stated in writing on your sales receipt, and be sure to take the stone to a gemologist-appraiser to confirm its identity.

Misleading Names

Another form of misrepresentation occurs when colored stones are called by names that lead the buyer to believe they are something they are not. This practice occurs frequently, especially outside the United States. When any stone is described with a qualifier, as in "Rio topaz," be sure to ask whether the stone is a genuine, natural stone. Ask why there is a qualifier.

Let's examine two examples: "Japanese amethyst" and "Ceylon sapphire." In the case of Japanese amethyst, the stone is not genuine but synthetic, and the name, therefore, is clearly misleading. However, in the case of the Ceylon sapphire, *Ceylon* refers to the location from which that gem was mined, and most Ceylon sapphires are always a particular tone of blue (a light shade, and very lively). Their color makes them much more desirable than certain other varieties, such as Australian or Thai, which are often overly dark and less brilliant. Therefore, in this case, *Ceylon* is very important to the stone's complete description.

Let's look at one more example, Ceylon-*colored* sapphire. In this case, the qualifier is the word *colored*. A Ceylon-colored sapphire is not a Ceylon sapphire but a sapphire that resembles the color of a Ceylon sapphire. In most cases, although there are rare exceptions, this qualifier also implies some type of color alteration or treatment.

There is nothing wrong with selling "Japanese amethyst" or "Ceylon-colored sapphire" or other similarly named stones, as long as you are told what they really are and pay the right price. Then the decision is yours: either you like it or you don't; it meets your emotional need for an amethyst or Ceylon sapphire or it doesn't; and the price is right or it isn't. The following tables provide some examples of names to be aware of: "descriptive" names that are important to the stone's complete description; and misnomers—misleading names that are meant to do exactly that, mislead.

Descriptive Names	Misnomers (And What They Really Are)
Emerald	
African emerald (emerald mined in Africa)	*Chatham emerald* (synthetic)
Brazilian emerald (emerald mined in Brazil)	*Esmeralda emerald* (green tourmaline)
	Evening emerald (peridot)
Colombian emerald (emerald mined in Colombia; the best quality is considered by connoisseurs to be the finest; rare and very expensive)	*Lannyte emerald* (doublet)
	Mascot emerald (doublet)
	Oriental emerald (green sapphire)
	Soudé emerald (doublet)
Indian emerald (emerald mined in India)	
Pakistan emerald (emerald mined in Pakistan)	
Zambian emerald (emerald mined in Zambia)	
Jade	
Ax stone (nephrite jade)	*African jade* (green massive garnet)
California jade (both jadeite and nephrite jade)	*Australian jade* (chrysoprase quartz)
	Colorado jade (amazonite feldspar)
Greenstone (nephrite jade, New Zealand)	*Fukien jade* (soapstone)
	Honan jade (soapstone)
Imperial jade (fine, gem-quality jadeite jade)	*Indian jade* (aventurine quartz)
	Korea jade (serpentine [bowenite])
Kidney stone (nephrite)	*Manchurian jade* (soapstone)
Maori (nephrite jade, New Zealand)	*Mexican jade* (dyed green calcite)
Spinach jade (nephrite jade)	*New jade* (serpentine [bowenite])
	Oregon jade (dark green jasper [quartz])
	Soochow jade (serpentine or soapstone)
	Swiss jade (dyed green jasper [quartz])
	Virginia jade (amazonite feldspar)
Opal	
Andamooka opal (a type of opal from Andamooka, Australia)	*Gilson opal* (imitation or synthetic)
	Japanese opal (plastic imitation)
Black opal (a rare type of genuine opal with a dark body color)	*Slocum opal* (imitation)

Opal (*cont.*)

Boulder opal (genuine opal in which brown host rock may be seen)

Fire opal (opal with strong reddish or orangish color, mostly from Mexico)

Harlequin opal (very rare genuine opal that exhibits a "harlequin" pattern)

Jelly opal (a transparent type of opal that has a jellylike appearance)

Ruby

African ruby (ruby from Africa)

Burmese ruby (ruby from Myanmar [Burma]; the finest considered by connoisseurs to be the most desirable; rare and costly)

Ceylon ruby (ruby from Sri Lanka [Ceylon])

Thai ruby (ruby from Thailand)

Almandine ruby (garnet)
Australian ruby (garnet)
Balas ruby (spinel)
Bohemian ruby (garnet)
Cape ruby (garnet)
Chatham ruby (synthetic)
Ramaura ruby (synthetic)
Ruby spinel (spinel)
Siberian ruby (tourmaline)

Sapphire

Australian sapphire (sapphire from Australia)

Burmese sapphire (sapphire from Myanmar [Burma]; in fine quality, rare and expensive)

Ceylon sapphire (sapphire from Sri Lanka [Ceylon]; lighter blue than Burmese; fine quality also rare and expensive)

Kashmir sapphire (sapphire from Kashmir; fine-quality stones considered by connoisseurs to be the finest; rare and costly)

Montana, or Yogo, sapphire (sapphire from Montana)

Oriental sapphire (old term to denote "genuine")

Thai sapphire (sapphire from Thailand)

Brazilian sapphire (blue tourmaline; Brazil also has sapphire, called simply sapphire)
Chatham sapphire (synthetic)
Lux sapphire (iolite)
Water sapphire (iolite)

Descriptive Names	Misnomers (And What They Really Are)
Topaz *Precious (imperial) topaz* (usually fine apricot orange)	*Madeira topaz* (citrine quartz)[*] *Occidental topaz* (citrine quartz) *Palmeira topaz* (citrine quartz) *Rio topaz* (citrine quartz) *Saffranite topaz* (citrine quartz) *Scottish topaz* (citrine quartz) *Smoky topaz* (smoky quartz) *Spanish topaz* (citrine quartz)
	[*]Much of the citrine quartz seen on the market today is produced by heating the purple variety of quartz (amethyst). This heating alters the color from purple to shades of yellow, yellow-brown, or golden yellow.

Other Names You Might See

Names	What They Really Are
Aquagem	Light-blue synthetic spinel
California moonstone	Chalcedony quartz
California turquoise	Variscite
Chortanite	Imitation tanzanite (yttrium aluminum garnet [YAG])
Cortanite	Imitation tanzanite (YAG)
Esmeralda	Green tourmaline
Forsterite	Imitation tanzanite
German lapis	Dyed blue jasper (quartz)
Goldstone	Artificial glass with copper crystals
Imperial yu stone (*yu* is the Chinese word for jade)	Fine green aventurine quartz
Japanese amethyst	Synthetic amethyst
Mystic topaz	Topaz treated with partial chemical coating to create iridescence (never seen in natural topaz)
Oriental chrysoberyl	Yellow-green sapphire
Oriental topaz	Yellow sapphire
Rose zircon	Synthetic pink spinel
South Sea cat's-eye	Operculum, "door" of a univalve shellfish
Swiss lapis	Dyed blue jasper (quartz)
Tavalite topaz	Cubic zirconia (CZ), or crystal spheres chemically treated on entire surface to create iridescent colors (not seen naturally)
Tsavolite	Imitation tsavorite (synthetic corundum)

CHAPTER SEVEN

Colored Gemstone Certificates

Systems for grading colored gemstones are not yet established world-wide. As a result, certificates or grading reports for colored gem-stones vary widely in the information provided. Reports for colored stones have a more limited value in some respects than diamond reports, which are widely relied on to describe and confirm diamond quality using precise, universally accepted standards. Nonetheless colored stone reports are *very* important.

Today's new-type synthetics, newly discovered gemstone materials, and increased use of treatments are creating a need for reports that verify *identity* (the type of gem), *genuineness* (whether it is synthetic or not), whether *natural* or *treated*, and, if treated, the *type* and *degree of treatment*.

If considering the purchase of any expensive colored gemstone today, especially gems of unusual size or exceptional quality and rarity, I recommend purchasing a gem that is accompanied by a report from a recognized laboratory (see appendix) or making the sale contingent upon getting a report. The most widely recognized reports for colored gemstones include those issued in the United States by American Gemological Laboratories (AGL), the American Gem Trade Association (AGTA) Gemological Testing Center, and the Gemological Institute of America (GIA) Gem Trade Laboratory (GTL); in Belgium, Hoge Raad voor Diamant (HRD); in Japan, the Gemological Association of All Japan (GAAJ); in Liechtenstein, Gemlab Laboratory for Gemstone Analysis and Reports; in Switzerland, Gübelin Gem Lab and the Swiss Gemological Institute (SSEF); in Thailand, the Asian Institute of Gemological Sciences (AIGS) and the Gem and Jewelry Institute of Thailand (GIT); in the United Kingdom, the Gemological Association (Gem-A) and Gem Testing Laboratory of Great Britain.

At the least, colored gemstone reports should identify the gemstone and verify whether it is natural or synthetic. You can also request a *grading report,* which will provide, in addition to identity, a full description of the stone and a rating of the color, clarity, brilliance, and other important characteristics. Just keep in mind that there is no universally accepted grading system, so each lab uses its own. Nonetheless, they provide important information pertaining to the stone's quality. This information is always useful for insurance purposes and can also be helpful if you are comparing several stones with an eye toward purchase. Also, depending on the information the gemologist can obtain from the gemstone during examination, some laboratories will indicate country of origin, if requested. The AGL, the AGTA lab, GAAJ, Gemlab (Liechtenstein), and Gübelin Gem Lab will indicate origin when possible; GIA will indicate country of origin on a limited number of stones only.

Treatment disclosure is essential. Whether or not a gem has been treated and, if so, the degree of treatment, affect value and durability as well as appearance. Furthermore, it is important to know whether or not the treatment is permanent and whether it necessitates special care. Regardless of the type of report, treatment information should be included. *"Quality" or "origin" reports that omit information related to treatments do not provide sufficient data to make sound decisions.*

In the past few years we have begun to see "treatment" or "enhancement" reports. These reports confirm identity and genuineness and also include important information pertaining to treatments. They indicate whether or not the color and clarity have been enhanced. In addition, laboratories such as AGL include the degree of enhancement—such as faint, moderate, extensive, or a similar description. In cases where heat treatment is present, SSEF also indicates "Amount of Residue" since glassy residues sometimes result from heating techniques. However, some labs, such as the GIA lab, do not always indicate degree of treatment ("minor," "moderate," "significant"). On emerald reports, for example, the degree of treatment is *not* provided in *identification* reports, but only on *full* gemstone reports. It is important to understand this and request the *"full emerald report"* in order to have the essential treatment information necessary to know for sure the quality of what you are buying. In some cases, the report will indicate the type of treatment or filler if there are sufficient gemological data, but sometimes these data are not available without very sophisticated equipment that many labs do not have. For reports from AGL, AIGS, Gemlab, GIT, and SSEF, an "enhancement" report alone, rather than a full quality report, is often sufficient to make a purchase decision, since they provide the degree of treatment in all reports, and thus your own eye may be able to provide the rest of the information you need—especially if you have taken sufficient time to look at and compare lots of stones.

Fees for colored gemstone reports vary depending on the type of gem; the type of report requested; and the time, skill, and gemological equipment necessary to perform conclusive tests. An estimate can usually be obtained by making a telephone call to the laboratory. When you are considering a colored gemstone that is accompanied by a report, keep in mind the different types of reports available. Also keep in mind that the information provided on the report is only as reliable as the gemologist performing the evaluation, so be sure the report is issued by a respected laboratory; if in doubt, check with one of the labs listed in the appendix to see if they are familiar with the laboratory in question. Next, ask yourself what the report is really telling you—is it confirming identity and genuineness only? If so, remember that *quality* differences determine value—a genuine one-carat ruby, sapphire, or emerald can sell for $10 or $10,000 or more, depending on the quality of the particular stone. *Being genuine doesn't mean a stone is valuable.*

Take time to look at many stones, ask questions, and make comparisons. In this way you can develop a good eye and an understanding of the differences that affect quality rating, beauty, and value.

Note: Reports issued by the AGTA are respected reports and are still in circulation, but the AGTA lab closed its doors in 2009. Information on old reports cannot be verified, so you may need to obtain a new report.

The Gemological Association of Great Britain (Gem-A) now offers only educational courses and conferences; its Gem Testing Laboratory no longer offers laboratory services, but it can verify information on old reports.

A sample American Gemological Laboratories colored-gemstone report providing identification and a full quality evaluation, country of origin, and information pertaining to the *absence* of any significant treatment.

Gemmological Association of All Japan GAAJ-ZENHOKYO
Emerald Identification Report

Report No.	**ZR000000**
Date	**1, January 2009**
Weight	**8.000 ct**
Measurement	**12.50 × 11.50 × 8.55 mm**
Shape	**Octagonal**
Cutting Style	**Emerald cut**
Colour	**Green**
Transparency	**Transparent**

Size of the stone may differ from its photo image

CONCLUSION

Species	**NATURAL BERYL**
Variety	**EMERALD**
Comments	**Indications of minor clarity modification (F1)**＊

SPECIMEN

Origin	**Colombia**

Special notes

· Treatment identification is obtained based on the current knowledge at the time of examination. Results given for the same gemstone may lead to different results with continuing research.
· Conclusion of as to the Geographic Origin is regarded as the professional opinion of the laboratory only. The Origin result is drawn from comparisons of internal features, physical and chemical data with specimens from known localities, continuous to-date scientific research and reference information.

＊ This report has been prepared in accordance with the standardised language and criteria set out by the Laboratory Manual Harmonization Committee (LMHC) see table. All rights jointly reserved by:
AGTA-Gemological Testing Center, CISGEM S.p.A. Laboratory, GAAJ-ZENHOKYO Laboratory, GIA Laboratory, GIT-Gem Testing Laboratory, Gubelin Gem Lab Ltd., SSEF Swiss Gemmological Institute.

Status	No fissures present in stone	No or insignificant filler in fissures	Quantification and identification of filler in fissures		
Alpha numeric			F1	F2	F3
Text	None	No / Insignificant indications of clarity modification	Indications of minor clarity modification	Indications of moderate clarity modification	Indications of significant clarity modification
		Condition	Quantification and identification of filler in fracture(s) / cavity(ies)		
		Alpha numeric	C1	C2	C3
		Text	Minor amount of Resin / wax in cavities	Moderate amount of Resin / wax in cavities	Significant amount of Resin / wax in cavities

This report is designed for countries outside Japan. The wording used in English in this report may differ from the wording used in Japanese in reports issued in Japan by the GAAJ-ZENHOKYO Laboratory. For reports designed for the Japanese market, please use GAAJ-ZENHOKYO standard reports that apply to the wording set by JJA/AGL.

Gemmological Association of All Japan Co.,Ltd.

8F Daiwa-Ueno Bldg., 5-25-11 Ueno, Taito-ku, Tokyo 110-0005, Japan
TEL: +81-3-3835-2466 / FAX: +81-3-3839-0798 / www.gaaj-zenhokyo.co.jp

IMPORTANT LIMITATIONS ON THE REVERSE

A sample report from the Gemological Association of All Japan providing identification, treatment information, and country of origin.

GEMOLOGICAL INSTITUTE OF AMERICA®

5355 Armada Drive | Carlsbad, CA 92008-4602
T: 760-603-4500 | F: 760-603-1814

GIA Laboratories
Bangkok   Carlsbad   Gaborone
Johannesburg   Mumbai   New York

www.gia.edu

RUBY ORIGIN REPORT

GIA REPORT 1106513175

January 12, 2009

Weight .... 7.80 carat
Measurements .... 13.25 x 9.85 x 6.35 mm
Shape .... Oval

Cutting Style: Crown .... Brilliant Cut
Cutting Style: Pavilion .... Step Cut
Transparency .... Translucent
Color .... Purplish Red

CONCLUSION

Species .... NATURAL CORUNDUM
Variety .... NATURAL RUBY
Source Type .... CMT Type I
Geographic Origin .... KENYA

TREATMENT
No indications of heating (NTE).

Comments:
*SAMPLE *SAMPLE *SAMPLE *SAMPLE
Any statement on geographic origin is an expert opinion based on a collection of observations and analytical data.

Image is Approximate

1106513175

No Indications of Heating	Indications of Heating (no residue)	Indications of Heating with Residue in Fissures				
NTE	TE	TE1	TE2	TE3	TE4	TE5
No Indications of Heating	Indications of Heating	Minor Residue in Fissures		Moderate Residue in Fissures		Significant Residue in Fissures

210100759428

This Report is not a guarantee, valuation or appraisal and contains only the characteristics of the article described herein after it has been graded, tested, examined and analyzed by the laboratory providing this Report ("GIA") and/or has been inscribed using the techniques and equipment used by GIA at the time of the examination and/or inscription. Inscriptions reported in this document are not a guarantee, validation or warranty of an article's quality, country of origin or source; or that the article will be identifiable by the inscription in the future (since inscriptions can be removed). GIA makes no representation concerning any trademark, word, or symbol which is inscribed by GIA or which is identified on this Report. The recipient of this Report may wish to consult a credentialed jeweler or gemologist about the information contained herein.

IMPORTANT LIMITATIONS ON BACK
© 2008 GEMOLOGICAL INSTITUTE OF AMERICA, INC.

SOURCE: © GEMOLOGICAL INSTITUTE OF AMERICA, REPRINTED BY PERMISSION

This sample report from the Gemological Institute of America provides identification of the gemstone, country of origin, and *geologic* origin, and indicates the stone has not undergone any treatment. Treatment codes are explained on the bottom of the report.

GÜBELIN
GEM LAB

EDELSTEIN-BERICHT · RAPPORT DE PIERRE PRECIEUSE
GEMSTONE REPORT

No.	**SPECIMEN**
Datum · Date	
Gegenstand · Objet · Item	One faceted gemstone
Gewicht · Poids · Weight	**15.25 ct**
Schliff · Taille · Cut	
Form · Forme · Shape	cushion-shape
Stil · Style · Style	brilliant cut / step cut
Abmessungen · Dimensions · Measurements	17.09 x 14.06 x 7.28 mm
Transparenz · Transparence · Transparency	transparent
Farbe · Couleur · Colour	**blue**

IDENTIFIKATION · IDENTIFICATION

Spezies · Espèce · Species
NATURAL CORUNDUM

Varietät · Variété · Variety
SAPPHIRE

Gemmological testing revealed characteristics
consistent with those of sapphires originating from:

Burma (Myanmar)

Bemerkungen · Commentaires · Comments

No indications of thermal enhancement (NTE).
Sapphires which have not been enhanced by
heat are scarce.

GEMMOLOGISCHES LABOR · LABORATOIRE GEMMOLOGIQUE · GEMMOLOGICAL LABORATORY
Maihofstrasse 102 · 6006 Lucerne · Switzerland · Tel. (41) 41 - 429 17 17 · Fax (41) 41 - 429 17 34
www.gubelinlab.com · info@gubelingemlab.ch

Dr. D. Schwarz, Dipl.-Min   C. Dunaigre, A.G., DUG

Wichtige Anmerkungen und Einschränkungen auf der Rückseite · Remarques au verso · Important notes and limitations on the reverse.
Copyright © 2003 Gübelin Gem Lab Ltd.

A sample report from Gübelin Gem Lab providing identification and confirmation that the stone has not been color enhanced by heating techniques.

SCHWEIZERISCHES GEMMOLOGISCHES INSTITUT

INSTITUT SUISSE DE GEMMOLOGIE

SWISS GEMMOLOGICAL INSTITUTE

Falknerstrasse 9
CH-4001 **Basel** / Switzerland

Telephone +41 061 262 0640
Telefax   +41 061 262 0641
e-mail   gemlab@ssef.ch
homepage www.ssef.ch

TEST REPORT No. XXXX

on the authenticity of the following gemstone,
mounted in a ring with diamonds

Shape & Cut:	octagonal, step cut
Total weight:	approximately 8.5 grams (including mounting and diamonds)
Measurements:	approximately 8.95 x 7.65 x 9.65 mm
Calculated weight:	approximately 2.9 ct
Colour:	green of medium strong saturation
Identification:	E M E R A L D (variety of natural beryl)
Comments:	The analysed properties confirm the authenticity of this transparent emerald. Indications of clarity modification. Moderate amount of oil in fissures.

Origin: Colombia

Text	Minor amount of filler in fissures	Moderate amount of filler in fissures	Significant amount of filler in fissures	Filler in cavities		
Alphanumeric system	F1	F2	F3	C1	C2	C3

Correspondence table for filler quantification

Important note: The conclusions on this Test Report reflect our findings at the time it is issued. A gemstone can be modified and / or enhanced at any time. Therefore, the SSEF can reconfirm at any time that the stone is in accordance with the Test Report.

Please see comments on reverse side.

SSEF - SWISS GEMMOLOGICAL INSTITUTE
Gemstone Testing Division

Basel, 28 August 2009 cy

P. Lefèvre, MSc, DUG

Dr. M.S. Krzemnicki, FGA

A sample Swiss Gemological Institute colored-gemstone report providing identification,
treatment information, country of origin, and explanation of their treatment codes.

GEM IDENTIFICATION REPORT

Report No.:	**SAMPLE**	Date:	**25th December 2009**
Sample Type:	**1 cut stone**	Weight:	**8.92 ct**
Cut:	**Brilliant/Step**	Dimensions:	**13.11 x 11.78 x 6.91 mm**
Shape:	**Oval**	Colour:	**Red**

Magnification 1x

IDENTIFICATION RESULT

Species: **NATURAL CORUNDUM**

Variety: **RUBY**

Comment(s): **Indications of heating with significant residue in fissures.**

Remark(s): Natural rubies and sapphires are commonly enhanced by heat to improve their colour and/or clarity, the results of which are stable and permanent.

Instruments Used for Identification

[x] Refractometer	[x] Polariscope	[x] SG Balance	[x] Microscope
[ ] Visual Spect.	[x] LW/SW UV Lamp	[ ] UV/VIS/NIR Spect.	[x] FTIR Spect.
[x] EDXRF	[ ] Laser Raman Spect.	[x] X-Radiography	[ ] LIBS
[ ] Diamond Tester	[ ] Cathode Lumin.	[x] Others	

Please see the back side for additional information
The original report with signatures and the grand palace hologram is the only valid identification document.

Thanong Leelawatanasuk

M.Sc. (Geology), Graduate Gemologist (GIA)

Monruedee Thawornmongkolkij

B.Sc. (Gemology), FGA, CDG (HRD)

The Gem and Jewelry Institute of Thailand (Public Organization)
GIT is the National Institute for Testing, Research and Development of Gem and Jewelry
Gemological Research and Testing Building.
Located at the Faculty of Science, Chulalongkorn University, Phyathai Road, Patumwan, Bangkok 10330, Thailand
Tel : (662) 218-5470-4 Fax : (662) 218-5474 Email : jewelry@git.or.th http://www.git.or.th

Sample report from the Gem and Jewelry Institute of Thailand providing identification, treatment information, and details showing instruments used to test the stone.

GEMLAB

LABORATORY FOR GEMSTONE AND PEARL ANALYSIS
AND REPORTS

Administration: Landstrasse 75, FL-9491 Ruggell (Liechtenstein)
Laboratory: Gewerbestrasse 3, FL-9496 Balzers (Liechtenstein)

Gemstone Report No. 2000/10

Varietät / Spezies / Gruppe
Variety / Species / Group...

Natural Ruby/Corundum, filled with lead glass; composite material

Schliff
Cut....................

Rectangular emerald cut

Messwerte und Gewicht
Measurements and weight..................................

11.22 x 9.68 x 5.93 mm, 6.84 ct

Farbe
Colour..

Very slightly brownish (saturation), dark (tone), purplish red (hue)

Behandlungen
Treatments.................

Fractures and cavities of this ruby are filled by lead glass; indications of heat treatment. The volumetric content of glass is roughly estimated to be near 15 to 20 %, and therefore the sample has been described as a "composite" material

Ursprungsland
Country of origin...............................

Not determined

Analyse Details
Analysis details:..................................

Explanation of the image: The X-ray image above visualizes the distinct quantities of lead glass (lighter zones) in the corundum (darker zones). The X-ray images led - In combination with further analysis methods - to the conclusions in this gemstone report.

Erklärung des Bildes: Das abgebildete Röntgenbild macht die deutlichen Anteile an Bleiglas (hellere Zonen) in dem Korund (dunklere Zonen) sichtbar. Die Röntgenbilder führten - in Kombination mit weiteren Analysemethoden - zu den Schlussfolgerungen in diesem Edelstein Gutachten.

Balzers, am 12.02.2010

Für die Richtigkeit des Gutachtens:
For the correctness of this report:

Thomas Hainschwang, DUG, GG, FGA, Experte SGG

Administration +423 3732464   Laboratory +423 2622464   +423 3732243   www.gemlab.net   gemlab@gemlab.net   VAT Nr. 54087

A sample report from Gemlab (Liechtenstein) providing identification and
very clear treatment and durability information…

Erklärung der verwendeten Terminologie für den GEOLOGISCHEN KONTEXT von Korund/Explanation of the used terminology for the GEOLOGICAL CONTEXT of corundum:*

RUBIN/RUBY Metamorph/Metamorphic

Typ/Type	Wichtige Vorkommen/Important Sources	Typische Einschlüsse/Typical Inclusions
Metamorphic A	Mogok (Myanmar), Vietnam, Sri Lanka, Madagaskar (Ejeda-Fotadrevo, Andilamena, Vatomandry, Ilakaka), Nepal	Kurze bis lange feine Rutilnadeln, rundliche Kristalle (Calcit, Apatit oder Zirkon), Boehmit Nadeln / Short to long fine rutile needles, rounded crystals (calcite, apatite, or zircon), boehmite needles
Metamorphic B	Vietnam, Sri Lanka, Nepal (Maltevi), Afghanistan (Jegdalek)	Oft bläulich erscheinende (Tyndall Effekt) Trübungen bestehend aus winzigen, submikroskopischen Partikeln / Often bluish appearing (Tyndall effect) clouds of tiny submicroscopical Particles
Metamorphic C	MongHsu (Myanmar), Vietnam, Afghanistan (Jegdalek)	Pinselstrich-, Streifen- und Schnurartige aus winzigen Partikeln bestehende Trübungen / Brush-, stroke- and cord-like clouds consisting of tiny particles
Metamorphic D	Tansania (Karalani, Umba, Songea)	Boehmit Nadeln und punktförmige Entmischungen, punktförmige Rutil-Entmischungen , kurzprismatische Rutilkristalle / Boehmite needles and pinpoint-like exolutions, pinpoint-like rutile exolutions, short prismatic Rutile crystals
Metamorphic XY	Nicht bestimmbar / Not determineable	Keine typischen Einschlüsse vorhanden / No typical inclusions present

RUBIN/RUBY Magmatisch/Magmatic

Typ/Type	Wichtige Vorkommen/Important Sources	Typische Einschlüsse/Typical Inclusions
Magmatic	Thailand, Kambodia	Fluide Filme - oft irisierend, Boehmit Nadeln an Zwillingslamellen, gerundelte z.T. glasige Mineraleinschlüsse umgeben von Fahnen / Fluid thinfilms - often iridescent, Boehmite needles on twinning planes, rounded sometimes glassy mineral inclusions surrounded by healed fractures

BLAUER SAFIR/BLUE SAPPHIRE Metamorph/Metamorphic

Typ/Type	Wichtige Vorkommen/Important Sources	Typische Einschlüsse/Typical Inclusions
Metamorphic A	Mogok, Sri Lanka, Madagaskar (Ilakaka)	Kurze bis lange feine Rutilnadeln, rundliche Kristalle (Calcit, Apatit oder Zirkon), Boehmit Nadeln / Short to long fine rutile needles, rounded crystals (calcite, apatite, or zircon), boehmite needles
Metamorphic B	Kashmir, Madagaskar (Andranondambo)	Schleier und Trübungen aus feinsten Partikeln, nicht als Nadeln definierbar / Clouds consisting of finest particles, not being definable as needles
Metamorphic C	Kashmir, Madagaskar (Andranondambo)	Pinselstrich-, Streifen- und Schnurartige aus winzigen Partikeln bestehende Trübungen / Brush-, stroke- and cord-like clouds consisting of tiny particles
Metamorphic D	Tansania (Umba, Tunduru)	Boehmit Nadeln und punktförmige Entmischungen, punktförmige Rutil-Entmischungen , kurzprismatische Rutilkristalle / Boehmite needles and pinpoint-like exolutions, pinpoint-like rutile exolutions, short prismatic Rutile crystals
Metamorphic XY	Nicht bestimmbar / Not determineable	Keine typischen Einschlüsse vorhanden / No typical inclusions present

BLAUER SAFIR/BLUE SAPPHIRE Magmatisch/Magmatic

Typ/Type	Wichtige Vorkommen/Important Sources	Typische Einschlüsse/Typical Inclusions
Magmatic	Thailand, Australien, Kambodia, China, Kenya, Laos, Nigeria, Madagaskar (Ambondromifehy, Diego Suarez), Vietnam, Rwanda	Feinkörnige Trübungen (Partikelgrösse generell submikroskopisch), feine Rutilnadeln , Pinselstrich-, Streifen- und Schnurartige aus winzigen Partikeln bestehende Trübungen / Fine-grained clouds (grain size generally submicroscopic), fine rutile needles, brush-, stroke- and cord-like clouds consisting of tiny particles

*Modified System, based on the "Source Type Classification" system by C.P. Smith et al. (2004) / Modifiziertes System, abgeleitet vom "Source Type Classification" System von C.P. Smith et al. (2006)

EINSCHRÄNKUNKEN ZUR GÜLTIGKEIT DES GUTACHTENS: Nur das komplette Original des gemmologischen Gutachtens, versehen mit Unterschrift(en) von einem oder zwei Repräsentanten von Gemlab kann als authentisch angesehen werden. Die Schlussfolgerungen des Laboratoriums beschreiben den Zustand und die Natur der Proben zur Zeit der Expertise. Jegliche mögliche darauf folgende Modifikation der Steine, durch Behandlung oder sonstigem Prozess, kann nicht in Betracht gezogen werden. Die von Gemlab formulierten Schlussfolgerungen basieren auf Techniken und gemmologischen Kenntnissen, welche zum Zeitpunkt der Analyse aufgrund erhältlicher Fachpublikationen generelle Akzeptanz erhalten haben. Diese Schlussfolgerungen können in einer Art und Weise jegliche zukünftige Evolution dieser Kenntnisse berücksichtigen. Daraus folgt, dass Gemlab keinerlei Verantwortung für eine mögliche Ungültigmachung seiner Schlussfolgerungen aufgrund von Entwicklungen neuer Techniken oder der Evolution von Kenntnisse [...] ausdrücklich keinerlei Verantwortung für S[...] verursacht werden oder daraus entstehen, [...] oder von Nachlässigkeit. Wir beschreiben all[...] Rahmens unserer analytischen Methodologie [...] von oder der Handel mit jeglichem vom Gem[...] strengstens untersagt. Einsprüche oder Stre[...] Dienstleistung des Gemlab Laboratoriums f[...] Liechtenstein.

NOTIZEN ZU BEHANDLUNGEN: Natürliche Kor[...] behandelt. Durch Hoch-Temperatur Erhitzen [...] Substanzen werden oftmals Risse und Vertief[...] und Korund zu Rekristallisierung angeregt [...] Behandlung werden von uns z. T. nicht zer[...] Allgemeinen mit Öl oder mit auch mit Kunsth[...] ist oft nicht sehr stabil und Steine müssen mit V[...]

NOTIZEN ZU GEOLOGISCHEM KONTEXT / URS[...] Korunde und für Smaragd bestimmt werde[...] praktisch allen Fällen bestimmen, da er sich [...] Steine widerspiegelt. Die Vielzahl an Vorko[...] Gegebenheiten, vor allem von Korund, las[...] Ursprungslandes oftmals nicht mehr zu. Das L[...] wenn die Eigenschaften ganz klar nur auf ein[...]

RESTRICTIONS TO THE VALIDITY OF THE REPORT: Only the original complete report of gemmological analysis bearing the signature(s) of one or two members of Gemlab shall be deemed authentic. The laboratory's conclusions render an account of the nature of the material at the time of the expert evaluation. They do not take into account any possible subsequent modifications of the material, due to treatment or otherwise. The conclusions formulated by Gemlab are based on techniques and gemmological knowledge accepted in the available specialised publications, at a given time. These conclusions cannot in any way take into consideration any evolution of this knowledge. Consequently, the possible invalidation of the conclusions formulated by Gemlab as a result of the development of these techniques or advancement of knowledge does not in any way entail the responsibility of the laboratory. Gemlab expressly declines

NOTES CONCERNING TREATMENTS: Natural corundum is commonly heat treated. High temperature heat treatment with addition of Borax or similar substances will lead to a filling of fractures and cavities with glass- like substances and to the re-crystalisation of corundum. Corundum suspected of being beryllium treatment is in some cases not certified by us. Natural emeralds are commonly clarity treated by oils or resins; this treatment is often not very stable and stones need to be treated with care.

NOTES CONCERNING GEOLOGICAL CONTEXT / COUNTRY OF ORIGIN: This information can only be determined for corundum and emerald. The geological context can be determined in practically all cases, since it is reflected within the inclusions and chemistry. The multitude of deposits and their often similar geological context, especially of corundum, are responsible that the unambiguous determination of country of origin is frequently not possible today. Therefore the country of origin is only indicated when all properties point towards one deposit only.

Foto des Steines - Photo of the stone

GEMLAB

LABORATORY FOR GEMSTONE AND PEARL ANALYSIS AND REPORTS

Edelstein Gutachten ~ Gemstone Report
No. 2000/10

…The reverse side of the Gemlab report provides general treatment comments and an important explanation of *country of origin* and the difficulties present in making this determination. Note Gemlab's laboratory policy pertaining to country of origin.

AIGS

GF

**ASIAN INSTITUTE
OF GEMOLOGICAL
SCIENCES**

919/1 Silom Rd, Jewelry Trade Center, 6th Fl, Bangkok 10500 Thailand
Tel : 662-267-4325-7 Fax : 662-267-4327
E-mail : info@aigslaboratory.com

Gemstone Identification Report

16 Feb 2009

Weight : **2.53 Carats**

Shape : Oval

Cut : Faceted

Measurements : 8.78 x 6.57 x 5.12 mm

Color : Red

Mounted : No

Photographs of item(s) tested - not actual size

Probable Origin : Myanmar (Burma)

Result(s) : **Natural Ruby**

Comment(s) : No indication of heat process.

Unless otherwise indicated, the item(s) described above has/have been examined by at least two qualified AIGS staff gemmologists and the stated result obtained. This report is limited in accordance with the agreement printed on its inside front cover, the cover being an integral part of this report.

Copyright © 2008 Asian Institute of Gemological Sciences   www.aigslaboratory.com

Identification report from the Asian Institute of Gemological Sciences
indicating origin and treatment.

CHAPTER EIGHT

Buying Colored Gems

When you go to buy colored gemstones today, you will find your-self immersed in color—every hue, every shade of the spectrum. There has never been a more exciting time to search for a colored gem because there have never been so many alternatives.

Today you will find "new" gems only recently discovered: emerald-green garnets (tsavorite), blue and green tanzanite (technically, the green variety should be called green zoisite, the mineral name for this gemstone, since *blue* zoisite is what we know as "tanzanite"), and "neon" tourma-lines from Paraiba, Brazil (also called Hetorita, after the man who discov-ered them) in blue and green shades never seen before. Even diamond can be seen in a wide variety of natural "fancy" colors, some at very "fancy" prices (see *Diamonds: The Antoinette Matlins Buying Guide*).

Whatever color you prefer, and whatever your budget, there is a sparkling natural gem awaiting your discovery. If you want an emerald-green stone but can't afford a fine emerald, you might choose a green gar-net (tsavorite), a green tourmaline, chrome diopside, or green tanzanite; if you like ruby red, but can't afford ruby, you might choose from red spinel, red tourmaline, or red garnet; if you prefer blue, choices now include blue spinel, iolite, tourmaline, and tanzanite. And we've just begun to scratch the surface.

Before getting started, just remember that with so many gemstones available in similar colors, the risk of erroneous identification increases; bas-ing identification on color alone is too often the cause. Unfortunately, most people still don't realize how many gems look alike in color. And even professionals in the trade can be misled or caught off-guard. Increasingly, inexpensive gems are mixed in with parcels of more costly gems of similar color and passed off as the more costly gem. These can get passed on to unsuspecting manufacturers, designers, jewelers, and, thus, ultimately to consumers. This is just one more reason why it is especially important to seek a knowledgeable, reputable jeweler when purchasing any colored gemstone, and to verify the authenticity of any significant gem purchase with an independent gem-testing laboratory or gemologist-appraiser.

In the following pages I will present some of the most popular gemstone alternatives by color; a table that indicates the effect of treatments on gemstone value; a list of gemstones that are not routinely treated; and a guide to how they compare in terms of price, availability, and wearability. Then the gems will be discussed individually in chapter 9.

Gem Alternatives by Color

Color Family	Popular Name of Stone	Gem Family
Red— *from red to shades of pink*	Andalusite—pink to reddish brown	Andalusite
	Diamond*—all shades of pink and red	Diamond
	Garnet—several red color varieties	
	Almandine—violet to pure red	Garnet
	Malaya—brownish red to orangy red	Garnet
	Pyrope—brownish red to red	Garnet
	Rhodolite—red to violet	Garnet
	Kunzite—violet-pink to pink-violet	Spodumene
	Morganite—pink to orange-pink	Beryl
	Pink sapphire—pinkish red	Corundum
	Red "emerald"—red	Beryl
	Rose quartz—pure pink	Quartz
	Rubellite—red to violet-red and pink	Tourmaline
	Ruby—bluish red to orange-red	Corundum
	Scapolite—light red	Scapolite
	Spinel—red to brownish red and pink	Spinel
	Sunstone—rich red to orange-red	Feldspar
	Zircon—brownish red to deep, dark red	Zircon
	Zultanite—pinkish to deep pink in incandescent light	Diaspore
Orange	Diamond*—various shades including yellow-orange to brownish orange	Diamond
	Garnet—a few orange varieties	
	Hessonite—orange-brown to brown-orange	Garnet
	Malaya—red-orange to orangy brown	Garnet
	Spessartite—orange to red-orange to brown-orange	Garnet
	Morganite—pale orange to orangy pink	Beryl
	Padparadscha sapphire—pinkish orange	Corundum
	Scapolite—orange	Scapolite

	Spinel—brown to orange	Spinel
	Sunstone—rich orange to orange-red	Feldspar
	Topaz—brownish orange, yellow-orange, pinkish orange	Topaz
	Tourmaline—all shades of orange	Tourmaline
	Zircon—orange to golden brown	Zircon
Yellow	Beryl (heliodor)—golden yellow	Beryl
	Chrysoberyl—yellow, yellow-green, yellow-brown	Chrysoberyl
	Citrine—yellow to yellow-brown	Quartz
	Diamond*—all shades of yellow to chartreuse	Diamond
	Garnet—a couple of yellow varieties	
	Andradite—honey yellow to greenish yellow	Garnet
	Grossularite—yellow to greenish yellow to brownish yellow	Garnet
	Sapphire—yellow	Corundum
	Scapolite—yellow	Scapolite
	Sphene—green-yellow to golden yellow to brown	Sphene
	Sunstone—orangy yellow, yellow, greenish yellow	Feldspar
	Topaz—brownish yellow to yellow	Topaz
	Tourmaline—all shades	Tourmaline
	Zircon—yellow to yellow-brown	Zircon
Green	Alexandrite—daylight: bluish to blue-green; artificial light: violet-red	Chrysoberyl
	Apatite—green to blue-green	Apatite
	Chrome diopside—green to yellow-green to blue-green	Diopside
	Diamond*—blue-green to yellow-green to gray-green	Diamond
	Emerald—yellowish green to bluish green	Beryl
	Garnet—a couple of green varieties	
	Demantoid—yellow-green to emerald green	Garnet
	Tsavorite—yellowish green to bluish green	Garnet
	Peridot—yellow-green to green	Peridot
	Sapphire—yellow-green to blue-green to gray-green	Corundum
	Scapolite—greenish gray	Scapolite
	Sphene—grass green to yellow-green	Sphene
	Sunstone—yellowish, grayish, brownish green	Feldspar
	Tanzanite—gray-green to blue-green	Zoisite
	Tourmaline—several green color varieties	
	Chrome—rich green to slightly yellow-green	Tourmaline
	Paraiba—light to deep green to blue-green	Tourmaline
	Verdelite—all shades of green	Tourmaline
	Zircon—green to yellow-green to gray-green	Zircon
	Zultanite—greenish in daylight or outdoor light	Diaspore

Blue	Apatite—blue to gray-blue to greenish blue	Apatite
	Aquamarine—blue to blue-green	Beryl
	Diamond*—all shades	Diamond
	Iolite—violet to gray-blue	Iolite
	Sapphire—cornflower blue to greenish blue to inky blue	Corundum
	Spinel—blue, gray-blue, greenish blue	Spinel
	Tanzanite—violet-blue	Zoisite
	Topaz—blue to blue-green	Topaz
	Tourmaline—a couple of blue color varieties	
	Indicolite—inky blue, greenish blue	Tourmaline
	Paraiba—intense blue to violet-blue to green-blue	Tourmaline
	Zircon—pastel blue	Zircon
Violet	Amethyst—lilac to violet to reddish purple to brownish purple	Quartz
	Benitoite—blue to violet-blue to gray-blue	Benitoite
	Diamond*—all shades	Diamond
	Kunzite—pinkish violet to red-violet	Spodumene
	Morganite—pinkish violet	Beryl
	Paraiba—violet to blue-violet	Tourmaline
	Rhodolite—red-violet	Garnet
	Sapphire—purple to violet	Corundum
	Scapolite—violet-blue, to greenish to bluish gray, lilac to violet	Scapolite
	Spinel—grayish violet to pure purple	Spinel

*For information on colored diamonds see *Diamonds: The Antoinette Matlins Buying Guide*.

The Effect of Treatments
on the Value of Gemstones

The following table provides an indication of price adjustment for *natural* versus *treated* ruby, sapphire, and emerald. Keep in mind that untreated sapphire and ruby from certain locations, such as Burma or Kashmir, command a premium greater than indicated. Also, note that there are rare gems of exceptional quality above the extra fine rating, and such stones will command a much greater premium if untreated.

How Treatments Affect Prices of Colored Gems*

Emerald	GOOD	FINE	EXTRA FINE
Untreated	N/A	+50% to +100%	+100% or more
Slight treatment	+5% to +20%	+5% to +30%	+10% to +50%
Moderate treatment	0%	0%	0%
Extensive treatment	–10% to –30%	–10% to –30%	N/A
Ruby			
Unheated	+5% to +20%	+20% to +40%	+40% to +75% and up
Moderate heat	0%	0%	0%
High heat with slight to moderate glass residue	0% to –5%	–8% to –12%	–10% to –15%
High heat with moderate to extensive glass residue	0% to –5%	–10% to –15%	–15% to –20%
Glass-filled cavity†	–10% to –50%	–10% to –50%	–10% to –50%
Sapphire			
Unheated	+5% to +10%	+10% to +20%	+20% to +30% and up
Heated	0%	0%	0%
Oiled (no data; often goes undetected)			

*The information presented above is based on information from several sources, including *The Guide* (Gemworld International) and *Jewelers' Circular Keystone*.
†These discounts do not apply to rubies that have such a high percentage of glass as to be considered *composite ruby*—their prices should be dramatically lower than what is shown here.

The Rarest of Them All—The Natural Gems

There has been so much focus on the extensive use of treatments to enhance gems that it is easy to forget that there are also natural gems: those that have not been artificially enhanced in any way. Within every gemstone family there is the occasional beauty that is just as nature made it. Unfortunately, as I discussed earlier, sometimes we cannot distinguish what is natural from what is not. Such is the case with blue topaz, for example. Blue topaz does occur naturally, in lovely pastel shades. It is one of nature's rarest and loveliest gems, but alas, we do not yet have the means to definitively distinguish what is natural from what has been irradiated. Thus, regardless of its rarity and true preciousness (and value), it commands a very low price.

There are also natural rubies, sapphires, and emeralds. Most are not the color and clarity we've come to expect (from the standards applied to the treated gems), but we are starting to see interest in a wider range of qualities, especially for stones in the lighter shades of color. And exceptionally fine-quality rubies, sapphires, and emeralds also exist. Fortunately, where ruby, sapphire, and emerald are concerned, it is usually possible to distinguish the natural from the treated, and as the natural stones become even rarer and rarer, prices are starting to reflect their preciousness, as you've seen in the table on page 101.

There is yet another group of gems about which little has been said until recently: gemstones and gemstone families that are not routinely treated to alter color or clarity at this time. When you buy one of the gemstones listed in the chart below, the color is generally natural, and in most cases these gemstones are not enhanced in any way. Included in the list are many beautiful choices in a rainbow of colors. If you are not familiar with them, there is more information in the following chapter. Whatever your color preference and budget, if you seek something truly "natural," you should be able to find the right gem from this list. If jewelers in your area don't have what you want, they can contact the American Gem Trade Association (AGTA) to arrange to get stones for you to see.

Gemstones That Are Not Routinely Enhanced*

Alexandrite	Iolite	Tourmaline (rare
Andalusite	Moonstone	chrome-green
Chrysoberyl	Fire opal	variety and cat's-
(all colors)	Peridot	eye tourmaline)
Chrysoprase	Spinel (all colors)	Zircon (brown and
Garnet (all colors)	Tanzanite (green)	green varieties)
Hematite		

*Historically the gemstones listed here have not been color or clarity enhanced. This remains the case with regard to color, but in some instances, surface-reaching fractures or cavities may be filled with oil, wax, or resin. In addition, the use of various fillers to reduce visibility of *internal* cracks or fissures is being encountered with greater frequency on an ever-increasing range of gemstones. Be sure to ask whether or not the stone has been checked for fillers.

How to Use the Following Guides

The purpose of the following price guides is twofold: to help you understand how prices for different gems in a given color compare with one another; and to demonstrate how significant the price range might be for a given type of stone, so that you will have a clearer understanding of the importance of quality differences.

The guides can be especially useful—and help you avoid mistakes—if you follow these steps:

- *Decide what color you want in a gem, and then make a list of the gems available in that color.* If you want an emerald-green gem, for example, and can't afford emerald itself, you would use the guide to see what other similarly colored emerald-green gems are available: tsavorite garnet, chrome tourmaline, green tourmaline, or green sapphire, for example.
- *Compare their prices* to get a sense of the relative cost of each. In comparing prices for these green gems, you would immediately see that tsavorite garnet is the most expensive (but still much more affordable than emerald), chrome tourmaline is next in cost, then green tourmaline, and finally the most affordable, green sapphire.
- *Note availability* to determine how easy or difficult it might be to locate the particular gem you think you want. In this example, you would see that of the choices, green sapphire is not as readily available as several other choices and might be difficult to find.
- *Note the range in price* for the stones that interest you. *The larger the price range in a given stone, the more critical any differences in quality become.* A wide price variance would indicate that you must be especially careful to spend time comparing and learning about the stone, developing an eye to spot subtle differences in quality.
- *Read about each gem individually.* Now turn to chapter 9 and read about each of the gems you're considering individually. You may find that there is something about the stone or its history, mythology, or wearability that makes it an even more interesting choice for you. Here you will also learn if there is anything special you need to know, to look for, or to look out for as you shop.

Now you're ready to embark on a sparkling search. But always remember: *being genuine doesn't mean a stone is a "gem" or that it is "valuable."* There are genuine rubies, sapphires, and emeralds that can be bought for a couple dollars per carat, and some you couldn't pay me to take! A gem must be beautiful and rare, attributes that are related to *quality.* The finer the quality, the more beautiful, and the more rare. The quality of the individual stone is what determines whether or not it is a "gem," and it is the *quality* that determines its value. The range in price for any colored gemstone is directly related to quality differences—and it can be enormous. Be sure you have read chapter 4 carefully, and understand the factors that determine quality before making any decision.

After reading these chapters, you will know what to ask the jeweler to show you. But don't forget to do a lot of window-shopping, looking, and asking questions until you really have developed a feel for that particular stone and its market.

Price Guides to Popular Gems

The prices quoted in these price guides are for fine-quality faceted gemstones unless otherwise noted. Cabochon-cut stones often cost less. Gems used in mass-produced jewelry sold in many jewelry stores are often of commercial quality and may cost significantly less than the prices indicated here. Also, it is rare to find gems sold by jewelry retailers that exceed the prices shown for extra-fine quality. Rare gems in exceptionally fine quality and rare stones of unusual size can sell for much more than the prices indicated here. If the price of a gem you are considering is higher than what I indicate, I strongly recommend taking extra steps to confirm its exceptional quality before purchase; in some cases I would recommend having the seller obtain a quality grading report from a laboratory such as the American Gemological Laboratories (AGL).

The prices shown for gems that are routinely treated or enhanced in some way—ruby, sapphire, emerald, topaz, tourmaline, and so on—reflect prices for treated material (showing evidence of "moderate" treatment). For natural or heavily treated emerald, ruby, and sapphire, see price-adjustment chart on page 101.

Guide to Popular Gems and Their Prices*

Family	Popular Name	Color(s)	Approx. Retail Cost Per Carat	Brilliance	Wearability	Availability
Ammolite	Ammolite or ammonite	Orange, red, green, yellow, blue, purple	25 to under 35 cts: $1,875–5,250 *per stone*	Good	Poor to good	Most colors: good; blue and purple: poor
Andalusite	Poor man's alexandrite	Changes color from grayish green to reddish brown, emerald green to bright yellow	1 to under 5 cts: $150–415 5 to under 10 cts: $350–565	Good	Good	Large: poor; smaller: fair
Apatite	Apatite	Various shades of blue and green varieties	1 to under 3 cts: $90–190 3 to under 5 cts: $115–200	Fair	Fair; soft, scratches easily	Good
Benitoite	Benitoite	Blue, violetish blue, bluish violet	½ to under 1 ct: $1,565–1,940 1 to under 2 cts: $2,125–4,500 2 to under 3 cts: $4,500–6,250	Very good	Fair to good	Up to 1 ct: good; larger: fair to poor
Beryl[1]	Aquamarine	Pastel blue to medium deep blue	1 to under 5 cts: $200–815 5 to under 10 cts: $500–1,000	Good	Good	Good
	Golden beryl (heliodor)	Yellow, brownish yellow	1 to under 5 cts: $100–200 5 to under 10 cts: $150–225	Good	Good	Good
	Green beryl	Pastel grayish green to yellowish green or bluish green	1 to under 5 cts: $90–190 5 to under 10 cts: $150–215	Good	Good	Good
	Emerald[2]	Yellow-green to blue-green	1 to under 2 cts: $3,340–10,000 2 to under 4 cts: $4,750–13,750	Fair to good	Fair to good	Very fine Colombian: rare; others: good

*Prices compiled from *The Guide*, Gemworld International, Inc., and adjusted to retail. The unprecedented global recession has caused wide variation in colored gemstone pricing. Prices indicated serve as a relative guide to the impact of quality differences in pricing.

[1]Beryl also comes in green (different from emerald green), lilac, salmon, and orange. Most colors are still not readily available, but some, such as the lovely orange variety, can be found for under $150 per carat and offer excellent value.

[2]Cabochon-cut rubies, sapphires, and emeralds usually cost much less; the finest gems can cost much more.

Chart continues on next page.

Family	Popular Name	Color(s)	Approx. Retail Cost Per Carat	Brilliance	Wearability	Availability
Beryl (cont.)	Morganite	Pink to orange-pink	1 to under 5 cts: $90–225 5 to under 10 cts: $140–415	Good	Good	Fine: rare; medium: good
	Red beryl[3] (Red Emerald™)	Light to deep orangish red to purplish red	under 1 ct: $10,000–12,500 1 to under 2 cts: $16,000–50,000 2 to under 2½ cts: $50,000–60,000	Fair to good	Fair to good	Very fine: rare; medium: good
Chrysoberyl	Alexandrite	Changes from greenish in daylight to reddish in incandescent light	½ to under 2 cts: $5,500–13,750 2 to under 5 cts: $8,250–18,750	Good	Excellent	Large: poor; small: fair
	Chrysoberyl	Yellow to yellow-brown to yellow-green	1 to under 5 cts: $100–275 5 to under 10 cts: $225–350	Good	Excellent	Fair
	Precious cat's-eye	Greenish to brownish yellow with "cat's-eye" effect	1 to under 3 cts: $1,500–3,500 3 to under 5 cts: $2,250–4,500	Negligible	Excellent	Fair to good
Corundum	Ruby[2]	Red to bluish or purplish red to yellow-red	½ to under 1 ct: $2,375–3,875 1 to under 2 cts: $3,250–5,500 2 to under 4 cts: $4,750–13,000	Fair to good	Excellent	Fine, natural color: rare; others: good
	Blue sapphire[2]	Bright blue to inky blue	½ to under 1 ct: $675–1,650 1 to under 2 cts: $1,425–4,125 2 to under 4 cts: $2,125–7,000	Good	Excellent	Natural color: rare; others: good
	Blue star sapphire[2]		½ to under 1 ct: $250–500 1 to under 3 cts: $1,500–3,000 3 to under 5 cts: $2,500–4,500	Fair to good	Good to excellent	Fine color and strong star: rare; others: good
	Colorless sapphire	White (colorless)	½ to under 1 ct: $75–125 1 to under 2 cts: $125–250	Good	Very good	Fair

[2]Cabochon-cut rubies, sapphires, and emeralds usually cost much less; the finest gems can cost much more. Fine-quality natural Burmese sapphire and ruby are very rare and command much higher prices than those shown here. *Composite ruby* should sell for under $75 *for the stone* in sizes up to 5 carats.
[3]Prices are based on information provided by Equatorian Imports, Inc. (Dallas, Texas).

		Color	Price / sizes			
Corundum (*cont.*)	**Green sapphire**	Clear green to brownish or bluish green	1 to under 3 cts: $340–690; 3 to under 5 cts: $550–1,000	Good	Excellent	Clear green: rare; others: good
	Pink sapphire	Light to very dark pink (almost red)	1 to under 3 cts: $750–2,250; 3 to under 5 cts: $875–3,000	Good	Excellent	Fair; good in sizes under 1 ct
	Yellow sapphire	Yellow (most are heat-treated; natural yellow usually less brilliant)	1 to under 5 cts: $250–1,500; 5 to under 10 cts: $750–1,565	Good	Excellent	Large: poor; others: fair
Feldspar	**Labradorite**	Deep gray-blue to brownish blue with strong iridescent play of color	16" strand of 8mm beads: $182–245	Not applicable	Good	Good
	Moonstone	Milky white to blue-white	1 to under 5 cts: $20–125	Not applicable	Good	White: good; blue: fair
	Sunstone[4]	Red, orange, green	under 1 ct: $250–500; 1 to under 5 cts: $300–1,315	Fair to good	Good	Small sizes: good; others: fair
Garnet	**Almandine** (**common garnet**)	Purplish red to pure red	1 to under 5 cts: $30–40; 5 to under 10 cts: $40–65	Fair to good	Good	Fair
	Demantoid	Yellow-green to emerald green	1 to under 2 cts: $2,250–4,500; 2 to under 3 cts: $3,750–6,250	Very good	Good	Good
	Grossularite	Yellow to yellowish green to yellowish brown	1 to under 5 cts: $175–750; 5 to under 10 cts: $375–1,125	Fair to good	Good	Good
	Malaya	Pink-orange to brownish red	1 to under 5 cts: $50–110; 5 to under 10 cts: $80–175	Good	Good	Poor
	Pyrope (**common garnet**)	Yellowish red to dark red	1 to under 5 cts: $20–40; 5 to under 20 cts: $30–70	Fair to good	Good	Good

Chart continues on next page.

[4]Bicolor, tricolor, and color-change sunstones also occur but are rare. Prices for these are much higher than indicated for other colors of sunstone.

Family	Popular Name	Color(s)	Approx. Retail Cost Per Carat	Brilliance	Wearability	Availability
Garnet (cont.)	Rhodolite	Red-violet	1 to under 5 cts: $55–175 5 to under 20 cts: $115–275	Good	Very good	Good
	Spessartite	Brownish orange to reddish brown to brownish red	1 to under 5 cts: $65–115 5 to under 30 cts: $90–175	Good	Very good	Good
	Spessartite—Nigerian	Brownish orange to red-orange	1 to under 3 cts: $315–565 3 to under 10 cts: $565–1,000 10 to under 30 cts: $750–1,375	Good	Very good	Good
	Mandarin	Intense orange to fiery reddish orange	1 to under 5 cts: $565–1,250 5 to under 10 cts: $1,000–1,550	Fair to very good	Very good	Large: rare; others: good
	Tsavorite	Yellowish green to bluish green	1 to under 3 cts: $2,000–3,125 3 to under 5 cts: $3,500–4,750 5 to under 10 cts: $5,500–6,875	Good	Very good	Good
Iolite	Iolite	Violet-blue to gray-blue	1 to under 5 cts: $75–150 5 to under 10 cts: $115–190	Good	Fair	Fair
Peridot (olivine)	Peridot	Yellow-green to deep green to rich chartreuse	1 to under 5 cts: $90–175 5 to under 10 cts: $165–275	Fair to good	Fair: will scratch easily	Large: poor; small: good
Quartz	Amethyst	Purple, reddish purple to brownish purple	1 to under 5 cts: $25–75 5 to under 10 cts: $40–90 10 to under 25 cts: $55–115	Fair to good	Good	Very good
	Ametrine	Shades of yellow and purple in same stone	1 to under 5 cts: $20–50 5 to under 25 cts: $30–75	Good	Good	Good
	Citrine	Yellow to yellow-brown	1 to under 5 cts: $20–65 5 to under 25 cts: $40–75	Good	Good	Good
	Rose quartz & Smoky quartz	Pure pink; some murky; some clear, transparent; brown shades	most sizes: $6–20 per stone	Good	Good	Good

Group	Variety	Color	Price			
Spinel	Blue spinel	Medium gray-blue to deep blue to violet	1 to under 3 cts: $675–1,125 3 to under 5 cts: $750–1,500	Good	Very good	Good
	Pink spinel	Lively or bright pink to brownish pink	1 to under 3 cts: $1,250–2,750 3 to under 5 cts: $1,625–3,750	Very good	Very good	Fair
	Red spinel	Red to brownish red	1 to under 3 cts: $1,125–3,000 3 to under 5 cts: $1,500–5,000	Very good	Very good	Ruby red: poor; others: good
Spodumene	Kunzite	Lilac, violet, pink	1 to under 5 cts: $40–165 5 to under 20 cts: $150–240	Good	Poor for rings	Good
Topaz	Blue topaz	Blue	1 to under 5 cts: $15–25 5 to under 20 cts: $20–30	Good	Fair	Good
	Imperial topaz	Golden with pinkish/reddish overtone	1 to under 3 cts: $340–1,225 3 to under 5 cts: $840–1,565	Good	Fair	Fair to good except in very large sizes
	Pink topaz	Pink (red also available, but very rare and much more expensive)	1 to under 3 cts: $1,125–2,000 3 to under 5 cts: $1,375–2,250	Good	Fair	Fair to good
	Yellow/golden topaz	Yellow/golden (no pink/red overtone)	1 to under 5 cts: $190–590 5 to under 20 cts: $375–690	Good	Good	Good
Tourmaline	Chrome	Deep green	1 to under 3 cts: $500–1,065 3 to under 5 cts: $875–1,125	Good	Fair to good	Poor
	Indicolite	Inky blue to blue-green	1 to under 5 cts: $340–750 5 to under 10 cts: $440–875	Good	Fair to good	Good
	Paraiba (neon)	Wide range of "neon" blue, green, blue-green, and purplish blue	under 1 ct: $1,500–10,000 1 to under 3 cts: $11,250–30,000	Excellent	Fair to good	Under 1 ct: fair; over 1 ct in fine quality: scarce
	Pink	Pink or rose	1 to under 5 cts: $175–500 5 to under 10 cts: $225–625	Good	Fair to good	Good
	Rubellite	Red to violet	1 to under 5 cts: $200–675 5 to under 10 cts: $450–750	Good	Fair to good	Good

Chart continues on next page.

Family	Popular Name	Color(s)	Approx. Retail Cost Per Carat	Brilliance	Wearability	Availability
Tourmaline (cont.)	Verdelite (green)	Green—all shades except chrome	1 to under 3 cts: $125–175 3 to under 5 cts: $250–415 5 to under 20 cts: $315–500	Good	Fair to good	Good
	Golden	Yellow, orange, and brown varieties	1 to under 5 cts: $190–500 5 to under 10 cts: $550–815	Good	Fair to good	Fair
	Bicolor, tricolor	Red/black, red/green, red/green/colorless	1 to under 5 cts: $165–565 5 to under 10 cts: $250–625	Good	Fair to good	Good
Zircon	Zircon	Pastel blue (usually heat-treated)	1 to under 5 cts: $150–300 5 to under 10 cts: $225–565	Good	Fair: zircon is not recommended for rings	Large: poor
		Brown to pinkish-brown	1 to under 5 cts: $90–215 5 to under 10 cts: $165–250	Good		Good
		All other colors	1 to under 5 cts: $100–165 5 to under 10 cts: $175–225	Good	"	True red: poor; other colors: good
Zoisite	Tanzanite (blue-violet)	Strong blue to weak violet, blue-violet	1 to under 3 cts: $750–1,065 3 to under 10 cts: $1,125–1,190 10 to under 20 cts: $1,190–1,250	Good	Poor for rings	Good

Opal Retail Price Guide*
Approximate Retail Cost *Per Carat*

There are numerous varieties of opals and wide ranges in quality. Quality differences are often difficult for the amateur to distinguish, but they may significantly affect price. The following prices provide only a guide. For more detailed information, see Selected Readings.

Popular Opal Varieties

Type	Size	Good	Fine	Extra Fine
White base, jelly opal	1 to under 15 cts	$25–75	$75–200	$200–1,000
Crystal, white	1 to under 15 cts	$30–85	$85–225	$225–1,120
Semi-crystal, gray base	1 to under 15 cts	$40–90	$150–875	$625–2,500
Fire (faceted)	5 to under 10 cts	$115–275	$275–590	$590–1,125

Black and Crystal Black Opal

Color	Size	Good	Fine	Extra Fine
Red-orange	1 to under 15 cts	$125–1,250	$940–6,250	$5,375–20,000
Green-blue	1 to under 15 cts	$90–590	$500–3,125	$2,750–12,000
Crystal	1 to under 15 cts	$65–475	$450–2,250	$2,125–8,750

Boulder Opal—Price *per stone*

	Size	Good	Fine	Extra Fine
Small	1 to 5 cts	$75–1,250	$1,250–3,750	$3,750–7,500
Medium	5 to 10 cts	$500–2,125	$2,125–5,000	$5,000–13,000
Large	10 to 15 cts	$750–2,750	$2,750–6,250	$6,250–20,000
Very large	15 to 30 cts plus	$1,125–4,500	$3,750–14,000	$12,500–80,000

*Prices compiled from *The Guide*, Gemworld International, Inc., and adjusted to retail. The unprecedented global recession has caused wide variation in colored gemstone pricing. Prices indicated serve as a relative guide to the impact of quality differences in pricing.

Synthetic Gemstone Retail Price Guide*

Common Synthetics
Prices are *per stone* in U.S. dollars.

Shape	Cubic Zirconia (CZ)	Synthetic Spinel	Synthetic Sapphire	Synthetic Spinel Triplet
Oval				
8x6 mm	$10	$10	$10	$20
10x8 mm	$10	$15	$15	$30
12x10 mm	$15	$15	$20	$35
Round				
4 mm	$5	$5	$10	$10
6 mm	$5	$10	$10	$20
8 mm	$10	$10	$15	$25

Flux-Grown Synthetics
Prices are *per carat* in U.S. dollars and are for all shapes.

Gemstone	Gem+ (flawless)	Gem Quality (eye clean)	Fine (slightly included)	A (moderately included)
Chatham created emerald (5–10 carats)		$565	$440	
Chatham created ruby (5–10 carats)		$540	$375	
Chatham created blue, pink, and padparadscha sapphire and alexandrite (5–10 carats)†		$375		
Ramaura™ cultured ruby (3–5 carats)	$750	$600	$285	$225
Empress™ cultured emerald (5–10 carats)	$375	$275	$225	$180
Nicholas™ created alexandrite (all weights)		$180		

*Prices are compiled from synthetic-gemstone producers and adjusted to retail.

†Chatham created alexandrite and sapphire are only available in gem quality.

Hydrothermal and Pulled Synthetics

Prices are *per carat* in U.S. dollars.

Gemstone	All Qualities
Lannyte lab-grown ruby and rose sapphire (round)*	
2+ mm	$145–180
4+ mm	$105–130
6+ mm	$55–80
Lannyte lab-grown alexandrite (round)*	
4+ mm	$130–155
6+ mm	$105–120
8+ mm	$70–95
Lannyte lab-grown emerald (square)*	
4–5.5 mm	$155
6–7.5 mm	$145
8–10 mm	$120–130

*Add $5 per carat for radiant, trilliant, and cushion cuts.

Recrystallized Ruby and Sapphire

Prices are *per carat* in U.S. dollars.

Larger than 1 carat	Top Quality
Recrystallized ruby	$630
Recrystallized sapphire	$690

Gilson Lab-Created Opal

Prices are *per gram* in U.S. dollars and are for all shapes.

All Weights	All Qualities
White Gilson opal	$30–100
Crystal Gilson opal	$30–115
Black Gilson opal	$40–165

Composite Gemstone Retail Price Guide

Ammolite Triplets

Prices are *per stone* in U.S. dollars.

Size	Good	Fine	Extra Fine
8x6 mm	$130	$260	$420
10x8 mm	$220	$435	$720
12x10 mm	$335	$655	$1,080

Glass-Ruby Composites

Prices are *per carat* in U.S. dollars.

Size	Approx. Retail Cost
1 to under 5 cts	$10–15
5 to under 10 cts	$15–20

Lannyte Emerald Doublets

Prices are *per carat* in U.S. dollars.

Shape	Top Quality Only
Round	
4 mm	$225
8 mm	$290
12 mm	$300
Emerald cut	
4x6 mm	$225
8x10 mm	$275
10x12 mm	$300
Oval	
4x6 mm	$225
8x10 mm	$275
12x14 mm	$325

Opal Triplets—Price *per piece*

Size	Good	Fine	Extra Fine
8x6 mm	$24–40	$50	$100
10x8 mm	$45–80	$100	$150
12x10 mm	$60–120	$160	$230
14x10 mm	$80–175	$220	$325

CHAPTER NINE

Colorful Choices in Colored Gemstones

The Big Three—Emerald, Ruby, and Sapphire

Emerald

Emerald is a green variety of the mineral beryl. One of the rarest members of the beryl family, it is one of the most highly prized of all the gems. There is only one member of the beryl family that is rarer—the *red* variety, also known as Red Emerald™. Aside from being the birthstone for May, it was historically believed to bestow on its wearer faithfulness and unchanging love, and was thought to enable the wearer to forecast events.

Contrary to popular belief, emerald is *not soft.* It ranks 7½ to 8 on Mohs' scale—an internationally recognized standard that ranks hardness on a scale from 1 to 10, with 1 being the softest and 10 the hardest. It is more fragile than other varieties of beryl and other gems, however, because it is more brittle and under more stress from fractures resulting from the violent geologic conditions under which it formed. This is why it is important to exercise care when you are wearing and handling emerald.

The highest-quality emerald has the color of fresh, young green grass—an almost pure spectral green, possibly with a very faint blue tint. Flawless emeralds are so rare that they are immediately suspect; thus, flaws have come to serve as "fingerprints" of genuineness. Connoisseurs seek fine emeralds from Colombia, which is known for its intensely rich, vivid-colored emeralds. Colombia is one of the most important emerald sources historically, but other sources now include Afghanistan, Brazil, India, Pakistan, Russia, and Zambia. It is also worth noting that a new emerald discovery in the United States, in Hiddenite, North Carolina, has produced some major crystals with fine color and clarity, and may provide an important new source of fine emerald.

Because of emerald's popularity and value, imitations are abundant. Glass, manufactured complete with "flaws," and doublets or triplets, such as two pieces of pale emerald or aquamarine fused together with a deep-green coloring agent (see chapter 6), are often encountered. New products such as the Lannyte emerald doublet are also entering the market; when properly represented, they can make an interesting jewelry choice, but a second or third party may fail to mention that they are doublets.

Also, fine synthetic emeralds are being produced (see chapter 5) that are indistinguishable from the natural with the eye alone. They not only look like natural emerald in their outward appearance, but the internal characteristics can so closely resemble the natural that it is sometimes necessary to send the stone to a major gem-testing laboratory to determine whether it is natural or synthetic. These synthetics are not inexpensive themselves, except by comparison with a genuine emerald of equivalent quality.

Techniques to enhance color and reduce the visibility of flaws are also frequently used. A common practice is to fill surface-reaching cracks with oil (sometimes tinted green)—a practice that goes back to early Greek times. Today emeralds are oiled by use of a vacuum/heat technology. This is a widely accepted trade practice, since it is actually good for the stone in light of its fragile nature. Oiling hides some of the whitish flaws, which are actually cracks, filling the cracks so they become less visible. The oil becomes an integral part of the emerald unless it is subjected to some type of degreasing procedure. The development and use of the ultrasonic cleaner has brought to light the extensiveness of this practice. *Never clean emeralds in an ultrasonic cleaner.* (An ionic cleaner is fine for emeralds as well as for all other jewelry.)

A good friend of mine took her heirloom emerald ring to her jeweler for a "really good cleaning." Luckily for the jeweler, she never left the store and was standing right there when the ring was put into the cleaner and removed. She couldn't believe her eyes. She was shocked by the loss of color and the sudden appearance of more flaws. The ultrasonic cleaner had removed the oil that had penetrated the cracks, and an emerald several shades lighter and more visibly flawed emerged. Had she not been there, she would never have believed the jeweler hadn't pulled a switch.

Oiling is considered an acceptable practice, but be sure the price reflects the actual quality of the stone. If necessary, most emeralds can be re-oiled.

Epoxy-resin fillers are a recent newcomer, but this treatment is gaining popularity and is now used on many emeralds mined in many parts of the world, including Colombia and Brazil.

As with all highly desired gems, the greater the value and demand, the greater the occurrence of fraudulent practices. Examples of almost every type of technique to simulate emerald can be found: color alteration by using green foil on closed backs; use of synthetics; substitution of less valuable green stones, doublets, or other composites. Therefore, be especially cautious of bargains, deal with reputable jewelers when planning to purchase, and *always* have the purchase double-checked by a qualified gemologist-appraiser. Any very fine emerald purchased today should have a laboratory report or be submitted to a lab to obtain one.

An American gem gains world recognition—Red Emerald™. Gemologists prefer calling this gem *red beryl* or *bixbite* (after Maynard Bixby, the man who discovered it) rather than red "emerald," but whatever the name, it is a beautiful gem and one of the world's rarest.

As I discuss in greater detail later, the beryl family offers us many beautiful gems: the blue variety is known as *aquamarine,* the pink variety as *morganite* (named after the wealthy twentieth-century philanthropist J. P. Morgan), a colorless variety as *goshenite,* and the deep-green variety as *emerald.* There is also a more common variety that occurs in a range of yellow shades that is known simply as *golden beryl* or *yellow beryl.* And another fairly common variety known simply as *green beryl* occurs in a light-to-medium bluish, yellowish, or grayish green.

The only known source of gem-quality red beryl is the United States. The mine is located in the Wah Wah Mountain range in Utah. Red beryl from this mine is marketed under the name Red Emerald™. For years it was known only to gemologists and rock hounds; jewelers were unaware of it because there was insufficient supply to meet any significant demand, so it remained obscure. This began to change when a major pocket was discovered in the 1980s, and red beryl is now sought by designers for unique and precious jewelry sold in the finest jewelry salons.

Until red beryl became available, the rarest variety of beryl was the deep-green variety known as emerald. The red variety is even rarer, and in an effort to communicate its rarity, preciousness, and value, many prefer to call it red "emerald." In fact, apart from its color, it more closely resembles emerald than any other member of the beryl family, especially in terms of internal features such as inclusions and fractures (resulting from the stressful geological conditions under which it is created). In light of this and the fact that it is even rarer than the green variety we call emerald, most people agree that referring to it as "red emerald" most clearly communicates to the layperson what it is. Furthermore, in terms of value, the association with emerald does not create a misleading perception of value or rarity; it is rarer and can be costlier than emerald itself.

Red Emerald™ remains rare in sizes over 2 carats. The world's largest Red Emerald™ weighs 8.03 carats; the second-largest weighs 4.50 carats. In sizes up to 2 carats, the price of fine-quality Red Emerald™ can be comparable to fine ruby, and the price often exceeds that of green emerald.

USEFUL FACTS

Emerald Composition: beryllium aluminum silicate   **Hardness**: 7.5–8.0
Weight: light (specific gravity: 2.69–2.76)   **Wearability**: fair to good
Brilliance: moderately high

Ruby

Prized through the ages as, in the words of the Roman historian Pliny, the "gem of gems . . . surpassing all other precious stones in virtue," ruby is the red variety of the mineral corundum. Historically, it has been symbolic of love and passion, considered to be an aid to firm friendship, and believed to ensure beauty. Today's birthstone for July, ruby has a color that ranges from purplish or bluish red to a yellowish red. The finest color is a vivid, almost pure spectral red with a very faint undertone of blue, as seen in Burmese rubies, which are considered the finest among ardent collectors. Other sources of fine ruby are Thailand, Vietnam, Cambodia, Kenya, Madagascar, Malawi, Tanzania, and Azad Kashmir in Pakistan, and new deposits have recently been discovered in Australia, Greenland, and Mozambique. The ruby is very brilliant and very hard, ranking 9 on Mohs' scale.

Ruby is also very durable and wearable—characteristics that make it an unusually fine choice for any piece of jewelry.

Translucent varieties of ruby are also seen, and one variety exhibits a six-ray star effect when cut as a cabochon. This variety is called *star ruby* and is one of nature's most beautiful and interesting gifts. But, as with so many other beautiful gifts once produced only in nature, these lovely gems are now duplicated in synthetic star rubies, and numerous faked star rubies are also the products of human beings' attempts at mimicry.

Here again, remember that the greater the value and demand, the greater the use of techniques to "improve" or to simulate. Among rubies, as among other gemstones, examples of almost every type of deceptive technique can be found—color enhancement, synthesis, substitutes, doublets, triplets, misleading names, and so on. Be especially alert to the possibility of diffusion treatment, oiling of reflective fractures, and "composite ruby" (see chapters 5 and 6).

The newest laboratory-grown synthetic rubies, like those made by Ramaura and Chatham, are so close to natural ruby in every aspect that many are actually passing for genuine, even among gemologists. When you are getting a very fine, valuable ruby, be sure to verify genuineness with a gemologist who has both many years' experience in colored gems and an astute knowledge of the marketplace today. I would recommend having the jeweler or gemologist also obtain a colored-gemstone report from a major gem-testing laboratory.

Here again, be especially cautious of bargains. Deal with reputable jewelers when planning to purchase, and have the purchase double-checked by a qualified gemologist-appraiser.

USEFUL FACTS

Ruby Composition: aluminum oxide   **Hardness**: 9.0
Weight: heavy (specific gravity: 3.97–4.05)   **Wearability**: excellent
Brilliance: high

Sapphire

The "celestial" sapphire—symbol of the heavens, guardian of innocence, bestower of truth and good health, preserver of chastity—is in fact the mineral corundum. While we know it best in its blue variety, which is highly prized, it comes in essentially every color; red corundum is ruby. As with ruby, its sister stone, sapphire is characterized by hardness (9 on Mohs' scale), brilliance, and availability in many beautiful colors, all of which make corundum probably the most important and most versatile of the gem families.

Blue sapphires can be among the most valuable members of the sapphire family—especially stones from Burma (Myanmar) and Kashmir, which are closest to the pure spectral blue. Fine, brilliant, deep-blue Burmese sapphires will surely dazzle the eye and the pocketbook, as will the Kashmir, which is a fine, velvety-toned deep blue.

The Ceylon (Sri Lanka) sapphires are a very pleasing blue but are a less deep shade than the Burmese or Kashmir, instead tending to fall more on the pastel side.

I am also seeing many Australian sapphires, which are often a dark blue but with a slightly green undertone, as are those from Thailand; both sell for much less per carat. They offer a very affordable alternative to the Burmese, Kashmir, or Ceylon, and can still be very pleasing in their color. Blue sapphires also come from Tanzania, Brazil, Africa, and even the United States. Montana sapphires are very collectible because of their unusual shades of color and because many are *natural* color—that is, not subjected to any treatment. For those who want a gem that is truly "natural," Montana sapphire may be the choice for you.

With sapphire, origin can have a significant effect on price, so if you are purchasing a Kashmir, Burmese, or Ceylon sapphire, that should be noted on the bill of sale.

Like ruby, the blue sapphire may be found in a translucent variety that may show a six-rayed star effect when cut into a cabochon. This variety is known as *star sapphire,* of which there are numerous synthetics (often referred to in the trade as Linde, pronounced *Lin′dee*).

In addition to blue sapphire, we are now beginning to see many other color varieties in the latest jewelry designs—especially yellow and pink (Madagascar has recently emerged as an important source of pink sapphires) and in smaller sizes, some beautiful shades of green. These are known as *fancy* sapphires. Compared with the costly blue sapphire and ruby, these stones offer excellent value and real beauty.

A beautiful and rare variety called *padparadscha* (a type of lotus flower) is also in demand. The true padparadscha should exhibit a *pink and orange color simultaneously.* Depending on the richness of color, brilliance, and size, these can be very expensive. A lovely but more common and more affordable variety available today is really a rich orange color. It is often sold as padparadscha, but the rarer and more costly gem will always exhibit a strong pink with the orange.

Many sapphires today tend to be too dark, however, because of the presence of too much black and poor cutting (cutting deep for additional weight), but the deep blues can be treated to lighten the color. Inevitably, evidence abounds of every technique known to imitate and improve the perceived quality and value of sapphire (see chapter 5). Be especially alert to the possibility of diffusion treatment (see chapter 5) and be aware that oil is being used increasingly to conceal fractures and reflective inclusions. New synthetics are also entering the market in a much wider range of color, including a vivid green color and the lovely orange-pink color of the very rare and costly padparadscha sapphire. Also, watch out for some very convincing doublets—composed of a thin sliver of real sapphire on the top bonded to a *synthetic* bottom—flooding the market. As always, I urge you to be especially cautious of bargains, deal with reputable jewelers, and have your stone double-checked by a qualified gemologist-appraiser.

USEFUL FACTS

Sapphire Composition: aluminum oxide   **Hardness:** 9.0
Weight: heavy (specific gravity: 3.97–4.05)   **Wearability:** excellent
Brilliance: high

Other Popular Colored Gems

Alexandrite

Alexandrite is a fascinating transparent gem that appears grass green in daylight and raspberry red under artificial light. It is a variety of chrysoberyl reputedly discovered in Russia in 1834 on the day the future Czar Alexander II reached his majority, and thus it was named in his honor. In Russia it is considered a stone of very good omen. It is also considered Friday's stone, or the stone of "Friday's child."

Unlike other stones, which humankind has known about and admired for thousands of years, alexandrite is a relatively recent gem discovery. Nonetheless, this rare beauty has come into its own; it is sought by connoisseurs and commands very high prices. The primary sources for alexandrite today include Russia, Brazil, Madagascar, and Sri Lanka. While I've seen gem-quality alexandrite in very large sizes (fifteen to twenty carats), they are usually small and are rare in sizes over three carats. A fine three-carat stone can cost $45,000 today. If you see an alexandrite that measures more than half an inch in width, be suspicious of a fake. Alexandrite is a hard, durable stone (8½ on Mohs' scale) and is normally cut in a faceted style, but some cat's-eye-type alexandrites, found in Brazil, are cut as a cabochon to display the eye effect. These are usually small; the largest I've seen was approximately three carats.

Before 1973, there were really no good synthetic alexandrites. While some varieties of synthetic corundum and synthetic spinel were frequently sold as alexandrite, they really didn't look like the real thing but were hard to differentiate, since so few buyers had ever seen genuine stones. They are, however, easy for a gemologist to spot. In 1973, a very good synthetic alexandrite was produced that is not easy to differentiate from natural stones. While a good gemologist today can identify the synthetics, when they first appeared on the market many were mistaken for the real thing. Be especially careful to verify the authenticity of your alexandrite, since it might have been mistakenly identified years ago and passed along to you today as authentic!

USEFUL FACTS

Alexandrite Composition: beryllium aluminum oxide   **Hardness**: 8.50
Weight: heavy (specific gravity: 3.70–3.72)   **Wearability**: excellent
Brilliance: high

Amber

Amber is not a stone but rather amorphous, fossilized tree sap. It was one of the earliest substances used for personal adornment. Modestly decorated pieces of rough amber have been found in Stone Age excavations and are assumed to have been used as amulets and talismans—a use definitely recorded throughout history before, during, and since the ancient Greeks. Because of its beautiful color and the ease with which it could be fashioned, amber quickly became a favorite object of trade and barter and personal adornment. Amber varies from transparent to semi-translucent and from yellow to dark brown in color; occasionally it's seen in reddish- and greenish-brown tones. In addition, amber can be dyed many colors. Occasionally, one can find "foreign" fragments or insects that were trapped in the amber, which usually increases its value because of the added curiosity factor. The best-known source of amber is in the Baltic region, primarily along the coastlines of Poland and Russia but also in Norway and Denmark. Amber is also found in Canada, the Czech Republic, the Dominican Republic, England, France, Germany, Italy, Mexico, Romania, and the United States.

Plastics are the most common amber imitations. But real amber, which is the lightest gem material, may be easily distinguished from most plastic when dropped into a saturated salt solution: amber will float, while plastic sinks. One other commonly encountered "amber" type is "reconstructed" amber—amber fragments compressed under heat to form a larger piece. An expert can differentiate this from real amber under magnification.

Amber can be easily tested by touching it in an inconspicuous place with a hot needle (held by tweezers). The whitish smoke that should be produced should smell like burning pine wood, not like medicine or disinfectant. If there is no smoke, but a black mark occurs, then it is *not* amber. Another test is to try to cut a little piece of the amber with a sharp pointed knife, at the drill hole of the bead; if it cuts like wood (producing a shaving), it is *not* amber, which would produce a sharp, crumbly deposit.

With the exception of those pieces possessing special antique value, the value of amber fluctuates with its popularity, which in part is dictated by the fashion industry and the prevalence of yellow and browns in one's wardrobe. Nonetheless, amber has proved itself an ageless gem and will always be loved and admired.

USEFUL FACTS

Amber Composition: organic plant resins
Weight: very light (specific gravity: 1.05–1.09)
Brilliance: moderate

Hardness: 2.0–2.5 (soft)
Wearability: Good

Amethyst

Amethyst, a transparent purple variety of quartz, is one of the most popular of the colored stones. Once believed to bring peace of mind to the wearer, it was also thought to prevent the wearer from getting drunk. If the circle of the sun or moon was engraved thereon, amethyst was believed to prevent death from poison.

Available in shades from light to dark purple, this February birthstone is relatively hard (7 on Mohs' scale), fairly brilliant, and overall a good, versatile, wearable stone, available in plentiful supply even in very large sizes (although large sizes with deep color are now becoming scarce). Amethyst is found in many countries. Some of the finest comes from Bolivia, Brazil, and Russia (which has a slightly reddish undertone to the purple), but it is also found in Australia, Canada, Germany, India, Madagascar, Namibia, Sri Lanka, Uruguay, the United States, and Zambia.

Amethyst is probably one of the most beautiful stones available at a moderate price; buyers should be careful, however, because "fine" amethyst is being produced synthetically today. Most synthetics can be identified by a skilled gemologist.

Amethyst may fade from heat and strong sunshine. Guard your amethyst from these conditions, and it should retain its color indefinitely. We are hearing stories from customers across the country, however, complaining of newly purchased amethyst jewelry fading over just a few months, from *deep purple* to *light lavender*. This should not happen and may result from an unacceptable color treatment. If your stone fades this quickly, return it to your jeweler.

USEFUL FACTS

Amethyst Composition: silicon dioxide   **Hardness**: 7.0
Weight: light (specific gravity: 2.65)   **Wearability**: good
Brilliance: moderate

Ammolite

Ammolite, also called ammonite, is a very interesting, vibrantly colored material that has entered the jewelry scene in recent years. Known to Native Americans of the last century—and believed to be a good-luck stone that would assure wealth and abundance—it has only been since 1981, following the discovery of a new source in Alberta, Canada, that there has been a sufficient supply of fine-quality ammolite to make it available for jewelry.

Ammolite is actually fossilized ammonite, an extinct shellfish that ceased to exist millions of years ago. The fossil has a coiled shape and is popular among fossil collectors. The name is derived from the ancient Egyptian god Ammon, who is depicted with the head of a ram and twisted spiral horns, similar to the coiled shell of the ammonite mollusk.

Ammolite, the gem, results when the calcium in the fossil is replaced with other minerals such as pyrite, iron, calcite, and so on. This, combined with light interference passing through the multiple layers of the gemstone, which is refracted into a rainbow of colors reflected back to the eye, is what causes the unusual coloration and iridescent character of this gem. Ammolite forms with very distinctive markings. While it resembles black opal in some ways, the surface reveals a unique pattern, an almost "crackled" effect that looks something like a snakeskin. It exhibits a melange of bright colors, including orange, red, green, and yellow. It also occurs with blue and purple, but these colors are rare and highly prized. The finest material exhibits three or more colors and, like fine opal, the color shifts back and forth from one to another as you tilt the stone back and forth.

The *intensity* of color, *range* of color, and *pattern* of color are the most important factors related to quality. The separations between the colors, the dark areas, must also be evaluated. Fine material will have very few or minimal separations, or separations that form a distinct and interesting pattern; if the patterns have special allure, they can increase value. If the separations are pronounced and unsightly, they diminish the value.

Sometimes ammolite is so thin that it is too delicate to use alone in jewelry. Ammolite triplets topped with synthetic spinel are common. Triplets sell for about half the price of natural ammolites. Prices are based on size (number of square millimeters), individuality, and overall quality. Typically, a triplet will range from $80 to $1,500 per stone; natural, free-form stones weighing 25 to 35 carats range from $750 to $6,125 per stone.

USEFUL FACTS

Ammolite Composition (fossilized ammonite): varies depending on replacement mineral
Weight: varies

Brilliance: high
Hardness: 3.5–4.5 (soft)
Wearability: poor to good

Ammolite is relatively soft (3.5–4.5 depending upon chemical composition) and special care is recommended. Wrap it in a soft cloth or tissue before placing it in a jewelry case, or keep it in a separate compartment to protect it from being scratched. Avoid exposing ammolite to acids, ammonia, hairspray, and perfumes. Clean with a soft brush, using mild soap and water or a pearl cleaner.

Andalusite (Poor Man's Alexandrite)

Andalusite is now offering interesting new possibilities for jewelry. Brazil is the primary source of these fascinating, fairly hard (7 to 7½ on Mohs' scale), and fairly durable stones. Andalusite is very interesting because it may exhibit several colors: an olive green from one direction, a rich reddish brown from another direction, and grayish green from yet another direction. In an emerald cut, it may look primarily green while exhibiting an orange color at the ends of the emerald shape. In a round cut, you may see the green body color with simultaneous flashes of another color. One benefit andalusite has over alexandrite is that you don't have to change the light in which it is being seen to experience its colors; merely changing the perspective does the trick. A rare and sometimes expensive emerald-green variety may exhibit a bright yellow simultaneously, or when viewed from different angles. A pink variety does not exhibit this kind of color phenomenon. While andalusite is not readily available yet, it is finding a market, especially among men. Andalusite is found primarily in Brazil and Sri Lanka but other sources include Australia, Canada, Russia, Spain, and the United States.

USEFUL FACTS

Andalusite Composition: aluminum silicate   Hardness: 7.0–7.5
Weight: moderately heavy (specific gravity: 3.10–3.2)   Wearability: good
Brilliance: moderate

Apatite

Apatite is a lovely stone that occurs in a range of colors including almost every shade of yellow, blue, green, purple, and pink. Unfortunately it is very soft and doesn't wear well. For this reason, it has not been used in jewelry until recently. It has become very popular in the past few years because in its unusual green, blue, and violet colors it is very similar to the newcomer Paraiba tourmaline (see pages 161–162). This very rare variety of tourmaline, discovered in the 1990s, occurs in what has been described as neon colors, colors never seen before in jewelry. The colors are so electric that it became popular overnight. Demand increased while supply dwindled, and prices for Paraiba soared, reaching prices comparable to gem-quality sapphire and emerald! As Paraiba tourmaline exceeded the reach of most people, apatite suddenly came into its own as a gem that is readily available, offering amazingly similar colors and costing a fraction of the price. An apatite in the one- to two-carat size range might cost $200 to 300 per carat compared to $10,000 to $15,000 per carat for a one- to two-carat Paraiba.

Apatite is abundant and is found in many countries, including Myanmar (Burma), Sri Lanka, Brazil, Russia, Canada, East Africa, Sweden, Spain, and Mexico. A yellowish-green variety found in Spain is often called *asparagus stone*. In addition to its transparent variety, a more translucent variety is available that may exhibit a strong cat's-eye effect when cut as a cabochon. It is readily available in all sizes, but stones larger than five carats often contain visible inclusions.

While similar in color to Paraiba tourmaline, apatite has much less brilliance and is much softer. Apatite can be used to make very lovely earrings, pendants, and brooches, but I do not recommend it for rings or bracelets because it scratches too easily and its appearance can quickly become dull-looking. Take special precautions to avoid scratching it with harder substances. I recommend keeping apatite jewelry in a separate compartment or section of your jewelry case, and also wrapping it in a soft cloth or tissue to prevent the stones from rubbing against each other or getting scratched by the metal settings. Also keep in mind that if you ever need to repair a piece of jewelry containing apatite, or should you want to remount it, you must advise the jeweler that the stone is apatite and requires special care and handling.

USEFUL FACTS

Apatite Composition: calcium phosphate
Weight: moderately heavy (specific gravity: 3.17–3.23)
Brilliance: moderately high

Hardness: 5.0 (soft)
Wearability: fair (poor in rings/ bracelets)

Aquamarine

To dream of aquamarine signifies the making of new friends; to wear aquamarine earrings brings love and affection. Aquamarine, a universal symbol of youth, hope, and health, blesses those born in March. (Before the fifteenth century it was considered to be the birthstone for those born in October.)

Aquamarine is a member of the important beryl family, which includes emerald, but aquamarine is less brittle and more durable than its green counterpart (7½ to 8 on Mohs' scale). Aquamarine ranges in color from light blue to bluish green to deep blue, the latter being the most valuable and desirable. It is a very wearable gem, clear and brilliant, and unlike emerald is available with excellent clarity even in very large sizes, although these are becoming scarce today. Aquamarines are still widely available in sizes up to fifteen carats, but ten-carat sizes with fine color and clarity are becoming scarce and are more expensive. Long considered a beautiful and moderately priced gem, it is now entering the "expensive" classification for stones in larger sizes with a good deep-blue color. The finest aquamarine is found in Brazil, but other important sources include Afghanistan, India, Madagascar, Nigeria, Pakistan, and Russia.

Several words of caution for those interested in this lovely gem. First, you may want to think twice before buying a pale or shallow-cut stone, since the color will become paler as dirt accumulates on the back. These stones need constant cleaning to keep them beautiful. Second, be careful not to mistake blue topaz for aquamarine. While topaz is an equally beautiful gem, it is usually much less expensive, since it is usually treated to obtain its desirable color. For those who can't afford an aquamarine, however, blue topaz is an excellent alternative as long as it is properly represented and priced. Finally, note that many aquamarine-colored synthetic spinels are erroneously sold as aquamarine.

USEFUL FACTS

Aquamarine Composition: beryllium aluminum silicate
Weight: light (specific gravity: 2.68–2.90)

Brilliance: moderate
Hardness: 7.5–8.0
Wearability: very good

Benitoite

This exquisitely beautiful and rare gem is seldom seen in jewelry but is very popular among collectors and connoisseurs. San Benito, California, where it was discovered (hence the name *benitoite*) remains the only source of this gemstone. It was recently selected as the official state stone of California, and we are beginning to see more of it in fine jewelry houses there.

Benitoite ranges from colorless to dark blue (often with a violet tint) to violet. A rare pink variety has also been identified. Benitoite can display fire, the dispersion of white light into the rainbow colors, comparable to a diamond, and is also very brilliant. Some might easily mistake it at a glance for a blue diamond. It lacks diamond's incredible hardness, however, and is more comparable to amethyst in hardness (6½ on Mohs' scale). It is difficult to find benitoite in sizes over 1 carat; only about five stones per year are cut that weigh 2 carats or more; only one in every five years yields a stone 5 carats or more. Benitoite's rarity keeps it very expensive—a fine 1-carat stone could easily cost $3,000—and 2-carat sizes with fine color are extremely rare and even more costly. A large, fine benitoite weighing just over 7¾ carats is on display at the Smithsonian Institution in Washington, D.C.; the largest known faceted benitoite weighs 15.42 carats.

For jewelry, benitoite is a relatively wearable stone if set in a protective mounting so that it is not easily subjected to accidental scratching or wear.

USEFUL FACTS

Benitoite Composition: barium titanium silicate   **Hardness**: 6.5
Weight: heavy (specific gravity: 3.65–3.68)   **Wearability**: fair to good
Brilliance: high to very high

Beryl (Golden Beryl and Morganite)

As early as 1220 CE, the virtues of beryl were well established in legend. Beryl provided help against foes in battle or litigation, made the wearer unconquerable but at the same time friendly and likable, and also sharpened the wearer's intellect and cured laziness. Today beryl is still considered important, but primarily for aesthetic reasons. The variety of colors in which it is found, its wonderful clarity (except for emerald), its brilliance, and its durability (7½ to 8 on Mohs' scale; again with the exception of emerald) have given the many varieties of beryl tremendous appeal.

Most people are familiar with the blue variety of beryl, aquamarine, and the green variety, emerald. Few as yet know the pink variety, morganite, and the beautiful yellow to yellow-green variety, referred to as golden beryl. These gems have only recently found their place in the jewelry world but are already being shown in fabulous pieces made by the greatest designers. While not inexpensive, they still offer excellent value and beauty. The finest golden beryl (also called *heliodor*) is found in Russia and Madagascar, but it is also found in Brazil, Namibia, the United States, and Ukraine. Fine pink morganite is primarily found in Madagascar and Brazil, but it is also found in Italy, Mozambique, Namibia, Pakistan, the United States, and Zimbabwe.

Beryl has also been found in many other colors—lilac, salmon, orange, sea green—as well as colorless. While most of these varieties are not as yet available to any but the most ardent rock hound, the orange varieties are fairly common and can still be found for under $125 per carat. Some orange varieties are heated to produce the more popular pink color and then sold as morganite. The rarest color is red, which is even more rare than emerald and is comparable in cost. It is often called *red emerald* (see the *Emerald* section above).

A new gem mineral related to the beryl family, known as *pezzottaite,* was discovered in 2002. For more on this gem, see page 149.

USEFUL FACTS

Beryl Composition: beryllium aluminum silicate   **Hardness**: 7.5–8.0
Weight: light (specific gravity: 2.68–2.90)   **Wearability**: good to very
Brilliance: moderately high   good

Bloodstone (Heliotrope)

Believed by the ancient Greeks to have fallen from heaven, this stone has held a prominent place throughout history, and even into modern times, as a great curative. It was (and still is in some parts of the world) believed capable of stopping every type of bleeding, clearing bloodshot eyes, acting as an antidote for snakebite, and relieving urinary troubles.

Today there are people who wear bloodstone amulets to prevent sunstroke and headache and to provide protection against the evil eye.

The birthstone for March, bloodstone is a more or less opaque, dark-green variety of quartz with specks of red jasper (a variety of quartz) spattering red throughout the dark green field. Particularly popular for men's rings (perhaps they need more protection from illness?), bloodstone is most desirable when the green isn't so dark as to approach black and the red flecks are roundish and pronounced. It is moderately durable (7 on Mohs' scale), and is fairly readily available and inexpensive. India is the major source of bloodstone, but it is also found in Australia, Brazil, China, and the United States.

USEFUL FACTS

Bloodstone Composition: silicon dioxide   **Hardness**: 7.0
Weight: light (specific gravity: 2.61)   **Wearability**: good
Brilliance: moderate

Chrysoberyl and Cat's-Eye

The chrysoberyl family is very interesting because all three of its varieties—alexandrite, cat's-eye, and chrysoberyl—while chemically alike, are quite distinct from one another in their optical characteristics and bear no visible resemblance to one another.

Chrysoberyl in its cat's-eye variety has long been used as a charm to guard against evil spirits. One can understand why, given the pronounced eye effect: the eye, so legend has it, could see all, and it watched out for its wearer. But it was also believed that to dream of cat's-eye signified treachery. On still another level, it symbolized long life for the wearer, perhaps as a result of being protected from the evil eye.

Cat's-eye chrysoberyl (8½ on Mohs' scale) is a hard, translucent gem ranging in color from a honey yellow or honey brown to yellowish green to an almost emerald green. It has a velvety or silklike texture and, when properly cut, displays a brilliant whitish line of light right down the center, appearing almost to be lighted from inside. Genuine cat's-eye should not be confused with the common quartz variety, which is often yellow-brown (tiger's-eye) or bluish (hawk's-eye). The quartz variety has a much less striking eye and weaker color altogether. This phenomenon is produced only in cabochons.

To see the effect properly, the stone should be viewed under a single strong light source, coming if possible from directly overhead. If the line is not exactly in the center, the stone's value is reduced. The line does shift from side to side when the stone is moved about—probably another reason ancient people believed it capable of seeing all and guarding its wearer.

The stone called chrysoberyl, on the other hand, is a brilliant, transparent, very clear, and very durable stone (8½ on Mohs' scale) found in yellow, yellow-green, and green varieties. The finest chrysoberyl comes from Russia, but Sri Lanka is also an important source. It is also found in Brazil, Madagascar, Myanmar, Tanzania, and Zimbabwe. Cat's-eye is found in Brazil, China, and Sri Lanka.

This is another stone that still offers excellent value. It's a real beauty, very moderately priced, and just beginning to be appreciated and used in contemporary jewelry.

USEFUL FACTS

Chrysoberyl Composition: beryllium aluminum oxide **Hardness**: 8.5
Weight: heavy (specific gravity: 3.71–3.72) **Wearability**: excellent
Brilliance: high

Chrysocolla

(See *Quartz*—true chrysocolla is a very soft copper-related mineral too soft for jewelry use.)

Chrysoprase and Carnelian

Chrysoprase has long been the subject of marvelous stories. In the 1800s, it was believed that a thief sentenced to be hanged or beheaded would immediately escape if he placed a chrysoprase in his mouth. Of course, it might be hard to obtain the stone unless he just happened to carry one around! And Alexander the Great was believed to have worn a "prase" in his girdle during battle, to ensure victory.

Chrysoprase is an inexpensive, highly translucent, bright, light-green to dark-green variety of quartz. While its color is often very uniform and can be very lovely in jewelry, for many years these gems have been dyed to enhance their color, where necessary. Chrysoprase is another stone that is usually cut in cabochon style. It has become very popular for jewelry as a fashion accessory. Do not confuse it with jade, however. It is sometimes called Australian jade and is sometimes misrepresented as real jade.

If you're the timid sort, carnelian is the stone for you. "The wearing of carnelians is recommended to those who have a weak voice or are timid in speech, for the warm-colored stone will give them the courage they lack so that they will speak both boldly and well," reports G. F. Kunz, a turn-of-the-century gemologist and historian.

This stone is especially revered by Muslims, because Muhammad himself wore a silver ring set with a carnelian engraved for use as a seal.

Napoleon I, while on a campaign in Egypt, picked up with his own hands (apparently from the battlefield) an unusual octagonal carnelian upon which was engraved the legend "The Slave Abraham Relying upon the Merciful [God]." He wore it with him always and bequeathed it to his nephew.

Carnelian, one of the accepted birthstones for August, is a reddish-orange to brownish-orange variety of quartz. A moderately hard (7 on Mohs' scale), translucent to opaque stone, its warm uniform color and fair durability have made it a favorite. It is often found in antique jewelry and lends itself to engraving or carving, especially in cameos. Today the best chrysoprase is found in Australia, but it is also found in Austria, Brazil, the Czech Republic, Poland, Russia, and the United States. The major source of carnelian is India. It is still a relatively inexpensive stone with great warmth and beauty and offers an excellent choice for jewelry to be worn as an accessory with today's fashion colors.

USEFUL FACTS

Chrysoprase and Carnelian Composition: silicon dioxide
Weight: light (specific gravity: 2.60–2.65)

Brilliance: moderate
Hardness: 7.0
Wearability: Good

Citrine

(See *Quartz*.)

Coral

Coral, which for twenty centuries or more was classed with precious gems and can be found adorning ancient amulets alongside diamond, ruby, emerald, and pearl, had been "experimentally proved" by the sixteenth century to cure madness, give wisdom, stop the flow of blood from a wound, calm storms, and of course enable the traveler to safely cross broad rivers. It was also known to prevent sterility. This was certainly a powerful gem!

Red coral symbolizes attachment, devotion, and protection against plague and pestilence. And one unique quality: it loses its color when a friend of the wearer is about to die! There is a catch to coral's potency, however. To effectively exercise its power, it should not be altered by the human hand but should be worn in its natural, uncut state. This perhaps is why one often sees this stone in necklaces or pins in its natural state.

Coral lost its popularity for a while but has been steadily gaining in popularity in recent years. It is a semitranslucent to opaque material, formed from a colony of marine invertebrates, that is primarily a skeletal calcium-carbonate gem. The formations as seen in the water look like tree branches. Coral occurs in a variety of colors—white, pink, orange, red, and black. One of the most expensive varieties, very popular in recent years and used extensively in fine jewelry, is angel-skin coral. This is a whitish variety highlighted with a faint blush of pink or peach. Today the rarest variety, and the most expensive, is blood coral, also called noble or oxblood coral. This is a very deep-red variety and shouldn't be confused with the more common orangy-red varieties. The best red comes from the Mediterranean Sea, near Italy. It is also found off the African coast, in the Red Sea, and off Malaysia and Japan (which also produces white coral). Black coral, which is chemically different from other coral, comes primarily from Hawaii and Mexico.

Coral is usually cabochon cut, often carved, but is also fairly frequently found in jewelry fashioned "in the rough" (uncut) in certain countries where the belief persists that coral's magical powers are lost with cutting. It is a fairly soft stone (3½ on Mohs' scale), so some caution should be exercised when wearing. Also, because of its calcium composition, you must be careful to avoid contact with acid, such as vinegar in a salad that you might toss with your hands.

In addition, be a cautious buyer for this gem as for others; glass and plastic imitations are commonplace.

USEFUL FACTS

Coral Composition: calcium carbonate or conchiolin   **Hardness**: 3.5 (soft)
Weight: light (specific gravity: 2.6–2.7)   **Wearability**: fair to good
Brilliance: low to moderate

Diaspore (Color-Change)

(See *Zultanite.*)

Diopside

Diopside is a mineral that was known primarily to rock hounds and mineral collectors until recently. Diopside is now entering the jewelry arena, but it is soft and needs special care. It occurs primarily in shades of green, including grayish green, brownish green, and yellowish green. It provides a very affordable alternative to other deep-green gems, but its color is often too dark, almost black, and these shades are not as desirable. A rarer variety, known as *chrome diopside*, can exhibit a very lively, bright-green to slightly bluish-green color that can be very pleasing. Diopside can also occur in a colorless variety, and a rare violet-blue diopside has been found in Italy and in the United States. Other sources for diopside include Austria, Brazil, Canada, India, Madagascar, Myanmar (Burma), Pakistan, Russia, South Africa, and Sri Lanka. Chrome diopside is readily available in sizes up to four carats, but stones over five carats are rare.

Diopside can be used to make very lovely earrings, pendants, and brooches, but I do not recommend it for rings or bracelets because it scratches too easily and, as is usually the case with softer stones, its appearance can quickly become dull-looking. Take special precautions to avoid scratching it with harder substances: store it in a separate compartment or section of your jewelry case, and also wrap it in a soft cloth or tissue to prevent the stones from rubbing against each other or getting scratched by the metal settings. Also keep in mind that if you ever need to repair a piece of jewelry containing diopside, or should you want to remount it, be sure the jeweler doesn't confuse it with tourmaline or other harder gemstones; be sure to tell the jeweler what it is, that it is soft, and that it requires special care and handling.

USEFUL FACTS

Diopside Composition: calcium magnesium silicate   **Hardness:** 5.5 (soft)
Weight: moderately heavy (specific gravity: 3.23–3.29)   **Wearability:** fair (poor in
Brilliance: moderate   rings/bracelets)

Feldspar

The feldspar group is an important group of minerals and includes some very popular gemstones. We will discuss individually those that are of particular interest in the jewelry world:

Andesine: Also known as andesine-labradorite, this very lovely gem is a variety of feldspar that occurs in vibrant shades of red, orange, green, and yellow, often with inclusions that create an interesting shimmering effect. It is a wearable stone (6 to 6½ on Mohs' scale) and is usually cut in the cabochon style because the material is rarely clean enough to facet. Most feldspar enthusiasts agree that the finest natural andesine comes from Oregon. The Oregon material possesses fine color, but stones with excellent transparency and brightness, in sizes over a few carats, are rare and costly. New sources of red-to-orange andesine have been documented in Tibet and Inner Mongolia, but most of this material is translucent to transparent and often lacks the intensity of color. We know that some of the yellow material from these regions, and yellow material from Mexico, can be diffusion-treated to create rarer, more desirable red and orange colors; we suspect that this is the case with the inexpensive faceted red-to-orange material now being sold, but it is often not possible for labs to determine whether or not the color is natural. If you want to purchase red or green andesine that you know is natural in color, we suggest you seek Oregon material, which has unique characteristics that identify it as "Oregon" material.

Labradorite, Sunstone, and Spectrolite: Labradorite is a fascinating stone that is starting to appear in some of the more distinctive jewelry salons, especially in beads and carved pieces, and is a member of the feldspar family (6 to 6½ on Mohs' scale). The most frequently seen variety is a grayish, almost opaque stone, within which startlingly brilliant flashes of peacock blue, greens, and/or yellows are visible at certain angles.

A beautiful, shimmering red-to-orange variety (and occasionally green or bicolor) known as *sunstone* is also beginning to enter the jewelry scene. Major United States retailers such as Tiffany are featuring this wonderful, truly American gem, mined in Oregon. Finland also produces a very lovely variety of labradorite, often called *spectrolite*, that occurs in colors resembling peacock hues or the colors seen on the wings of butterflies. It can also exhibit a cat's-eye effect.

Labradorite is usually cut in cabochon style, but sunstone also occurs in a transparent material that makes a beautiful faceted gem. There are some glass imitations, but they don't come close to the real thing. This is a stone that is still relatively inexpensive and one to consider seriously if you want something striking and unusual.

Moonstone: Moonstone is definitely a good-luck stone, especially for lovers. As a gift the moonstone holds a high rank, for it is believed to arouse one's tender passion and to give lovers the ability to foretell their future—good or ill. To get this information, however, legend has it that the stone must be placed in the mouth while the moon is full. Perhaps a more important use, however, was in amulets made of moonstone, which would protect wearers from epilepsy and guarantee a greater fruit-crop yield when hung on fruit trees. The stone, in fact, assisted all vegetation.

The name *moonstone* is probably derived from the myth that one can observe the lunar month through the stone—that a small white spot appears in the stone as the new moon begins and gradually moves toward the stone's center, getting always larger, until the spot finally takes the shape of a full moon in the center of the stone.

Moonstone is a member of the feldspar family (6 to 6½ on Mohs' scale). It is a transparent, milky-white variety in which a floating opalescent white or blue light within the stone's body can be seen. It is a popular stone for rings because as the hand moves, the effect of the brilliant light color is more pronounced. The bluer color is the finer and more desirable, but it is becoming rare in today's market, particularly in large sizes.

There are some glass imitations of moonstone, but compared with the real thing they are not very good.

USEFUL FACTS

Feldspar Composition (Andesine): sodium calcium aluminum silicate
Weight: light (specific gravity 2.57–2.77)
Brilliance: moderately high
Hardness: 6.0–7.0
Wearability: good

Feldspar Composition (Labradorite, Sunstone, and Spectrolite): sodium calcium aluminosilicate
Weight: light (specific gravity: 2.68–2.70)
Brilliance: moderately brilliant; highly iridescent
Hardness: 6.0–6.5
Wearability: good ("tougher" than some harder gems)

Feldspar Composition (Moonstone): potassium aluminum silicate
Weight: light (specific gravity: 2.57)
Brilliance: moderate
Hardness: 6.0–6.5
Wearability: good

Garnet

If you are loyal, devoted, and energetic, perhaps the garnet is your stone. Or if not, perhaps you should obtain some! Red garnets were known to promote sincerity, stop hemorrhaging or other loss of blood, cure inflammatory diseases, and cure anger and discord. And if you engrave a well-formed lion image upon a garnet, it will protect and preserve health, cure the wearer of all disease, bring him honors, and guard him from all perils in traveling. All in all, quite a worthwhile stone.

The garnet family is one of the most exciting families in the gem world. One of the few untreated gems, it is moderately hard (ranging from 6½ to7½ on Mohs' scale), durable, and brilliant. It is available in many colors (greens, reds, yellows, oranges) and offers far greater versatility and opportunity for the jewelry trade than has yet been capitalized upon. Depending on the variety, quality, and size, lovely garnets are available for under $40 per carat or more than $5,000 per carat. Garnet can also be mistaken for other, usually more expensive, gems. Green garnet (tsavorite) is one of the most beautiful, and all but a few would assume it was an emerald of the finest quality. In fact, it is clearer, more brilliant, and more durable than emerald itself. There is also a rarer green garnet, called demantoid, which costs slightly more than tsavorite but which, although slightly softer, has more fire (it should be noted that low-temperature heating may be used to enhance the color of demantoid garnet). These gems offer fine alternatives to the person desiring a lovely green gem who can't afford emerald. While still rare, expensive gems themselves, these garnet varieties are far less expensive than emeralds of comparable quality. Garnet also occurs in certain shades of red that have been mistaken for some varieties of ruby. And in yellow it has been confused with precious topaz.

Garnet is found in almost every color and shade, including a rare color-change variety that appears red in incandescent light and blue (the only color not normally seen in garnet) in daylight or fluorescent light. It is best known in a deep-red variety but is commonly found in orangish brown shades and brilliant wine-red shades as well. Other colors include orange—the new mandarin garnet being an intense, fiery red-orange—red-purple, violet, and pink. A nontransparent variety, grossularite, resembles jade and may be mistaken for jade in cabochons and carvings.

USEFUL FACTS

Garnet Composition
- Almandine/Uvarovite: iron aluminum silicate
- Hessonite/Tsavorite/Grossularite: calcium aluminum silicate
- Pyrope/Spessartite: magnesium aluminum

Weight: moderately heavy to heavy (specific gravity: 3.49–4.16)

Brilliance: fairly high to very high
Hardness: 6.5–7.5
Wearability: good to very good

Garnet is found in many parts of the world. The rare green variety called tsavorite is found in Kenya (it is named after Tsavo National Park in Kenya) and Tanzania. The finest, fiery mandarin-orange garnet is from Namibia, but other sources now include Madagascar and Pakistan. An orangy-brown variety is found in the United States. A reddish- to purple-colored *star* garnet found in the United States displays a faint four-ray or six-ray star, similar to a six-ray star ruby but not as pronounced.

Hematite and Marcasite

Hematite is a must for the lawyer, for it ensures its wearer "alertness, vivacity, and success in litigation," claimed an unknown source from ages past. It is also believed to ensure sexual impulse, so if you know of someone with a problem, this may make a "thoughtful" gift.

Hematite is an iron oxide (like iron rust), a metallic, opaque stone found in iron-mining areas. It takes a very brilliant, metallic polish that can look almost like silver, or almost pure black, or gunmetal blue. It was and is popular for use in carving hollow cameo portraits known as *intaglio*. Cuttable hematite is found in Brazil, Canada, Elba (Italy), England, Germany, and Venezuela.

Marcasite, the tiny, glittering stone with a brassy-colored luster often seen in old belt buckles and costume jewelry, is a relative of hematite. Most "marcasite" seen in jewelry is not marcasite, but pyrite (fool's gold)—another brassy-colored metallic mineral.

USEFUL FACTS

Hematite Composition: iron oxide
Weight: very heavy (specific gravity: 5.20)
Brilliance: very high; intense shine

Hardness: 6.5
Wearability: fair (easy to mar surface with wear)

Iolite

This is a transparent, usually very clean blue gem, ranging from deep blue to light gray-blue to yellowish gray. It is sometimes called *dichroite* or *cordierite*, and in its sapphire-blue color is sometimes referred to as *water sapphire* or *lynx sapphire*. It is a lovely, brilliant stone but not as durable as sapphire (7 to 7½ on Mohs' scale). Sources of iolite include Burma (Myanmar), Finland, Germany, India, Madagascar, Namibia, Norway, Sri Lanka, and Tanzania. We are just beginning to see this stone in jewelry, and it is still a good value. It is abundant, still very low priced, and one of the most attractive jewelry options for the near future.

USEFUL FACTS

Iolite Composition: magnesium aluminum silicate   **Hardness**: 7.0–7.5
Weight: light (specific gravity: 2.57–2.66)   **Wearability**: fair to good
Brilliance: moderately high

Jade

Jade has long been revered by the Chinese. White jade (yes, white) was believed by the early Chinese to quiet intestinal disturbances, while black jade gave strength and power. A very early written Chinese symbol for "king" was a string of jade beads, and jade beads are still used in China as a symbol of high rank and authority. Jade is also an important part of the Chinese wedding ceremony (the "jade ceremony" holds a prominent place here), for jade is considered the concentrated essence of love.

Jade is a very tough, although not too hard, translucent to opaque gem, often seen in jewelry and carvings. There are really two types of jade—jadeite and nephrite—which are really two separate and distinct minerals differing from each other in weight, hardness, and color range. Both are called jade.

Jadeite, the more expensive and more desirable variety, was the most sought after by the Chinese after 1740. It is not found in China, however, but in Burma (Myanmar). Some fine jadeite also comes from Guatemala. It is found in a much wider range of colors than nephrite: green, mottled green and white, whitish gray, pink, brown, mauve, yellow, orange, and lilac. In fact, it occurs in almost every color. But with the exception of green, which comes in shades that vary from light to a beautiful emerald green, colored jade is usually pale and unevenly tinted. The

Colored Gemstones and Great Design—
A Natural for Endless Possibilities

Timeless Ring Designs...

Variations on the Classic Oval

Classic softness created by using pear-shape diamonds with oval.

Elegant effect created by *half-moon* cut diamonds with oval.

Classic yet contemporary feeling created by using three tapered baguettes scrolled across the ring shoulder.

Straight baguette and tapered baguette define and lead eye toward the center.

Distinctive Designs for a Traditional Emerald Cut

Counterclockwise from top left: Emerald-cut ruby flanked on each side by two parallel straight-baguette diamonds; emerald-cut ruby with *trapezoid* diamond and *trapezoid* ruby on each side; classic emerald cut with triangular diamonds; a classic square emerald-cut emerald with unusual *bullet*-shaped diamonds.

The Ageless Cushion

Three distinctively different rings highlight a cushion-cut center stone.

Left: A classic cushion-cut sapphire accentuated by modern trilliant-cut diamonds.

Center: A modified, contemporary cushion-cut tourmaline surrounded by round, brilliant-cut diamonds that extend from the top into the ring shank.

Right: A cushion-cut emerald in an elegant diamond baguette frame.

Princess Takes Center Stage

Princess-cut diamond, sapphire, and aquamarine move to center stage in these contemporary two-tier geometric designs by Chris Correia.

...And New Classics by Modern Designers

Simon G's green tourmaline and diamond ring is a lovely, modern interpretation of a classic heirloom design, while his tanzanite and rubellite ring shows bold, innovative design.

Meticulous detail captures an heirloom feeling in this modern diamond and sapphire ring by Brian Sholdt.

Classic Colored Stone Bands...

...Infinite Possibilities

Richard Krementz's innovative use of color creates stunning results.

Color Story® artfully combines ancient motifs with a contemporary diamond surround, a distinctive setting for the equally distinctive cutting of the peridot it highlights.

In this contemporary ring, designer Steve Dangler uses exotic color-change Zultanite to add irresistible allure.

Bold New Looks in Colored-Stone Rings...

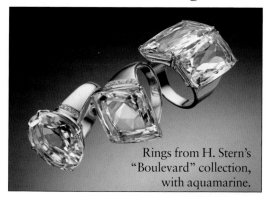

Rings from H. Stern's "Boulevard" collection, with aquamarine.

Sapphire rings for the woman who loves bold color and bold design, by award-winning designer Claude Thibaudeau.

Imperial jadeite deserves this regal setting by Nikolai Tsang.

Jean-Francois Albert balances strong color with strong design.

Distinctive cutting is the perfect complement to Stephen Webster's distinctive designs using amethyst with green tsavorites, and morganite with diamond pavé.

Prince Dimitri's ring creations make artful use of agate, chalcedony, and onyx, into which faceted stones such as citrine, amethyst, and aquamarine are set.

...A Natural Fit

Using precious stones such as ruby and sapphire for pavé work, combined with larger stones such as blue topaz and amethyst, Raymond Hak creates a melodic blend of color for the fashion-forward woman.

The simplicity of ancient design and warmth of 24-karat gold sets Gurhan's creations apart. Befitting important gems such as this black opal, yet also perfect for simple stacking rings worn alone or in multiples.

Designs by Gadi use classic materials—18-karat white or yellow gold and diamonds—with stones such as garnet, blue topaz, citrine, tourmaline, and aquamarine to create a variety of daring, contemporary new looks.

The "Corset" collection by Stefan Hafner combines diamonds and colored gemstones to create a soft, sensual, undulating effect.

Designer Tamara Comolli loves to combine color in a variety of ways, and in stacking rings, the possibilities are endless.

Colorful Creations from Winning Designers...

Colored gemstones are more popular today than ever before. Unique cutting styles and unusual colors and color combinations provide top designers with limitless possibilities to create distinctive jewelry, from the traditional to the avant-garde.

PHOTO: LEE-CARRAHER

Gordon Aatlo uses yellow sapphires, white diamonds, and peridot to create a dramatic contemporary pendant.

PHOTO: HELEN KIM

Innovative design is the focus of a sundial, and innovative cutting is the focus of a ring in these creations by John David Cooney.

AGTA Spectrum Award winners add dramatic flair: stylized orbit ring with pink spinel and spessartite garnets by James W. Currens; morganite, zircon, and spinel drops by Ashok Sancheti.

PHOTO: ROBERT WELDON

Designers Blend Old and New in Upcoming Collections

PHOTOS: AARON CHENEY

PHOTO: HAP SAKWA

PHOTO: LEHRER DESIGNS

Glenn Lehrer's TorusRing™ cut is a hit with designers: ring by Glenn Lehrer *(above)*; pendant/brooch by Kent Raible *(left)*.

Classic elegance is created in this necklace by Brian Sholdt, while use of the innovative *bar cut* produces a strikingly bold look in his ring.

Designer Karl Benz puts the focus on the new square *Context*® cut, round *Spirit Sun*® cut, and the latest *marquise* cut, creating a simple but distinctive contemporary feel.

...To Suit Every Style

Right: Scott Keating's colorful use of *turret*, or *bar*, cuts.

Designer David Hrubec surrounds exceptional color-change Zultanites in rose gold and diamonds to create a stunning statement.

James Breski offers a range of classic styles, such as these mystery-set pendant and earrings—a technique requiring intensive labor and skill.

PHOTO COURTESY OF STULLER, INC.

Stuller's selection of finished jewelry provides a bold designer look, as in this lovely peridot ring, at more affordable prices.

Texture, color, and movement combine to create this unique brooch by Richard Kimball.

Checkerboard cut in convertible pendant/ring design creates a distinctive award-winner by Virginia Andersen.

Innovative combination of cabochons with faceted stones. Ring by William Richey *(right)* uses faceted citrine with cabochon amethyst for striking contrast. Peggy Stephaich Guinness *(left)* creates more subtle contrast, and a very different mood, using cabochon turquoise with faceted blue topaz.

More Winning Creations...

Stylish carnelian and blue sapphire earrings by Peggy Stephaich Guinness.

Cobblestone bracelet in amethyst, rose quartz, smoky quartz, and pink tourmaline is sophisticated yet casual. By H. Stern.

Stunning rare black opal and 24-karat gold necklace, and ruby, diamond, and 24-karat gold earrings by Gurhan.

Tom Trozzo's "floating bubbles" cut, seen here in ametrine earrings, is sure to bring smiles.

Elizabeth Rand's cabochon and faceted peridot and diamond earrings *(left)* move from day into evening.

Prince Dimitri's love for carved gems is evident in his cuff links and bracelets. *Above:* Bracelets featuring carved peridot and amethyst.
Left: Cuff links in green quartz with diamond, and amethyst with chrome diopside.

...And "Suite" Possibilities

Left: This delightful suite by Bellarri™ offers a palette of colors that goes with everything, anytime, anywhere.

Stephen Webster's "wild rose" rubellite tourmaline and diamond pendant and earrings are simply stunning. A ring to complete the suite is also available.

PHOTO: KELLY ALLEN

PHOTO: LEE CARRAHER

Blossom-cut ametrine pendant and matching rings by Gordon Aatlo make a strong contemporary statement.

Tamara Comolli's colorful earrings and fanciful *Candy Mikado Flamenco* bracelet using bullet-shaped cabochons bring smiles to all.

Cabochons of Every Type...

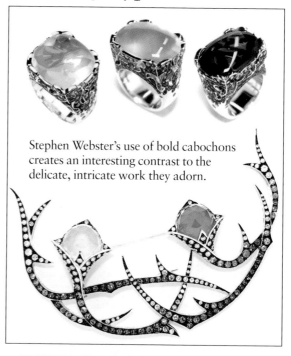

Stephen Webster's use of bold cabochons creates an interesting contrast to the delicate, intricate work they adorn.

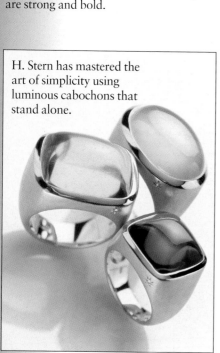

De Vroomen loves cabochons. Here his tourmaline and garnet "forest brooch" and earrings are soft and sensual, while his sugarloaf cabochon amethyst, gold, and green enamel bracelet and earrings are strong and bold.

H. Stern has mastered the art of simplicity using luminous cabochons that stand alone.

Moonstone and tanzanite pendant and earrings by Murphy Designs evoke an ancient feeling while his combination cabochon amethyst and faceted blue topaz pendant creates a striking contemporary contrast.

...Simply Captivate Designers

Cabochons are enjoying renewed popularity, as seen in rings from Gumuchian Fils, Ltd.

Richard Krementz's blue moonstone cabochon creates a sensual classic surrounded by pavé diamonds.

Striking use of interesting cabochon shapes and contrasting colors by Raymond Hak.

Right: Rodney Rayner's lush orange mandarin garnet cabochon is embraced by small orange sapphires and colorless diamonds. *Above:* Intense green tsavorite garnets protectively hug the soft green prehnite cabochon.

Colored Gemstones...
A Natural for Whimsical Jewels

Rodney Rayner takes off with his bold, fun "space rings." *Top:* graduated pink sapphire and amethyst. *Lower left:* graduated tsavorite and smoky quartz. *Lower right:* graduated blue sapphire and blue topaz.

Artfully created by H. Stern, this one-of-a-kind lizard brooch is pure delight! 18-karat yellow gold, tourmaline, and ruby.

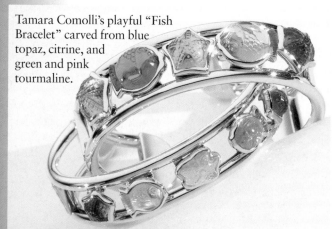

Tamara Comolli's playful "Fish Bracelet" carved from blue topaz, citrine, and green and pink tourmaline.

Nafco creates a world of fantasy in fancy-colored sapphires, tsavorite, chrome tourmaline, and diamonds.

"Pinwheel" rings in tsavorite, diamond, black sapphire, and ruby, by Stephen Webster.

Elizabeth Rand's playful nature comes through in her smiling moon-face, carved in moonstone, and her "Rosemary" necklace, a natural for the aquamarine it highlights, can't help but add some spice to life.

A sailor's dream in 14-karat gold, chrysocolla, and pink tourmaline, by Murphy Designs, with matching earrings.

most desirable color is a rich emerald green, sometimes referred to as *imperial jade*. Smooth, evenly colored pieces of this jadeite are highly prized and, in fact, can be classed as precious stones today. The mottled pieces of irregular green, often seen carved, are less valuable but are still more rare and valuable than nephrite jade.

Nephrite jade, the old and true Chinese jade, resembles jadeite but is slightly softer (jadeite is 7 on Mohs' scale; nephrite, 6½, yet slightly tougher and thus less easily broken) and has a much more limited range of color. Usually fashioned in cabochon cut, round beads, or in carvings, it is regularly seen in dark-green shades sometimes so dark as to look black—hence, black jade. Nephrite green is a more sober green than the apple-green or emerald-green color of good jadeite. It is closer in color to a dark sage green or spinach green. Nephrite may also be a creamier color, as in mutton-fat jade. Any fine Chinese carving that is more than 230 years old is carved from nephrite (jadeite was unknown to the Chinese before 1740).

Nephrite has been found in many countries, including the United States, where in the late nineteenth century Chinese miners panning for gold in California discovered large boulders of nephrite jade that they sent back to China to be cut or carved. It is also common in Wyoming, Alaska, and British Columbia.

Nephrite jade is much more common than jadeite and is therefore much less expensive. But it is a lovely, popular stone, used extensively in jewelry and carvings.

One must be careful, however, in purchasing jade. You will often see "imperial" jade that is nothing more than a cheap jade that has been dyed, or dyed quartz. Much jade is treated with polymers or is dyed to enhance its value. The dyeing, however, may be very temporary. Black

---

USEFUL FACTS

Jadeite Composition: sodium aluminum silicate   **Hardness**: 7.0
Weight: moderately heavy (specific gravity: 3.30–3.36)   **Wearability**: fair to good
Brilliance: moderately high; takes high polish

Nephrite Composition: calcium magnesium iron   **Hardness**: 6.5
   silicate   **Wearability**: fair to good
Weight: moderately heavy (specific gravity: 2.90–3.02)
Brilliance: moderately high; lower polish than jadeite

jade is either dyed or very dark-green nephrite that looks black. There are also numerous minerals that look like jade and are sold as jade under misleading names, such as "Korean jade," which is serpentine, a soft green stone similar in appearance to some varieties of jade (see the table of misleading names on page 81). In fact, much of the intricately and beautifully carved jade is actually serpentine, which can be scratched easily with a knife.

Soapstone may also look like jade to the amateur, especially when beautifully carved. This stone is so soft that it can easily be scratched with a pin, hairpin, or point of a pen. It is much less expensive than comparable varieties of jade, as well as softer and less durable.

Jade is a wonderful stone, and imperial jade is breathtaking; no wonder it was the emperor's stone! But jade has long been "copied"—misrepresented and altered. Just be sure you know you are buying what you think you are buying.

Lapis Lazuli

Lapis, a birthstone for December, has been highly prized since ancient Babylonian and Egyptian times. An amulet of "great power" was formed when lapis was worked into the form of an eye and ornamented with gold—in fact, so powerful that sometimes these eyes were put to rest on the limbs of a mummy. In addition, it was recognized as a symbol for capacity, ability, success, and divine favor.

Genuine lapis is a natural blue opaque stone of intense, brilliant, deep-blue color. It sometimes possesses small, sparkling gold-colored or silver-colored flecks (pyrite inclusions), although the finest quality is a deep, even blue with a purplish tint or undertone and no trace of those flecks. Occasionally it may be blue mottled with white. The finest lapis comes from Afghanistan and Argentina, but other sources include Russia, Chile, and Canada. Occasionally it is found in the United States.

Don't confuse genuine lapis with the cheaper "Swiss lapis" or "Italian lapis," which aren't lapis at all. These are natural stones (usually quartz)

USEFUL FACTS

Lapis Lazuli Composition: rock containing lazuli and other minerals **Brilliance**: high
Weight: light (specific gravity: 2.6–2.7) **Hardness**: 5.5
  Wearability: fair to good

artificially colored to look like lapis lazuli. Genuine lapis is often represented as "Russian lapis," although it doesn't always come from Russia. The finest lapis comes from Afghanistan.

Lapis has become very fashionable, and the finest-quality lapis is becoming more rare and more expensive. This has resulted in an abundance of lapis that has been "color improved." It is often fashioned today with other gems—pearls, crystal, coral—that make particularly striking fashion accessories.

Sodalite is sometimes confused with the more expensive, and rarer, lapis and is used as a substitute for it. However, sodalite rarely contains the silvery or golden flecks typical of most lapis. It may have some white veining, but more commonly it just exhibits the fine lapis blue without any markings. The lapis substitutes transmit some light through the edges of the stone; lapis does not, since it is opaque.

Dyed chalcedony (quartz), glass, and plastic imitations are common. One quick and easy test to identify genuine lapis is to put a drop of hydrochloric acid on the stones; this will immediately produce the odor of a rotten egg. This test should be administered only by a professional, however, since hydrochloric acid can be dangerous.

Malachite and Azurite

Malachite must have been the answer to a mother's prayer. According to legend, attaching malachite to the neck of a child would ease its pain when cutting teeth. Also, tied over a woman in labor, it would ensure an easier, faster birth. It could also cure diseases of the eye. More important, however, it was believed capable of protecting from the evil eye and bringing good luck.

Malachite is also popular today, but perhaps more because of the exquisite color and a softness (3½ on Mohs' scale) that makes it very

---

USEFUL FACTS

Malachite Composition: copper hydroxycarbonate   **Hardness**: 3.5 (soft)
Weight: heavy (specific gravity: 3.80)   **Wearability**: fair to poor
Brilliance: high

Azurite Composition: copper hydroxycarbonate   **Hardness**: 4.0 (soft)
Weight: heavy (specific gravity: 3.77)   **Wearability**: fair
Brilliance: high

popular for carving. Malachite is a copper ore that comes in a brilliant kelly green, marked with bands or concentric striping in contrasting shades of the same basic green. It is opaque and takes a good polish, but it is soft and should not be worn in rings. This softness, however, makes it a favorite substance for use in carved bases, boxes, beads, statues, spheres, and so on. It is also used in pins, pendants, and necklaces (usually of malachite beads). Malachite is often found in copper-producing areas. Russia was once a major source, but today Zaire is the major producer.

Azurite is also a copper ore, but it occurs in a very vivid deep blue, similarly marked. Occasionally one will come across both azurite and malachite intermingled in brilliant combinations of color and striking patterns. In Israel, "Eilat stone" is usually azurite and malachite together, although it can also contain chrysocolla.

A particular note of caution: Never clean malachite or azurite with any product containing ammonia. In seconds the ammonia will remove all the polish, which will significantly reduce the stone's beauty.

Obsidian

Obsidian was widely used by pre-Columbian Mexicans, probably because of its brilliant polished surface, for making images of their god Tezcatlipoca and for polishing into mirrors used to divine the future. It has also been found in Egypt, fashioned into masks. It has been used since prehistoric times to make tools and weapons as well, such as arrowheads and other projectiles.

Obsidian is a semitranslucent to opaque glass that is smoky brown to black and sometimes a mixture of both. It is natural glass, not artificial. It is formed by volcanic activity and is also called volcanic glass. One variety, snowflake obsidian, exhibits white spots resembling snowflakes against or mingled with the black; some obsidian exhibits a strong iridescence; and some obsidian exhibits a sheen from within, as seen in moonstone.

Jewelry made from obsidian, which is available in great quantity and is very inexpensive, is a popular fashion accessory. It is particularly pop-

---

USEFUL FACTS

Obsidian Composition: primarily silicon dioxide   **Hardness:** 5.0 (soft)
Weight: very light (specific gravity: 2.33–2.42)   **Wearability:** fair
Brilliance: moderately high

ular in Mexican and Native American jewelry and is seen fairly extensively in the West and in Mexico. Most obsidian jewelry today comes from North and Central America. One must exercise some caution, however, because obsidian is glass (5 on Mohs' scale) and can be scratched or cracked easily.

Onyx

Onyx is not a good-omen stone, and it is certainly not one for young lovers, since it is believed to bear an evil omen, to provoke discord and separate them. Worn around the neck, it was said to cool the ardors of love. The close union and yet strong contrast between the layers of black and white in some varieties may have suggested onyx's connection with romance. It was also believed to cause discord in general, create disharmony among friends, bring bad dreams and broken sleep to its wearer, and cause pregnant women to give birth prematurely.

But there isn't complete agreement as to its unlucky nature. Indians and Persians believe that wearing onyx will protect them from the evil eye, and that onyx placed on the stomach of a woman in labor will reduce the labor pain and bring on earlier delivery. So you choose—good or bad?

Onyx is a lovely, banded, semitranslucent to opaque quartz. It comes naturally in a variety of colors—reds, oranges, reddish orange, apricot, and shades of brown from cream to dark, often alternating with striking bands of white. The banding in onyx is straight, while curved bands occur in the variety of quartz known as agate. Onyx is used extensively for cameo and other carving work. It is also frequently dyed.

The "black onyx" that is commonly used in jewelry isn't onyx at all and isn't naturally black. It is chalcedony (another variety of quartz) dyed black. It is *always* dyed and may be banded or solid black.

Do not confuse the quartz variety of onyx with cave onyx, which is found in the stalactites and stalagmites of underground caves. Cave onyx is a different material altogether. It is much softer, lacks the color variety, and is much less expensive than quartz onyx.

USEFUL FACTS
Onyx Composition: silicon dioxide   **Hardness**: 7.0
Weight: light (specific gravity: 2.61)   **Wearability**: good
Brilliance: moderate

Opal

The opal has suffered from an unfortunate reputation as being an evil stone and bearing an ill omen. Ominous superstitions surround this wonderful gem, including the belief that misfortune will fall on those who wear it. But its evil reputation has never been merited and probably resulted from a careless reading of Sir Walter Scott's novel *Anne of Geierstein,* in which the ill-fated heroine received an opal before her untimely death.

Among the ancients, opal was a symbol of fidelity and assurance, and in later history it became strongly associated with religious emotion and prayer. It was believed to have a strong therapeutic value for diseases of the eye and, worn as an amulet, it would make the wearer immune from them, as well as increase the powers of the eyes and the mind. Further, many believed that to the extent the colors of red and green (ruby and emerald) were seen, the wearer would also enjoy the therapeutic powers of those stones: the power to stop bleeding from the ruby or the power to cure kidney diseases from the emerald. The black opal was particularly highly prized as the luck stone of anyone lucky enough to own one!

This stone, whose brilliance and vibrant colors resemble the colors of the fall, is certainly appropriate as a birthstone for October. When we try to describe the opal, we realize how insufficient the English language is. It is unique among the gems, displaying an array of very brilliant miniature rainbow effects, all mixed together.

Its most outstanding characteristic is an unusual, intense display of many colors flashing out like mini-rainbows. This effect is created by opal's formation process, which is very different from that of other gems. Opal is composed of hydrated silica spheres. The mini-rainbows seen in most opals result from light interference created by these spheres. The arrangement of the spheres, which vary in size and pattern, is responsible for the different colors.

Opal is usually cut flat or in cabochon, since there is no additional brilliance to be captured by faceting. In opals, color is everything. The more brilliant the color, the more valuable the gem. It is probably truer of opal than any other stone that the more beautiful the stone and its color, the more it will cost. But it is fairly soft (5½ to 6½ on Mohs' scale), so opals should be treated with care.

Opal is generally categorized based upon the body color—*light* or *dark*—and the degree of transparency. By body color we don't mean the rainbow colors, but rather its base tone, which can be colorless or white, various gray shades, or black. "Light opal" includes all the shades through medium gray; "dark opal" includes dark gray to black.

Opal can exhibit varying degrees of transparency from opaque to translucent to transparent. When an opal is transparent or very translucent and the clarity of the color is very sharp, it is called *crystal*—the play of color must be visible both on the surface and within the stone. When the color in such a stone is hazy, we refer to the opal as a *jelly opal*. You may also hear the terms *semi-crystal* or *semi-jelly* or *water opals* used to describe opals with such transparency. *Fire opal* is a crystal or jelly opal with an intense, fiery red-orange color.

The type of opal that first comes to mind when most people think of opal is white opal, but connoisseurs seek black opals, the rarest of all. Black opals are usually a deep gray or grayish black with flashes of incredibly brilliant color dancing around within and about the stones as they are turned. One must be careful when purchasing a black opal, however; be sure to ask whether or not it is a doublet or triplet (see pages 74–77). There are many doublets and triplets in the market because of black opal's rarity, beauty, and extremely high cost; a black opal the size of a lima bean could cost $25,000 today. Black opal doublets provide affordable options to those who love opal but can't afford a natural. But they also provide another opportunity for misrepresentation that can be very costly to the consumer.

Generally speaking, purity of color, absence of dead spots (called *trueness*), flawlessness, intensity or brilliance of color, and transparency are the primary factors affecting value. Opals with an abundance of red are usually the most expensive, whether a light or dark opal; those strong in blue and green are equally beautiful but less rare, so their price is somewhat less. One of the rarest is the harlequin opal, which displays color patterns resembling a checkerboard, and these can be incredibly costly. Australia is the leading producer of all types of opal, but other sources include Brazil, the Czech Republic, Ethiopia, Mexico, Nigeria, Tanzania, and the United States.

While there are imitations and synthetics, for the most part their quality is such that they are not yet worth considering. The synthetic opal, nonetheless, is being used extensively. Also, since the color of black opals can be improved by treatment, treated opals are encountered frequently. So the usual precautions are in order: make sure you know what you are

---

USEFUL FACTS

Opal Composition: hydrated silica gel
Weight: very light (specific gravity: 1.98–2.20)
Brilliance: ranges from low to high

Hardness: 5.5–6.5
Wearability: fair to good

---

getting, and before buying, shop around. This holds truer for opal, perhaps, than any other stone.

One word of caution must also be offered: opals require special care because some tend to dry and crack. Avoid exposure to anything that is potentially drying, and immerse your opal in water for several hours periodically to help preserve it. *Never wipe the surface of opals with oil or immerse them in oil;* soaking some opals in oil for only a few hours can cause them to lose some or nearly all of their fire. Furthermore, it was once thought that wiping the surface of an opal regularly with oil would protect it. *This is not true and will damage most opals.*

Peridot (Olivine)

Today's birthstone for August, peridot was also a favorite of the ancients. This lovely transparent yellowish-green to deep-chartreuse stone was quite a powerful gem. It was considered an aid to friendship and was also believed to free the mind of envious thoughts (which is probably why it was an aid to friendship). Because of its yellowish-green color, it was also believed to cure or prevent diseases of the liver and dropsy. If that's not enough, worn on the left arm it would protect the wearer from the evil eye.

Peridot is also popular today, but probably more for its lovely shade of green than its professed powers. While peridot is not particularly brilliant, the richness of its color can be exceptional and it is natural. Peridot is one of the few gems that is not routinely treated. It comes in shades of yellowish green to darker, purer green colors. Unfortunately, because of its rarity most people never see peridot in the deeper, purer green color that is so prized, but newly discovered sources may change this. Today sources of peridot include Arizona in the U.S., Mexico, Myanmar, Norway, Pakistan, Russia, and Sri Lanka.

Peridot is still widely available in small sizes, but larger stones are becoming scarce, so prices are now fairly high for good-quality material in higher carat weights.

USEFUL FACTS

Peridot Composition: magnesium iron silicate   **Hardness**: 6.5–7.0
Weight: moderately heavy (specific gravity: 3.34)   **Wearability**: fair to good
Brilliance: moderate to high

Some caution should be exercised in wearing peridot. It is moderately hard (6½ to 7 on Mohs' scale) but can chip and scratch easily. Also, some stones—like green sapphire or green tourmaline—can look like peridot and be mistaken or misrepresented.

Pezzottaite

If pink is your color, this is a gemstone to watch. Pezzottaite (pronounced pet-ZOH-tah-ite) is a new gem mineral discovered in 2002 in Madagascar. A source in Afghanistan has also now been identified. It was named pezzottaite in 2003 after Italian mineralogist Federico Pezzotta, one of the first to investigate this new gem, in recognition of his contributions to understanding the mineralogy of Madagascar.

This gem is a new variety of beryl and is very similar to other gemstones in the beryl family. It was initially thought to be morganite (pink beryl), but pezzottaite crystallizes differently and has different physical and optical properties; it is more brilliant and heavier. In some ways it is more similar to pink tourmaline and might be confused with this gem, but careful gemological testing will easily distinguish between the two. It occurs in lovely pink shades, usually with a slightly purplish undertone. Some stones display a strong chatoyant (cat's-eye) effect when cut as a cabochon. In terms of wearability, it is comparable to other gemstones in the beryl family. In terms of availability, supply is currently limited. This may change as more sophisticated production techniques are used, and other sources may also be discovered.

USEFUL FACTS

Pezzottaite Composition: cesium aluminum silicate   **Hardness**: 7.5–8.0
Weight: moderately heavy (specific gravity 3.09–3.14)   **Wearability**: fair to good
Brilliance: moderately high

Quartz

The most versatile of any of the gem families, quartz includes among its members more variety and a larger number of gems than any other three mineral families together. In the gem trade, the old saying "If in doubt, say quartz" still holds true.

The quartz minerals, for the most part, are relatively inexpensive gems that offer a wide range of pleasing color alternatives in both transparent and nontransparent varieties, from translucent to opaque. They are reasonably hard stones (7 on Mohs' scale) and, while not very brilliant in the transparent varieties, still create lovely, affordable jewelry.

Some of these gems have been discussed in separate sections, but I will provide a list here with brief descriptions of most of the quartz family members.

Transparent varieties. **Amethyst** (see page 124) is lilac to purple in color.

Citrine is often called quartz topaz, citrine topaz, or topaz, all of which are misleading. The correct name for this stone is citrine. It ranges in color from lemon yellow to egg-yolk yellow to an orangy amber or brownish amber. This is the most commonly seen "topaz" in today's marketplace and is, unfortunately, too often confused with precious topaz because of the careless use of the name. While a pleasing stone in terms of color and fairly durable, citrine is slightly softer and has less brilliance than precious topaz. It also lacks the subtle color shading, the pinker yellow or pinkish-amber shades, which lends to precious topaz a distinctive color difference. Much citrine is made by heating pale amethyst.

Citrine is much less expensive than precious topaz. It should never be represented as topaz, which technically is "precious" or "imperial" topaz. Unfortunately, it often is. For example, "topaz" birthstone jewelry is almost always citrine (or a worthless synthetic). So the question to ask the seller is, "Is this citrine or precious topaz?" Get the answer in writing if you are told, "Precious topaz."

Citrine is plentiful in all sizes and can be made into striking jewelry, especially in very large sizes, for a relatively small investment, while precious topaz of fine quality is scarce in sizes over seven carats and is *very* expensive.

Ametrine is a lovely, unusual bicolor quartz in which amethyst and citrine are both present in the same stone. The name is derived by taking the first three letters of amethyst and the last five letters in citrine. Bolivia is the source of natural ametrine, although "ametrine" can also be created in the laboratory.

Praseolite is a pale-green, transparent variety produced by heating amethyst.

Rock crystal is water clear. It was used in old jewelry for rondelles, a type of small bead resembling a doughnut. Faceted crystal beads were also common in older jewelry. Today, however, *crystal* usually refers to glass.

Rose quartz is light to deep pink. This stone has been very popular for many years for use in carved pieces—beads, statues, ashtrays, fine lamp bases, and pins and brooches. Rarely clear, this stone is usually seen in cabochon cuts, rounded beads, or carvings rather than in faceted styles. Once very inexpensive, it is becoming more costly, particularly in the finer deep pink shades. But the color of rose quartz is especially pleasing and offers an excellent choice for use in fashion accessory jewelry.

You must be somewhat cautious with rose quartz, however, because it tends to crack more easily than most other varieties of quartz if struck or exposed to a blow. The inclusions or internal fractures that are also responsible for the absence of clarity in this stone cause it to be slightly brittle.

Smoky quartz is a pale to rich smoky-brown variety, sometimes mistaken for or misrepresented as smoky topaz or topaz. It is also very plentiful and is becoming popular for use in very large sizes for beautiful brooches, large dinner rings, and so forth.

Translucent to opaque varieties. *Agate* and *chalcedony* are found in all colors, and all varieties of markings are seen in this wonderful ornamental gem. Among them you'll find, to mention a few, banded agate; moss agate, a fascinating white or milky agate that looks as though it actually has black, brown, or green moss growing within; eye agate, which has an eyeball effect; or plume agate, which looks as if it's filled with beautiful feather plumes. The colors and "scenes" in agate are infinite. While agate is usually an inexpensive stone, some varieties or special stones with very unusual scenes or markings can be quite expensive.

Carnelian, sard, and *sardonyx* are reddish, orange, apricot, and brown varieties of chalcedony and are often seen in cameo or other carving work. Black onyx is a dyed chalcedony; chrysoprase is green chalcedony, often dyed green; see page 133 for more about carnelian.

The unusual colors and markings of agate made it very highly regarded by the ancients and revered throughout history, even to the present day.

According to Pliny, it was believed to make wearers "agreeable and persuasive and give them God's favor." Other virtues claimed for agate wearers include giving the wearer victory and strength and also protection from tempests and lightning, guarding its wearer from all dangers, enabling him to overcome all terrestrial obstacles, and imparting to him a bold heart.

Wearing agate ornaments was also seen as a cure for insomnia and could ensure good dreams. In the middle of the 1800s, and continuing to the present in some parts of the world, amulets made from eye agate (brown or black agate with a white ring in the center) were so popular that agate cutters in Germany had time for cutting little else. The "eye" was believed to take on the watchfulness of one's guardian spirit and to protect the wearer from the evil eye by neutralizing its power. At one time these amulets commanded an incredible price.

Whatever their real power, these are fascinating stones, some quite mesmerizing in their unusual beauty. They are often seen in antique jewelry as well as in contemporary pieces. One must be careful, however, to exercise some caution in wear to protect from knocks, as some varieties are more fragile than others. Also, agate is frequently dyed, so it is important to ask whether the color is natural and to be sure that it is not another less valuable stone, dyed to look like a special variety of agate.

Aventurine is a lovely pale- to medium-green, semitranslucent stone with tiny sparkling flecks of mica within. This stone makes very lovely cabochon or bead jewelry at a very affordable price. It is occasionally misrepresented as jade; although the mica flecks are sometimes so small that they cannot be seen easily, they provide an immediate and reliable indicator that the material is aventurine quartz. Be aware, however, that there are some fairly good glass imitations in the marketplace.

Bloodstone (see page 130) is dark green with red spots.

Cat's-eye is a pale yellowish-green stone that when cut in cabochon style produces a streak of light down the center that creates an eye effect. This phenomenon is a result of the presence of fiberlike inclusions. This stone has a weaker center line, a paler color, and much lower cost than true cat's-eye from the chrysoberyl family. But it is nonetheless an attractive stone that makes attractive, affordable jewelry.

Chrysocolla—the true chrysocolla— is a very soft copper mineral, too soft for jewelry use. However, quartz that has been naturally impregnated or stained with chrysocolla has good hardness and the same brilliant blue-green, highly translucent color. Chrysocolla is becoming a very popular stone for jewelry, and its price is starting to reflect increased demand.

Chrysoprase (see page 132) is a bright light- to dark-green, highly translucent stone, often of very even color. It is sometimes misrepresented as or confused with jade.

Jasper is opaque red, yellow, green, and brown (or sometimes gray). It is usually strongly marked in terms of the contrast between the green and other colors in an almost blotchlike or veinlike pattern. The red and green combination is the most popular, although there are more than fifty types of jasper of various colors and patterns.

Jasper was believed in ancient cultures to bring rain and also to protect its wearer from the bites of poisonous creatures. It was believed to have as diverse a power as the colors and veins in which it came, so many uses and magical powers were associated with it.

Jasper offers interesting color contrast and variety and is being used increasingly in today's fashion accessory jewelry.

Petrified wood is sections of trees or limbs that have been replaced by quartz-type silica and transformed into a mineral after centuries of immersion in silica-rich water under extreme pressure. It is usually red, reddish brown, or brown and is not often seen in jewelry.

Tiger's-eye is a golden, yellowish, reddish, and sometimes bluish variety of quartz that produces a bright shimmering line (or lines) of light, which when cut in a cabochon will produce an eye. The eye will move when the stone is turned from side to side. It is inexpensive but very popular for fashion accessory jewelry and men's cufflinks and rings. The blue variety is often called *hawk's-eye*.

USEFUL FACTS

Quartz Composition: silicon dioxide   **Hardness**: 7.0
Weight: light (specific gravity: 2.61–2.65)   **Wearability**: good
Brilliance: moderately high

Rhodochrosite

Rhodochrosite is a newcomer to the jewelry business. While sought by rock hounds for many years and a favorite of beginning lapidaries, rhodochrosite appeared only occasionally outside of rock and mineral shows frequented by hobbyists. A member of the carbonate mineral group, rhodochrosite is a relatively soft stone occurring in a very rare transparent variety and a more common nontransparent variety. For practical purposes, I will discuss the latter, more readily available form.

A lovely red to almost white color, often with agatelike curved lines creating a design in contrasting shades of red or pink, rhodochrosite may occasionally occur in an orangy tone, but this is poorer-quality material. The finest color is a medium to deep rose, preferably with curved banding. It has long been popular for certain ornamental objects (spheres, boxes, eggs) but only recently for jewelry. Today, necklaces using rhodochrosite beads alternating with other stones or gold beads are becoming particularly popular. We will see more rhodochrosite on the market in coming years, but it is soft (4 on Mohs' scale) so care should be used when wearing it to avoid unnecessary abuse. The major source of this variety of rhodochrosite is the United States.

USEFUL FACTS

Rhodochrosite Composition: manganese carbonate   **Hardness**: 4.0 (soft)
Weight: very heavy (specific gravity: 5.20)   **Wearability**: fair to good
Brilliance: moderate

Scapolite

This is an interesting gem that is beginning to appear in more jewelry as it becomes more available. Found in Madagascar, Myanmar, and Canada, it was rediscovered in Brazil and also recently discovered in Kenya. Scapolite is a nice transparent, fairly durable stone (6 on Mohs' scale) occurring in a range of colors, from colorless to yellow, light red, orange, greenish, bluish gray, violet, and violet-blue. The orange, light-red, and whitish specimens may also occur as semitransparent stones, which may show a cat's-eye effect (chatoyancy) when cut into cabochons.

USEFUL FACTS

Scapolite Composition: complex silicate   **Hardness**: 6.0
Weight: light (specific gravity: 2.70)   **Wearability**: fair
Brilliance: moderate

The most likely to appear in jewelry are the violets and yellows, and possibly orange cat's-eyes. They might easily be mistaken for yellow beryl or certain quartz minerals like amethyst or citrine.

The bottom line here is that we will have to wait and see what trends evolve around this stone, as its availability will determine its future use and cost.

Serpentine

Serpentine derives its name from its similarity to the green, speckled skin of the serpent. Amulets of serpentine were worn for protection from serpent bites, stings of poisonous reptiles, and poison in general. A king was reputed to have insisted that his chalice be made of serpentine, as it was believed that if a poisoned drink were put into a serpentine vessel, the vessel would sweat on the outside. The effectiveness of medicine was increased when it was drunk from a serpentine vessel.

Serpentine is often used as a jade substitute. It is a translucent to semi-translucent stone occurring in light- to dark-yellowish green to greenish yellow. One variety is used for decorative wall facings and table and counter surfaces, but some of the more attractive green varieties so closely resemble jadeite or nephrite jade that they are used in carvings and jewelry and are often misrepresented as jade. Common serpentine is also sometimes dyed a jadelike color. One lovely green variety, williamsite, which is a very pleasing deep green, often with small black flecks within, is often sold as "Pennsylvania jade." It is pretty, but it is not jade. Another variety of serpentine, bowenite, is also sold today as "Korean jade" or "new jade." Again, it is pretty but is not jade. Serpentine is softer than jade, less durable, and much more common, which its price should reflect. Sources of serpentine include Afghanistan, China, England, Italy, New Zealand, South Africa, and the United States.

Serpentine is a lovely stone in its own right and makes a nice alternative to jade. While it has been around for a long time (too often, however,

---

USEFUL FACTS

Serpentine Composition: magnesium hydroxysilicate   **Hardness**: 5.0
Weight: light (specific gravity: 2.58–2.62)   **Wearability**: fair to good
Brilliance: moderate

represented as jade), we are just beginning to see this stone used frequently in necklaces and other fine jewelry under its own name.

Sodalite

This stone has already been discussed under *lapis lazuli*. It is a dark-blue semitransparent to semitranslucent stone, used frequently as a substitute for the rarer, more expensive lapis. While it may have some white veining, it does not have the golden or silver flecks that are characteristic of lapis. If you do not see these shiny flecks, suspect that the stone is probably sodalite. The major commercial source of sodalite is Ontario, Canada. It is sometimes called *Princess Blue* since it was discovered there during a visit by Princess Margaret. Other sources include Brazil, India, Namibia, and the United States.

USEFUL FACTS

Sodalite Composition: sodium aluminum silicate   **Hardness**: 5.5 (soft)
Weight: light (specific gravity: 2.27)   **Wearability**: fair to good
Brilliance: moderately high

Sphene (Titanite)

Sphene is another "new" gem (also known as *titanite*) that is beginning to appear and offers some interesting possibilities for the jewelry market. While it has been highly regarded for many years, its relative scarcity prevented its widescale use in jewelry. Today, however, new sources have been discovered, and we are beginning to see greater availability. Today it is found primarily in Brazil and Madagascar, but it can also be found in Austria, Canada, Mexico, and Switzerland.

Sphene is a beautiful, brilliant stone, with a diamondlike (adamantine) luster, and fire that is even greater than in diamond. Unfortunately, it is soft. Its colors range from grass green to golden yellow to brown.

USEFUL FACTS

Sphene Composition: calcium titanium silicate   **Hardness**: 5.0–5.5 (soft)
Weight: heavy (specific gravity: 3.53)   **Wearability**: fair
Brilliance: very high

There is need for some caution because of its softness (5 to 5½ on Mohs' scale). I suggest that it is especially suitable for pendants, earrings, brooches, and only in rings that offer a protective setting.

Spinel

Spinel is one of the loveliest of the gems, but it has only recently begun to enjoy the respect and admiration it deserves. It is usually compared to sapphire or ruby rather than being recognized for its own intrinsic beauty and value. There is also a common belief that spinel (and similarly zircon) is synthetic rather than natural, when in fact it is one of nature's most beautiful—and truly natural—creations. This misconception probably arose because synthetic spinel is seen frequently on the market, whereas genuine spinel is not often seen.

Spinel is one of the very few gems currently *not enhanced or treated.* It occurs in red-orange (flame spinel); light to dark orangy red; light to dark, slightly grayish blue; greenish blue; grayish green; and dark to light purple to violet. It also occurs in yellow and in an opaque variety—black. When compared with the blue of sapphire or the red of ruby, the color is usually considered less intense (although some red spinel can look very much like some ruby on the market now), yet its brilliance can be greater. If you appreciate these spinel colors for themselves, they are quite pleasing. The most popular are red (usually a more orange-red than ruby red) and blue (sometimes resembling a strong Bromo Seltzer–bottle blue).

One of the most famous of all stones—the "Black Prince's Ruby" that adorns the famous Imperial State Crown, part of the British crown jewels—was discovered to be a red spinel! Throughout history, natural spinel has been confused and misidentified as many other gemstones—some less valuable, some more valuable—including ruby, sapphire, zircon, amethyst, garnet, synthetic ruby/sapphire, and even glass. Then, to make matters more complex, synthetic spinel is used to make composite stones such as emerald doublets.

USEFUL FACTS

Spinel Composition: magnesium aluminum oxide **Hardness**: 8.0
Weight: heavy (specific gravity: 3.60) **Wearability**: good to very
Brilliance: high good

Spinel is a hard (8 on Mohs' scale), fairly durable stone with good brilliance and a lively personality. It occurs in many lovely colors and still offers very good value. The primary sources of spinel are Madagascar, Myanmar, and Sri Lanka, but others include Afghanistan, Australia, Brazil, Italy, Pakistan, Russia, Sweden, Turkey, and the United States.

As more and more people discover this lovely gemstone, however, prices may increase significantly. We are already seeing prices strengthen.

Spodumene (Kunzite and Hiddenite)

Spodumene is another gem relatively new to widespread jewelry use. The most popular varieties are kunzite and hiddenite. Kunzite was named after the famous American gemologist George Frederick Kunz, and hiddenite was named after an American gemologist, William Hidden, who discovered the green variety in North Carolina, in the area that now also bears his name, Hiddenite.

Kunzite is a very lovely, brilliant stone occurring in delicate lilac, pinkish, or violet shades. Its color can fade in strong light, so it has become known as an "evening" stone. Also, while a relatively hard stone (6 to 7 on Mohs' scale), it is nonetheless brittle and can break easily if it receives a sharp blow from certain directions. It is not recommended for rings for this reason unless set in a protective mounting. But it is a lovely gem, whose low cost makes it attractive in large sizes, and is an excellent choice for lovely, dramatic jewelry design.

Hiddenite is rarer. Light-green or yellow-green varieties are available, but the emerald-green varieties are scarce. As with kunzite, it is relatively hard but brittle, so you must be careful when wearing it.

Spodumene also occurs in many other shades of color, all pale but very clear and brilliant. Only blue is currently missing—but who knows what may yet be discovered in some part of the world? Primary sources of kunzite and hiddenite are Brazil, Madagascar, Myanmar, and Pakistan, but they are also found in Canada, Mexico, Russia, Sweden, and the United States.

USEFUL FACTS

Spodumene Composition: lithium aluminum silicate   **Hardness**: 6.0–7.0
Weight: moderately heavy (specific gravity: 3.18)   **Wearability**: fair to good
Brilliance: high

Spodumene is still fairly inexpensive and is an excellent choice for contemporary jewelry design. Be careful, however, as it can be confused with and sold as more expensive topaz, tourmaline, spinel, or beryl. Also, synthetic corundum or spinel can be mistaken for this gem.

Sugilite

Named for the Japanese petrologist who discovered it, Ken-ichi Sugi, sugilite first appeared on the jewelry scene in the late 1970s, sold as Royal Azel and Royal Lavulite. Best known today as sugilite, its lovely, deep, rich purple to purple-red color is unique. An opaque gem, it is usually cut in cabochons or beads, although it is also popular for inlay work (intarsia) by top artisans. Sugilite belongs to the manganese family, and most comes from Africa. The finest color is already becoming scarce, so it is difficult to predict the future for this interesting newcomer.

USEFUL FACTS

Sugilite Composition: sodium/lithium silicate   **Hardness:** 6.0–6.5
Weight: slightly heavy (specific gravity: 2.74–2.80)   **Wearability:** fair to good
Brilliance: moderate

Sunstone and Spectrolite
(See *Feldspar.*)

Tanzanite
(See *Zoisite.*)

Titanite
(See *Sphene.*)

Topaz

True topaz, symbol of love and affection, aid to sweetness of disposition, and birthstone for November, is one of nature's most wonderful and least-known families. The true topaz is rarely seen in jewelry stores. Unfortunately, most people know only the quartz (citrine) topaz, or glass, and in the past almost any yellow stone was called topaz. A very beautiful and versatile stone, topaz is a hard, brilliant stone with a fine color range, and it is much rarer and much more expensive than the stones commonly sold as topaz. It is also heavier than its imitators.

Topaz occurs not only in the transparent yellow, yellow-brown, orangy-brown, and pinky-brown colors most popularly associated with it, but also in a very light to medium red now found naturally in fair supply, although many are produced through heat treatment. It also is found in a very light to medium deep blue, also often as the result of treatment, although blue does occur naturally on a fairly wide scale. Other topaz shades include very light green, light greenish yellow, violet, and colorless. Diffusion-treated topaz is also available in medium to deep green and blue-green.

Blue topaz has become very popular in recent years, most of it treated; unfortunately, there is no way yet to determine which has been treated and which is natural. The blue form closely resembles the finest aquamarine, which is very expensive today, and offers a very attractive and much more affordable alternative to it. Some of the fine, deeper blue treated topazes have been found to be radioactive and, according to the Nuclear Regulatory Commission, may be injurious to the wearer. In the United States, all blue topaz must be tested for radiation levels; the Gemological Institute of America (GIA) now provides this service to the jewelry trade. However, be very careful when buying blue topaz outside the United States. If you do, you may be wise to have it tested when you get home.

There are many misleading names to suggest that a stone is topaz when it is not, for example, "Rio topaz," "Madeira topaz," "Spanish topaz," and "Palmeira topaz." They are types of citrine (quartz) and should be represented as such.

The true topaz family offers a variety of color options in lovely, clear, brilliant, and durable stones (8 on Mohs' scale). Precious topaz can be found in Africa, Australia, Brazil, Japan, Mexico, Myanmar, Pakistan, Russia, and Sri Lanka. The major sources of pink topaz are Brazil, Pakistan, and Russia. This family should become more important in the years ahead.

USEFUL FACTS

Topaz Composition: aluminum fluorohydroxysilicate   **Hardness**: 8.0
Weight: heavy (specific gravity: 3.54)   **Wearability**: good
Brilliance: high

Tourmaline

Tourmaline is a gem of modern times, but nonetheless it has found its way to the list of birthstones, becoming an "alternative birthstone" for October. Perhaps this honor results from tourmaline's versatility and broad color range, or perhaps from the fact that red and green tourmaline, in which red and green occur side by side in the same stone, is reminiscent of the turning of October leaves.

Whatever the case, tourmaline is one of the most versatile of the gem families. It is available in every color, in every tone from deep to pastel, and even with two or more colors appearing in the same stone side by side. There are bicolored tourmalines (half red and half green, for example) and tricolored (one-third blue, one-third green, and one-third yet another color). The fascinating "watermelon" tourmaline looks just like the inside of a watermelon: red in the center surrounded by a green "rind." A rare new "particolor" variety (more than three colors) called liddicoatite—named to honor American gemologist Richard Liddicoat—was discovered in Brazil and Madagascar. It is marked by multiple-color banding and a three-rayed star that resembles the Mercedes logo. Tourmaline can also be found in a cat's-eye variety.

One of the most exciting gemological discoveries of this century was the discovery of a unique variety of tourmaline in Paraiba, Brazil. These particular beauties, referred to as Paraiba or Hetorita after the man who discovered them, have colors so intense and come in such a wide range of green, blue, and lilac shades that they are referred to as the *neon* tourmalines. Unfortunately, demand has been unprecedented for these particular tourmalines, and supply has dwindled. The result is that many of the finest Paraibas are very expensive, and some rival the finest sapphires and emeralds in price. Many imitations are now on the market, and I have found apatite, a common, inexpensive stone that occurs in similar colors but is too soft for most jewelry use, being sold as "Paraiba" tourmaline.

It is indeed surprising that most people know of tourmaline simply as a common "green" stone. Nothing could be more misleading. Today,

USEFUL FACTS

Tourmaline Composition: complex borosilicate   **Hardness**: 7.0–7.5
Weight: moderately heavy (specific gravity: 3.06)   **Wearability**: good to
Brilliance: high   excellent

we are finally beginning to see other lovely varieties of this fascinating gem in the jewelry market. In addition to the exciting new Paraiba, other popular varieties include the following:

- Chrome—a particularly rare green hue
- Indicolite—deep indigo blue, usually with a green undertone
- Rubellite—deep pink to red, as in ruby

While many tourmalines are very inexpensive, the chrome, indicolite, and rubellite varieties are priced (depending on size and quality) anywhere from $200 to $1,000 per carat or more. And the incomparable Paraiba variety can sell for $10,000 to $20,000 per carat for a top-quality one-carat stone—up to $35,000 to $45,000 *per carat* for a three-carat stone, if you can find one. So much for the "common and inexpensive" myth!

Tourmaline is a fairly hard (7 to 7½ on Mohs' scale), durable, brilliant, and very wearable stone with a wide range of colors. Tourmalines can be found in Australia, Brazil, East Africa, Madagascar, Mexico, Myanmar, Nigeria, Pakistan, Russia, South Africa, Sri Lanka, Tanzania, and the United States (California and Maine are important sources of fine tourmaline).

Tourmaline is a stone that will, without question, play a more and more important role in jewelry in the years ahead.

Turquoise

A birthstone for December, and ranking highest among all the opaque stones, turquoise—the "Turkish stone"—is highly prized throughout Asia and Africa, not only for its particular hue of blue (a beautiful robin's-egg or sky blue) but especially for its supposed prophylactic and therapeutic qualities. The Arabs consider it a lucky stone and have great confidence in its benevolent action. Used in rings, earrings, necklaces, head ornaments, and amulets, it protects the wearer from poison, reptile bites, eye diseases, and the evil eye. It was also believed capable of warning of impending death by changing color. Also, the drinking of water in which turquoise has been dipped or washed was believed to cure bladder ailments. Buddhists revere turquoise because it is associated with a legend in which a turquoise enabled Buddha to destroy a monster. Even today it is considered a symbol of courage, success, and love. It has also long been associated with Native American jewelry and art.

Turquoise is an opaque, light- to dark-blue or blue-green stone. The finest color is an intense blue, with poorer qualities tending toward yellowish green. The famous Persian (Iranian) turquoise, which can be a very intense and pleasing sky blue to robin's-egg blue, is a very rare and valuable gem. In Tibet there is a greener variety, which is preferred there. The United States (Arizona and New Mexico) is an important source of fine turquoise, some of which is comparable to the highly prized sky and robin's-egg blue associated with Iranian turquoise. Mexico continues to produce turquoise, although it is typically greener. Turquoise is also found in Australia, Chile, China, Russia, and Turkestan.

All turquoise is susceptible to aging, turning greenish or possibly darker over time. Also, care must be taken to avoid contact with soap, grease, or other materials that might discolor it, and to protect it from abuse, since turquoise scratches fairly easily (6 on Mohs' scale).

But exercise caution when buying turquoise. This is a frequently simulated gem. Very fine glass imitations are produced that are difficult to distinguish from the genuine. Enhanced, coated, and "stabilized" stones, and reconstructed stones (from turquoise powder bonded in plastic), saturate the marketplace, as does synthetic turquoise. There are techniques to quickly distinguish these imitations and treated stones, so, if in doubt, check it out (and get a complete description on the bill of sale: "genuine, natural turquoise").

Radioactive inclusions in turquoise appear on the market. A new source of turquoise, reportedly from China, has recently been found to contain *radioactive inclusions.* These inclusions appear as bright yellow spots in heavily veined turquoise, and are usually visible to the eye. While thought to be harmless due to low-level emissions, this turquoise could be harmful if worn frequently. It might also pose a risk to anyone cutting this material and inhaling the dust. Turquoise-lovers should have stones tested for radioactivity by a gemologist-appraiser (see chapter 11).

USEFUL FACTS

Turquoise Composition: hydrated copper aluminum phosphate	**Brilliance**: moderately high **Hardness**: 6.0
Weight: light (specific gravity: 2.80)	**Wearability**: fair to good

Zircon

Known to the ancients as hyacinth, this gem had many powers, especially for men. While it was known to assist women in childbirth, for men it kept evil spirits and bad dreams away, gave protection against "fascination" and lightning, strengthened their bodies, fortified their hearts, restored appetite, suppressed fat, produced sleep, and banished grief and sadness from the mind.

Zircons are very brilliant, transparent stones that occur in several lovely colors. Unfortunately, many consumers suffer from a strange misconception that zircon is a synthetic or artificial stone rather than a lovely natural creation. Perhaps this is based on the fact that relatively inexpensive brown stones are routinely heated to transform them into colorless and blue. Despite the number of treated zircons in the market, they also occur naturally in a range of colors, including yellow, orange, red, green, and brown. Sri Lanka has been a source of gem-quality zircon for hundreds of years. It is also found in Australia, Brazil, Cambodia, France, Myanmar, Tanzania, Thailand, and Vietnam.

Many might mistake the colorless zircon for diamond because of its strong brilliance, which, coupled with its very low cost, makes colorless zircon an interesting alternative to diamonds as a stone to offset or dress up colored stones. But care needs to be exercised because zircon is only moderately hard (6½ to 7½ on Mohs' scale), and it is brittle, so it will chip or abrade easily. For this reason, zircon is recommended for earrings, pendants, brooches, or rings with a protective setting.

USEFUL FACTS

Zircon Composition: zirconium silicate
Weight: very heavy (specific gravity: 4.69)
Brilliance: very high

Hardness: 6.5–7.5
Wearability: fair

Zoisite (Tanzanite)

Zoisite was not considered a gem material until 1967, when a beautiful, rich blue to purple-blue, transparent variety was found in Tanzania (hence the name *tanzanite*). Today the primary sources of tanzanite are Tanzania and Kenya. Tanzanite can occur naturally in a rich sapphire-blue color, possibly with some violet-red or greenish-yellow flashes, but most have been heated to obtain the lovely blue and violet colors we see. A green variety has recently been discovered, which is being called green zoisite, green tanzanite, or chrome tanzanite. The green can be a very lovely shade, ranging from a slightly yellowish green to gray-green to bluish green, and the color is *natural*. The green variety is one of the few gems *not routinely treated*. Supply is still limited, so time will tell whether or not this green variety will be readily available to the public.

Tanzanite has become one of the most popular gems in the marketplace. As a result, many imitations are being produced. Double-check on the identity of any fine tanzanite with a gemologist-appraiser.

This lovely gem can cost over $2,000 per carat today in larger sizes. But one must exercise care when wearing this stone because, while moderately hard (6½ on Mohs' scale), it is brittle and can chip easily. For this reason, I don't recommend it for rings (unless the ring provides some protection for the stones) or for everyday wear in which it would be exposed to knocks and other abuse. The green variety is somewhat more durable since it is not heated (heating can increase brittleness).

USEFUL FACTS

Tanzanite Composition: calcium aluminum hydroxysilicate
Weight: moderately heavy (specific gravity: 3.35)

Brilliance: high
Hardness: 6.5
Wearability: blue: fair; green: good

Zultanite (Color-Change Diaspore)

Color-change gemstones have long fascinated collectors and connoisseurs, but it is only in recent years that we have started to see interest in the larger consumer marketplace. As more and more people seek unique or unusual gemstones, color-change gems—those that are one color in certain lighting environments but which turn a completely different color in a different type of light—are moving to center stage. We have already discussed the rare, highly sought gem called alexandrite, and mentioned color-change garnets, sapphires, and even diamonds. In recent years another exciting color-change gem was unearthed in Turkey: Zultanite, a color-change variety of a little-known material called diaspore.

While diaspore has been known for many years to gemologists and mineralogists, most of it was too heavily included to be considered a "gem." In the 1970s, some very clean specimens began to surface, and then a substantial deposit of beautiful color-change material was discovered in Turkey. *Zultanite* was introduced into the market, the name meant to conjure up images of the ancient *sultans* who ruled Turkey and the Ottoman Empire. (They had wanted to name it *"Sultan*ite," but that name was unavailable!)

Zultanite occurs in lovely, soft pastel colors, changing from a lovely pastel green in daylight to pink, brownish pink or pinkish beige in warm, indoor light. The green color is a beautiful shade but the pastel pink tones may be more difficult to see, depending upon the type of light in which they are viewed. As in alexandrite, there is often a brownish undertone to both the green and pink colors. Nonetheless, the color is very pleasing, and very wearable, even if less vivid than some other color-change gems. Some women prefer the colors of Zultanite because there is a more subtle contrast and the colors are an especially nice complement to earth tones (green, brown, gold). For some, the colors are more wearable than stones with stronger color and more extreme color change.

Zultanite is a gemstone worth seeking out. Its colors are very pleasing, it is a lively stone, and it is relatively hard. It is also available in a wide range of sizes, including 10+ carats, which is an advantage over other color-change stones that rarely exceed 2–3 carats.

All in all, Zultanite is a good choice for jewelry and remains more affordable than most other color-change gemstones. At the moment, prices for fine-quality stones (eye-clean and slightly included) range from about $300–$400 per carat in 2–3 carat sizes, $600–$700 per carat in 5–7 carat sizes, to around $800–$1,000 per carat in 7–10 carat sizes. Larger stones or stones of exceptional color and overall quality can cost more, sometimes much more. Keep in mind that pricing is a reflection of supply and demand; supply is still somewhat limited. If demand increases, prices could increase in the foreseeable future.

USEFUL FACTS

Color-Change Diaspore Composition: aluminum oxide hydroxide
Weight: moderately heavy (specific gravity ±3.39)

Brilliance: moderately high
Hardness: 6.5–7.0
Wearability: fair to good

PART ◆ THREE

Important Advice
Before & After You Buy

CHAPTER TEN

What to Ask When Buying the Stone

Asking the right questions is the key to knowing what you're getting when it comes to buying gemstones. It is also the only way you can be sure what you are comparing when considering gems from different jewelers. Be sure the jeweler can answer your questions or can get the answers for you. Then, be sure the jeweler is willing to put the answers *in writing* on your bill of sale. Finally, verify the facts—double-check that the stone is as represented—by having it examined by a qualified gemologist-appraiser. In this way you'll be able to make an informed choice about quality and value, you'll have no doubt about what you are getting, and you'll begin to develop a solid relationship with the jeweler from whom you make the purchase, based on confidence and trust. And, in the event the stone is not as represented, you'll know in time—and have the information you need—to get your money back.

What to Ask When Buying a Colored Gemstone

It is very important to ask the right questions to help you understand the differences in gems you may be considering. Asking the following questions should help you to gain a greater understanding of the differences, determine what's right for you, and have greater confidence in your decision.

1. *Is this a genuine, natural stone, or a synthetic?* Synthetic stones are *genuine* but not *natural* (see chapter 5).
2. *Is the color natural?* Most colored gemstones are routinely color enhanced (see chapters 5 and 6). However, stones such as lapis

should not be, and you must protect yourself from buying dyed material that will not retain its color permanently. See information on specific gems (chapters 8 and 9) to determine whether or not this is an important question for you to ask.

Be especially cautious when buying any blue sapphire; make sure you ask whether or not the stone has been checked for diffusion treatment and oiling. Today, with diffused sapphire being found mixed in parcels of natural sapphires and unknowingly set into jewelry, it's possible that one may be sold inadvertently (see chapter 5).

3. *Clarify what the name means.* Be particularly careful of misleading names (see chapter 6). When a stone is described with any qualifier, such as "Rio topaz" (which is not topaz), ask specifically whether or not the stone is genuine. Ask why the qualifier is being used.

4. *Is the clarity acceptable, or do too many inclusions detract from the beauty of the stone?* Are there any flaws, inclusions, or natural characteristics in this stone that might make it more vulnerable to breakage with normal wear? This is a particularly important question when you are considering a colored stone (see chapter 4). While visible inclusions are more common in colored gems than in diamonds, and their existence has much less impact on value than it has on diamond value, value is nonetheless reduced if the inclusions or blemishes affect the stone's durability, or are so numerous that they mar its beauty.

Be especially careful to ask whether or not any inclusion breaks the stone's surface, since this may weaken the stone, particularly if the imperfection is in a position normally exposed to wear, like the top of the stone or around the girdle. This would reduce the stone's value significantly. On the other hand, if the flaw is in a less vulnerable spot, where it can be protected by the setting, it may carry minimal risk and have little effect on value.

A large number of inclusions will usually detract noticeably from the beauty, especially in terms of liveliness, and will also generally weaken the stone and make it more susceptible to any blow or knock. Such stones should be avoided unless the price is right and you're willing to assume the risk.

Also, certain gems, as we've mentioned, are more brittle than others and may break or chip more easily, even without flaws.

These stones include opal, zircon, and some of the new and increasingly popular gems, such as tanzanite. This does not mean you should avoid buying them, but it does mean you should give thought to how they will be worn and how they will be set. Rings and bracelets are particularly vulnerable, since they are more susceptible to blows or knocks. Brooches, pendants, and earrings are less vulnerable.

5. *Do you like the color? How close is the color to its pure spectral shade? Is it too light? Too dark? How does the color look in different types of light?* Learn to look at color critically. Become familiar with the rarest and most valuable color of the gem of your choice. But after you do this, decide what you yourself really like. You may prefer a color that might be less rare and therefore more affordable. Be sure the color pleases you—don't buy what you think you *should* buy unless you really like it.

6. *Is the color permanent?* This question should be asked in light of new treatments (such as diffusion) and also because color in some stones is prone to fading. Two examples are amethyst and kunzite (one of the new and increasingly popular gems). Just which ones will fade and which ones won't, and how long the process might take, no one can know. This phenomenon has never affected the popularity of amethyst, and I see no reason for it to affect kunzite's popularity, but I feel the consumer should be aware of it. There is evidence that too much exposure to strong sunlight or intense heat contributes to fading in these stones, so I suggest avoiding sun and heat. It may be wise to wear these gems primarily for evening or indoor activities.

7. *Does the stone need a protective setting?* The setting may be of special importance when you are considering stones like tanzanite, opal, or emerald. They require a setting that will offer some protection—for example, one in which the main stone is surrounded by diamonds. A design in which the stone is unusually exposed, such as in a high setting or one with open, unprotected sides, would be undesirable.

8. *Does the stone have a pleasing shape? Does it have a nice "personality"?* This will be determined by the cutting. Many colored gems are cut in fancy shapes, often by custom cutters. Fine cutting can enrich the color and personality, and increase the cost. However, with colored gems, brilliance and sparkle are

less important than the color itself. The most critical considerations must focus on color, first and foremost. Sometimes a cutter must sacrifice brilliance in order to obtain the finest possible color. But if the color isn't rich enough or captivating enough to compensate for less brilliance, ask if the jeweler has something that is cut better and exhibits a little more sparkle. Keep in mind, however, that the more brilliant stone may not have the precise color you like, and that when you are buying a colored gem, *color* is the most crucial factor. Unless you find the stone's personality unappealing, don't sacrifice a beautiful color for a stone with a less appealing color just because it may sparkle more. Compare, and decide based on what you like and what you can afford.

When considering a pastel-colored gem, remember that if it is cut too shallow (flat), it can lose its appeal quickly (but only temporarily) with a slight buildup of greasy dirt on the back; the color will fade, and liveliness will practically disappear. This can be immediately remedied by a good cleaning.

9. *What are the colorless stones?* In a piece of jewelry where a colored stone is mounted with colorless stones to accentuate or highlight its color, ask, "What are the colorless stones?" Do not assume they are diamonds. They may be diamonds, zircons, artificial diamond imitations such as CZ or YAG, or synthetic white spinel (spinel is frequently used in Asia).

Special Tips to Remember
When Buying a Colored Stone

When looking at unmounted stones, view them through the side as well as from the top. Also, turn them upside down on a flat, white surface so they are resting on the table facet and you can look straight down through the stone from the back. Look for evenness of color versus color zoning—shades of lighter or darker tones that create streaks or planes of differing color.

Remember that color is the most important consideration. If the color is fine, flaws or inclusions don't detract from the stone's value as significantly as with diamonds. If the overall color or beauty is not seriously affected, the presence of flaws should not deter a purchase. But, conversely, flawless stones may bring a disproportionately higher price per carat because of their rarity, and larger sizes will also command higher prices per carat. In pastel-colored gems, or stones with less fine color, clarity may be more important.

Be sure to check the stone's color in several different types of light— a spotlight, sunlight, or fluorescent or lamplight—before making any decision. Many stones change color—some just slightly, others dramatically—depending on the light in which they are viewed. Be sure that the stone is a pleasing color in the type of light in which you expect to be wearing it most.

If you are considering a stone with rich, deep color—especially if it is for special occasions and likely to be worn mostly at night—be sure it doesn't turn black in evening light. Some stones, like sapphire, can look like black onyx in evening light.

Remember to give special attention to wearability. If you are considering one of the more fragile stones, think about how the piece will be worn, where, and how frequently. Also, pay special attention to the setting and whether the stone is mounted in a way that will add protection, or allow unnecessary, risky exposure to hazards.

Get the Facts on the Bill of Sale

If a colored stone is over one carat and is exceptionally fine and expensive, make the sale contingent on verification of the facts by a qualified gemologist, appraiser, or gem-testing lab such as American Gemological Laboratories (AGL) or the Gemological Institute of America (GIA). See appendix for a list of respected labs outside the USA.

Always make sure that any item you purchase is clearly described in the bill of sale exactly as represented to you by the salesperson or jeweler. For colored gems, essential information also includes the following:

- The identity of the stone or stones and whether or not they are genuine or synthetic, and not in any way a composite (doublet, triplet).
- A statement regarding whether or not the stone has been treated; if untreated, a statement that the stone has not been color or clarity enhanced; if treated, the type and degree of treatment.

- A statement that the color is natural, if it has been so represented; or, in the case of sapphire, a statement that the stone is either surface diffused or *not* surface diffused.
- A statement describing the overall color (hue, tone, intensity).
- A statement describing the overall flaw picture. This is not always necessary with colored stones. In the case of a flawless or nearly flawless stone, it is wise to note the excellent clarity. In addition, note any unusual flaw that might prove useful for identification.
- A statement describing the cut or make. This is not always necessary, but it may be useful if the stone is especially well cut, or has an unusual or fancy cut.
- The carat weight of the main stone or stones, plus total weight if there is a combination of main and smaller stones.
- If the stone is to be taken on approval, make sure that the *exact* dimensions of the stone are included, as well as any other identifying characteristics. The terms and period of approval should also be clearly stated.

Other Information That Should Be Included for Jewelry

- If the piece is being represented as being made by a famous designer or house (Van Cleef and Arpels, Tiffany, Caldwell, Cartier, etc.) and the price reflects this, the name of the designer or jewelry firm should be stated on the bill of sale.
- If the piece is represented as antique (technically, an antique must be at least a hundred years old) or as a period piece from a popular, collectible period like art deco, art nouveau, or Edwardian (especially if made by a premier artisan of the period), this information should be stated on the bill of sale, with the approximate age or date of manufacture and a statement describing the condition.
- If the piece is made by hand, or custom designed, this should be indicated on the bill of sale.
- If the piece is to be taken on approval, make sure millimeter dimensions—top to bottom, as well as length, width, or diameter—are provided, as well as a full description of the piece. Also, check that a time period is indicated, such as "two days." Before you sign anything, be sure that you are signing an approval form and not a binding contract for purchase.

CHAPTER ELEVEN

How to Select a Reputable Jeweler & Gemologist Consultant

It's very difficult to give advice on this matter, since there are so many exceptions to any rules I can suggest. Size and years in business are not always absolute indicators of the reliability of a firm. Some one-person jewelry firms are highly respected; others are not. Some well-established firms that have been in business for many years have built their trade on the highest standards of integrity and knowledge; others should have been put out of business years ago.

One point worth stressing is that for the average consumer, price alone is not a reliable indicator of the integrity or knowledge of the seller. Aside from variations in quality, which often are not readily discernible by the consumer, significant price differences can also result from differences in jewelry manufacturing processes. Many jewelry manufacturers sell mass-produced lines of good-quality jewelry to jewelers all across the country. Mass-produced items, many of which are beautiful, classic designs, are usually much less expensive than handmade, one-of-a-kind pieces, or those on which there is a limited production. The work of some designers may be available in only a few select establishments and may carry a premium because of skill, labor, reputation, and limited distribution. Handmade or one-of-a-kind pieces are always more expensive, since the initial cost of production is paid by one individual rather than shared by many, as in mass-produced pieces.

Furthermore, depending on the store, retail markups also vary based on numerous factors unique to each retailer, including differences in insurance coverage, security costs, credit risks, education and training costs, special services such as in-house design and custom jewelry production and repair, customer service policies, and more.

The best way to select wisely is by shopping around. Go to several fine jewelry firms in your area and compare the services they offer, how knowledgeable the salespeople seem, the quality of their products, and pricing for specific items. This will give you a sense of what is fair in your market area. As you do so, however, remember to ask the right questions to be sure the items are truly comparable, and pay attention to design and manufacturing differences as well. As part of this process, it may be helpful to consider these questions:

- *How long has the firm been in business?* A quick check with the Better Business Bureau may reveal whether or not there are significant consumer complaints.
- *What are the gemological credentials of the jeweler, manager, or owner?* Is there a gemologist on staff? Does the store have its own laboratory?
- *What special services are provided?* Are custom design services, rare or unusual gemstones, educational programs, Gemprint, or photographic services for your jewelry available?
- *How would you describe the store window?* Is the jewelry nicely displayed? Or is the window a melange of incredible bargains and come-on advertising to lure you in?
- *How would you describe the overall atmosphere?* Is the sales staff's manner professional, helpful, tasteful? Or hustling, pushy, intimidating?
- *What is the store's policy regarding returns?* Full refund or only store credit? How many days? What basis for return?
- *What is the repair or replacement policy?*
- *Will the firm allow a piece to be taken "on approval"?* It won't hurt to ask. Some jewelers will. However, unless you know the jeweler personally this is not often permitted today, since too many jewelers have suffered from stolen, damaged, or switched merchandise.
- *To what extent will the firm guarantee its merchandise to be as represented?* Be careful here. Make sure you've asked the right questions, and get complete and accurate information on the bill of sale, or you may find yourself stuck because of a technicality.

If the jeweler can't or won't provide the necessary information, I recommend that you go to another store, no matter how much you've fallen in love with the piece. If you're making the purchase on a contingency basis, put the terms of the contingency on the bill of sale.

Never allow yourself to be intimidated into accepting anyone's claims. Beware of the person who says "Just trust me" or who tries to intimidate you with statements such as "Don't you trust me?" A trustworthy jeweler will not have to ask for your trust; he or she will earn it through knowledge, reliability, and a willingness to give you any information you request—in writing.

Again, in general, you will be in a stronger position to differentiate between a knowledgeable, reputable jeweler and one who isn't if you've shopped around first. Unless you are an expert, visit several firms, ask questions, examine merchandise carefully, and then you be the judge.

Using a Gemologist Consultant

Somewhat new to the gem and jewelry field is the arrival of the gemologist consultant. People interested in acquiring a natural-color gemstone or a fine piece of period or antique jewelry that may be difficult to find in traditional jewelry stores are now seeking the professional services of experienced gemologist consultants. A gemologist consultant can provide a variety of services, including general consulting to help you determine what you really want, what it will cost, and how to best acquire it; how to dispose of jewelry you already own, or from an estate; how to design or redesign a piece of jewelry and have it made. A gemologist consultant can also provide the expertise needed to help you safely purchase gems or jewelry at auction, or from private estate sales. An experienced gemologist consultant can expand your view of the possibilities in terms of gemstones and also suggest ways to make jewelry more personal and distinctive.

As with all else in the sparkling world of gems and jewelry, be sure to check the credentials of anyone offering services as a gemologist consultant. Do they have a gemological diploma? How long have they been working in the field of gems? Do they have a laboratory? Can they provide references within the field? Can they provide client references? If you have jewelry you wish to sell, arrange meetings at a safe place, such as a bank vault.

Fees vary, depending on the gemologist consultant's level of expertise and experience and the nature of the assignment. For example, for general consulting about how to buy or sell gems or jewelry, you should expect to pay about $125 to $200 per hour for someone with good credentials.

For assistance in the acquisition or sale of specific gems or pieces of jewelry, some gemologist consultants work on a fixed fee for the project, some on a percentage of the purchase or sale amount, and some at an hourly rate. When I am retained by clients, my work is done on one of the bases noted above, or even a combination of them, depending on the nature of the work to be done and what best meets the client's needs.

If You Want to File a Complaint

If you have a complaint about a firm's practices or policies, please contact the Better Business Bureau in your city. In addition, if any jeweler has misrepresented what was sold to you, please contact the Jewelers Vigilance Committee (JVC), 25 West 45th Street, Suite 1406, New York, NY 10036; (212) 997-2002. This group can provide invaluable assistance to you, investigate your complaint, and take action against firms believed to be guilty of fraudulent activity in the jewelry industry.

CHAPTER TWELVE

Verifying & Insuring Your Purchase

Step One—Get an Appraisal!

If you have bought a colored gemstone or colored gemstone jewelry, getting a professional appraisal and keeping it updated is critical. *The most important reason to get an appraisal is to verify the facts about the jewelry you have purchased.* This is especially important with the abundance of new synthetic materials and treatments. There are also three other reasons to get an appraisal: (1) to obtain adequate insurance to protect against theft, loss, or damage; (2) to establish adequate information to legally claim jewelry recovered by the police; and (3) if items are lost or stolen, to provide sufficient information to make sure they are replaced with jewelry that actually is of comparable quality, if that is what your insurance policy provides.

The need for appraisal services has increased greatly because of the high incidence of theft and sharp increases in the prices of colored gemstones. It has become necessary to have any fine gem properly appraised—if possible, *before* a purchase decision—given today's costs and the potential for financial loss if the gem is not accurately represented.

It is also important, given recent rising prices, to update value estimations from old appraisals. This will ensure adequate coverage should gems that have been in your possession for several years or more be lost or stolen. In addition, current and accurate appraisals may be needed in connection with inheritance taxes, gifts, or the determination of your net worth.

How to Find a Reliable Appraiser

The appraisal business has been booming over the past few years, and many jewelry firms have begun to provide the service themselves. I must point out, however, that there are essentially no officially established guidelines for going into the gem appraising business. Anyone can represent himself or herself as an appraiser. While many highly qualified professionals are in the business, some others lack the expertise to offer these services. So it is essential to select an appraiser with care and diligence. Further, if the purpose of the appraisal is to verify the identity or genuineness of a gem as well as its value, I recommend that you deal with someone who is in the business of gem identification and appraising and not primarily in the business of selling gems.

To find a reliable gem-testing laboratory, see the appendix for a selected list of laboratories that issue internationally recognized reports. To find a reliable gemologist-appraiser in your community, contact:

Accredited Gemologists Association (AGA)
c/o G-Force Services, 3315 Juanita St., San Diego, CA 92105
(619) 501-5444 • Ask for a list of *Certified Gem Laboratories* or *Certified Master Gemologists.*

American Gem Society (AGS)
8881 W. Sahara Ave., Las Vegas, NV 89117
(866) 805-6500 • Ask for a list of *Certified Gemologist Appraisers* or *Independent Certified Gemologist Appraisers.*

American Society of Appraisers (ASA)
555 Herndon Pkwy., Ste. 125, Herndon, VA 20170
(703) 478-2228 • Ask for a list of *Master Gemologist Appraisers.*

International Society of Appraisers (ISA)
737 N. Michigan Ave., Ste. 2100, Chicago, IL 60611
(312) 981-6778 • Ask for a list of *Certified Appraisers of Personal Property.*

National Association of Jewelry Appraisers (NAJA)
P.O. Box 18, Rego Park, NY 11374
(718) 896-1536 • Ask for a list of *Certified Master Appraisers* or *Certified Senior Members.*

In addition, when selecting a gemologist-appraiser, keep the following suggestions in mind:

- *Obtain the names of several appraisers and then compare their credentials.* To be a qualified gemologist-appraiser requires extensive formal training and experience. You can conduct a preliminary check by telephoning the appraisers and inquiring about their gemological credentials.
- *Look for specific credentials.* The Gemological Institute of America (GIA) and the Gemological Association of Great Britain provide internationally recognized diplomas. GIA's highest award is G.G. (Graduate Gemologist) and the Gemological Association of Great Britain awards the F.G.A.—Fellow of the Gemological Association (F.G.A.A. in Australia; F.C.G.A., Canada). Some hold this honor "with distinction." In Germany, the D.G.G. is awarded; in Asia, the A.G. Make sure the appraiser you select has one of these gemological diplomas. In addition, when seeking an *appraiser,* look for the titles C.G.A. (Certified Gemologist Appraiser) or I.C.G.A. (Independent Certified Gemologist Appraiser), which are awarded by the American Gem Society (AGS), or M.G.A. (Master Gemologist Appraiser), which are awarded by the American Society of Appraisers. Some fine gemologists and appraisers lack these titles because they do not belong to the organizations awarding them, but these titles currently represent the highest awards presented in the gemological appraisal field. Anyone holding these titles should have fine gemological credentials and adhere to high standards of professional conduct.
- *Check the appraiser's length of experience.* In addition to formal training, to be reliable, a gemologist-appraiser needs extensive experience in the handling of gems, use of the equipment necessary for accurate identification and evaluation, and activity in the marketplace. The appraiser should have at least several years' experience in a well-equipped laboratory.
- *Ask where the appraisal will be conducted.* An appraisal should normally be done in the presence of the customer, if possible. This is important in order to ensure that the same stone is returned to you and to protect the appraiser against charges of "switching" or damaging the piece in any way.

If there are several pieces, the process can be very time-consuming. It normally takes about a half hour per item to get all of the specifications, and it can take much longer in some cases. Several appointments may be required for a proper job.

Appraisal Fees

This is a touchy and complex subject. As with any professional service, there should be a suitable charge. Fees should be conspicuously posted or offered readily on request so that the customer knows beforehand what to expect to pay for this service. Fees are essentially based on the expertise of appraisers and the time required of them, as well as the secretarial work required to put the appraisal in written form, since all appraisals should be done in writing. While it used to be standard practice to base appraisal fees on a percentage of the appraised value, this practice is no longer acceptable. Today, all recognized appraisal associations in the United States recommend that fees be based on a flat hourly rate or on a per-carat basis.

There is usually a minimum appraisal fee, regardless of value. The hourly rate charged by a professional, experienced gemologist-appraiser can range from $50 to $150, depending on the complexity of the work to be performed and the degree of expertise required. Find out beforehand what the hourly rate is and what the minimum fee will be.

For certification or special gemological consulting that requires special expertise, rates can easily be $125 to $150 per hour. Extra services such as photography, radiography, Gemprint, or spectroscopic examination of fancy-color diamonds will require additional fees.

Be wary of appraisal services offering appraisals at very low rates and of appraisers who continue to base their fee on a percentage of the "appraised valuation." The Internal Revenue Service, for example, will not accept appraisals performed by appraisers who charge a percentage-based fee.

Some appraisers can photograph jewelry, which I suggest. On the photo, the appraiser should note the approximate magnification and the date, along with your name as the owner. This provides a means of identifying merchandise that may have been stolen or lost and subsequently recovered by police. The photo can also be useful with the U.S. Customs Service should you take your jewelry with you on a trip outside the United States and find yourself having to prove that the jewelry was not purchased abroad.

Choosing an Insurer

Once you have a complete appraisal, the next step is to obtain adequate insurance. Most people do not realize that insurers differ widely in their coverage and reimbursement or replacement procedures. Many companies will not reimburse the "full value" provided in the policy, but instead exercise a "replacement" option by which they offer a *cash sum less than the amount for which the jewelry is insured,* or offer to replace it for you. Therefore, it is important to ask very specific questions to determine the precise coverage offered. I recommend asking at least the following:

- How do you satisfy claims? Do you reimburse the insured amount in cash? If not, how is the amount of the cash settlement determined? Or do you replace the jewelry?
- What involvement do I have in the replacement of an item? What assurance do I have that the replacement will be of comparable quality and value to the original?
- What is your coverage on articles that cannot be replaced?
- Exactly what risks does my policy cover? All risks? Mysterious disappearance? At all times?
- Does the policy have any geographic restrictions?
- Are there any exemptions or exclusions? What if the loss involves negligence?
- What are the deductibles, if any?
- What documentation do you expect me to provide?

To help with insurance claims, keep a photo inventory of your jewelry. Take a photo and store it in a safe place (a bank safe deposit box). In case of theft or fire, a photo will be useful in helping you describe your jewelry, and also in remembering other pieces that are missing, and in identifying them if recovered. A photo is also useful for insurance documentation. In addition, when planning a trip, whatever jewelry you will be taking should be photographed. Just put it on a table and take a snapshot.

CHAPTER THIRTEEN

Buying on the Internet
E-Commerce & Online Auctions

E-commerce is the current buzzword, and gem and jewelry websites are springing up almost daily, along with online auction sites. The Internet offers an endless array of merchandise from around the world—a virtual international flea market—and opens doors to more choices than ever imagined, often at prices much lower than what can be found in traditional jewelry stores. Buying on the Internet can be fun, and there are some good opportunities for knowledgeable buyers, possibly even a real "treasure" at a bargain price. But e-commerce and online auctions are not for everyone, and the risk of buying something that is not properly represented is very high. Before flying off into cyberspace, take a few moments to consider some of the pros and cons.

For many, the major attraction of shopping online is convenience. It is fast and easy, enabling you to make decisions in private, but without the assistance of salespeople. For those who live in remote areas far from fine jewelry stores, it provides an opportunity to see what is available, see what's new and exciting, and keep current about everything from gemstones to the latest award-winning designers. Many online vendors also provide educational sites to help you understand more about what you are buying. And for people who leave important gifts to the last minute, the Internet can bring the world of jewelry directly to the screen, in time to be a real lifesaver!

It is easy to see the allure of Internet shopping, but in all too many cases it is not all that it appears to be. Where gems and jewelry are concerned, the disadvantages may quickly outweigh the advantages, especially on auction sites.

The first disadvantage is the inability to see and compare gems and jewelry firsthand. As I hope you've learned from previous chapters, this is a serious shortcoming, since it is impossible to accurately judge beauty and desirability from a static photo. Furthermore, you can't determine how well-made a piece of jewelry might be or how it might compare with the alternatives. Be sure to ask about the vendor's return policy, and read the fine print. Find out how quickly merchandise must be returned and whether you will receive a refund. Be leery of vendors who will only give a credit toward future purchases.

Another serious problem is the absence of any screening mechanism to help you determine the reliability of information provided. Sales information pertaining to gems or jewelry being sold is often incomplete and inaccurate, and many "educational" sites are also filled with inaccurate, incomplete, or misleading information. It is also difficult to find reliable information about the competence or trustworthiness of many online vendors, and written representations may be meaningless unless you can work out a way to verify the facts before making payment to the vendor.

In general, everything I have warned about in previous chapters applies to purchases from an online vendor or auction. As I have stressed repeatedly, many of the factors affecting quality and value cannot be accurately judged without gemological training, experience, and proper equipment, and many online vendors are so deficient in requisite knowledge and skill that their representations may be unreliable.

I cannot emphasize too strongly the importance of taking every precaution to protect yourself and ensure you are getting what you think you are getting, at an appropriate price. Remember that many Internet companies and individual vendors are unknown entities, without reliable track records or well-established reputations. This means that problems might be more difficult or impossible to resolve satisfactorily, regardless of "guarantees" made before purchase. You must also remember that it may be difficult or impossible to find the seller offline, and you cannot rely on vendor ratings because they can be easily rigged by the unscrupulous.

Appraisals and Laboratory Reports Provide a False Sense of Security

Appraisals and gem-testing laboratory reports are being used increasingly by online sellers to increase confidence among prospective buyers.

Unfortunately, they are also being used increasingly by the unscrupulous. I am seeing an increase in bogus appraisals and fraudulent lab reports that have duped unsuspecting buyers into purchasing something that has been misrepresented. Be sure to get independent verification of any documentation provided by the seller before payment if possible.

Remember also that you cannot properly judge a gem on the basis of a lab report or appraisal alone. In other words, you really must see the stone along with the report.

Other problems that are surfacing on the web include the following:

- *Failure to comply with Federal Trade Commission (FTC) guidelines.* The FTC has found extensive failure to comply with its guidelines. Most notably, descriptions provided by sellers often omit critical information pertaining to quality factors, exact weight, and treatments used on colored gemstones.

- *Prices are often higher than fair retail.* Don't assume you will pay a lower price, and beware of fictitious "comparative retail" prices that lead you to believe you are getting a bargain. Prices are often no lower than those at a local jewelry store, and many e-retailers sell jewelry at prices significantly higher than what you would pay for comparable quality from knowledgeable, independent jewelers. Before buying on-line, check prices from a variety of sources, including your local jeweler.

- *"Wholesale" claims may be misleading.* "Wholesale" online offerings present even greater risks to consumers than buying in any wholesale jewelry district, because you do not see the actual gem or jewelry firsthand and have no guarantee you are buying from a bona fide wholesaler. Many people buying "wholesale" through online sources are not getting the bargains they believe they are getting, and many mistakes would have been avoided had the buyer seen the jewelry first or had an opportunity to compare it with alternatives.

   In some cases, arrangements can be made to allow you to view the stone before the vendor receives payment, using a local bank or gemological laboratory, for example, as an intermediary. I recommend this be done wherever possible.

- *Here today, gone tomorrow.* In numerous reported cases, buyers have never received the merchandise for which they paid, or received merchandise that was not as represented. Often there is no recourse because vendors cannot be located once the transaction is complete.

Online Auctions—Rewards and Rip-offs

Fine auction houses are an important source of exquisite jewelry from bygone eras, often exhibiting elaborate workmanship that cannot be duplicated today. They are also an important source of some of the finest, rarest, and most magnificent natural gemstones—gems that surpass even the best material being mined today—which are no longer available in the jewelry trade. Such gems may fetch handsome prices—possibly even a new record—or some knowledgeable buyer may recognize a treasure that others have missed and pay very little. This, for many, is what makes the auction arena so fascinating.

Items offered at auction may also come to the auction block to settle estates, or as a means to dispose of unclaimed property, and usually must be sold at whatever the highest bid might be, regardless of value. While this is no guarantee that you'll get a bargain, because knowledgeable buyers know the value of pieces on which they are bidding, sometimes these pieces are sold at very low prices because no one obtained proper certification and the pieces were overlooked, even by the pros!

Buying at auction can be a rewarding experience, but keep in mind that even at the best firms there is an element of risk. One must be very knowledgeable, or work with an expert consultant, to recognize opportunities and spot pitfalls. Over the years I've seen many pieces acquired from reputable auction firms that contained synthetic stones, fracture-filled stones, and diffusion-treated sapphires!

As I have stressed throughout this book, no one can properly judge any fine gem without seeing it firsthand and examining it with proper gem-testing equipment. Where auctions are concerned, proper examination is even more critical because the auction house has limited liability. I never bid on any item at auction without having personally viewed the piece and examined it with proper gem-testing equipment. Firms such as Antiquorum, Christie's, and Sotheby's provide opportunities to view the items at exhibitions held at various locations around the country before the auction, and bidding takes place both on-site and online, as a convenience to people who cannot be present. However, this is not the case with all online auction sites, and in many cases there is no opportunity to view the item before bidding on it. In such cases, more than anything else, success is dependent upon having incredible luck!

Protection May Be Illusion

Where some auction sites are concerned, you may be under the impression that you are protected against misrepresentation and have recourse should there be a problem, but this may be just an illusion. In reality, you may have no recourse at all. Never forget that in situations where proper examination is not possible, the risk is dramatically increased: you are bidding on a blind item from a blind source. Even among legitimate sources, not seeing the gem or jewelry before purchase can result in disappointment when you receive your purchase. Be sure to read the "terms and conditions" very carefully, especially the fine print pertaining to "representations, warranties, and limits of liability."

Buying at auction can be an exciting and exhilarating experience with compelling financial incentives, but there are always risks for the unknowledgeable, and buying through online auction sites poses even greater risk. The FTC has warned that Internet auction fraud has become a significant problem. According to the FTC, most consumer complaints center on these situations:

- Sellers who don't deliver goods
- Sellers who deliver something far less valuable than they described
- Sellers who don't deliver in a timely way
- Sellers who fail to disclose all the relevant information about the product or terms of sale

Form of Payment May Provide Protection

There are several payment options that might provide some protection against these risks. Credit cards offer the most consumer protection, usually including the right to seek a credit through the credit card issuer if the product isn't as promised. If the seller won't agree, other options include setting up an escrow arrangement (for which there is usually a nominal fee) or using a reliable third party for verification, such as a well-known gem-testing laboratory, before an exchange of products or money.

To sum up, whether you are buying or selling gems or jewelry online—from e-retailers, auction sites, or individuals—the rewards may be great, but the risks are much higher than buying from traditional sources. For additional information on how to reduce the risk in buying or selling online, or to file a complaint, write to the Federal Trade Commission, Consumer Response Center, 600 Pennsylvania Avenue, NW, Washington, D.C. 20580, or see their website: www.ftc.gov.

Online Sources of Information

There are many sources of online information, but there is not yet any screening mechanism to separate reliable from unreliable information. You must consider the source of the information and be wary of information provided by sellers of gems or jewelry. The following sites may provide helpful information:

1. www.ftc.gov (Federal Trade Commission)
2. www.jic.org (Jewelry Information Center)
3. www.gia.edu (Gemological Institute of America educational site)
4. www.ags.org (American Gem Society)
5. www.gem-a.info (Gemological Association of Great Britain)
6. www.accreditedgemologists.org (Accredited Gemologists Association)
7. www.gemstone.org (International Colored Gemstone Association)
8. www.cibjo.org (World Jewelry Confederation)
9. www.antoinettematlins.com (Antoinette Matlins, P.G.)

CHAPTER FOURTEEN

Caring for Your Gems & Jewelry

A key to enjoying your jewelry over the years is knowing how to care for it and protect it. I've come to realize, however, that most people don't know what proper care means. So, here are some tips that will help you derive even greater pleasure from your jewelry and gems—after you buy!

Store Jewelry Carefully

Store your jewelry carefully. Avoid *extremes* of temperature and humidity (places *very* hot or *very* cold; *very* humid or *very* dry).

Keep gemstone jewelry and gold and silver pieces separated from each other to prevent scratching. Keep fine jewelry in soft pouches or wrapped in soft cloth to help protect it.

Don't overcrowd your jewelry box. This can result in misplacing or losing pieces that might fall unnoticed from the case. Forcing jewelry into the box may cause damage, such as bending a fragile piece or cracking a fragile stone.

Handle and Wear Fine Jewelry with Care

Every twelve to eighteen months, have a reliable jeweler check each fine jewelry piece to make sure the setting is secure, especially the prongs. If you ever feel (or hear) the stone moving in the setting, it's a warning that a prong or bezel needs tightening. Failure to fix this may result in loss of or damage to the stone.

Get into the habit of removing jewelry before showering or bathing. Soap can deposit a film that can diminish the liveliness and beauty of your jewelry, and necessitate more frequent cleaning. Also, remove jewelry before putting on makeup or powder, and wash your hands after applying makeup (to remove dulling residues) before handling your jewelry.

Avoid wearing fine jewelry while doing any type of rough work, especially where abrasives or chemicals are used. Abrasives can scratch your jewelry—both the stones and the metal. Chemicals such as chlorine and ammonia can cause discoloration of metals used in settings and dull the polish on many stones (necessitating having the stone repolished to restore its full beauty). Chlorine (and chlorinated pool water) can cause settings to pit, discolor, and even break (especially 14K gold, or lower), causing lost stones. Ammonia will remove the polish on stones such as malachite (avoid cleaning any malachite "objets d'art" with any ammonia-based cleaner)!

Avoid exposing fine jewelry to intense heat (for example, while *cooking*). Exposure to extreme heat—from contact with a hot pot handle or from getting too near a flame or hot steam—can cause damage to many gems. *Note:* Enamel may be ruined by contact with heat. I know someone who ruined an antique ring with lovely enameling on the shank by picking up a pot with a very hot handle that caused the enamel to melt.

Avoid storing jewelry in safe deposit boxes for extended periods of time. While rubies, sapphires, and diamonds won't be adversely affected, other gems—such as opal and emerald—may suffer from the extreme dryness. With these gems, if long-term storage in a safe deposit box or bank vault is unavoidable, place a damp cloth in the box with the jewelry (check from time to time to be sure the cloth is still damp).

Avoid exposing fine jewelry to extreme temperature changes, such as might be encountered by putting jewelry in an in-the-ground safe in winter or in an automobile trunk while traveling, then removing it and wearing in a heated room. This is especially important with opals.

Never boil jewelry to clean it. Stones may crack or lose their color.

Special Tips on Opals and Emeralds

Immerse opals in water for a few minutes periodically to help prevent loss of moisture and subsequent cracking. Never immerse opals in oil; soaking some opals in oil for only a few hours can cause them to lose some or nearly all of their fire. *Note:* It was once thought that wiping the surface of an opal regularly with oil would protect it. *This is not true and will damage most opals.*

Avoid wearing emeralds while doing rough work or active sports. Emeralds are fragile and are susceptible to damage from a hard blow or a knock.

Never clean opals or emeralds in ultrasonic cleaners. Ultrasonic cleaners can worsen inclusions and weaken color.

A Few Special Words about Rings

Try not to touch the stones in your rings when putting them on or taking them off. Instead, take rings on and off by grasping the metal portion that encircles the finger (called the *shank*). Slipping rings on and off by grasping the metal shank rather than the stones will prevent a greasy buildup on the stone's surface, which greatly reduces the brilliance and sparkle of a stone.

To keep rings sparkling, get into the habit of "huffing" them. This is a little trick we use to remove the dirt and oily film on the stone's surface (which occurs from putting rings on and off incorrectly, or from occasionally fingering them—which most of us do without even realizing). Each time the stones are touched, a layer of oily film is applied to the top, and the stone's beauty is reduced. To restore its sparkle, simply hold the ring close to your mouth and "huff" on it with your breath—you'll see the stone fog up—and wipe it off with a soft, lint-free cloth, such as a handkerchief, scarf, or coat/blouse sleeve. You'll be amazed to see how much better jewelry can look simply by removing even the lightest film of oil from the surface!

Don't take rings off and lay them on the side of the sink unless you are sure the drain is closed. Also, never remove your rings to wash your hands when away from home (all too many have been forgotten and lost).

Take Extra Precautions When Traveling

If you take jewelry with you when traveling, don't pack it in luggage that you plan to check or in luggage to be given to the bell captain at a hotel or a ship's porters, etc. Keep it with you.

Never leave jewelry in your hotel room. Wherever possible, obtain a safety deposit box in which to store your jewelry, even for part of a day. Be wary of in-room safes that are operated by programming your own private code; professionals can quickly and easily override your code and remove the contents of the safe.

Purchase a "body pouch" that can be concealed under clothing for when you *must* carry a valuable piece. Never go sightseeing with valuables in a purse or pocket.

For customs purposes, it can be useful to take a photo of the jewelry pieces you take with you. Have the photo dated and notarized before departure, so you can prove that you did not purchase it abroad. Otherwise you may be asked to pay duty on it.

Keep a photo inventory of your jewelry. You don't need professional photos; simply lay your jewelry out on a flat surface and take several snapshots. They will be invaluable should there be a robbery, providing detectives with a visual record that will make it easier to recognize the stolen pieces and claim what is yours should the jewelry ever be recovered. Photos are also important for insurance purposes and can aid in replacement. Where a piece is one-of-a-kind, and you want to have someone make a replica, a photo can provide a custom jeweler with the necessary details in order to duplicate it.

Keep Your Jewelry Clean to Make It Sparkle

Keeping your gemstone jewelry clean is essential if you want it to sparkle to its fullest. Film from lotions, powders, and your own skin oils will dull stones and reduce their brilliance. You will be amazed at how much a slight film can affect the brilliance—and color—of your gems. So, learn how to keep them clean, and clean them on a regular basis.

How to Clean Your Jewelry

The simplest and easiest way to clean any kind of jewelry is simply to wash it with warm, sudsy water. Prepare a small bowl of warm, sudsy water, using any kind of *mild* liquid detergent. Soak the piece a few minutes and then brush gently with an eyebrow brush or soft toothbrush, keeping the piece submerged in the sudsy water. Rinse thoroughly under running water (make sure the drain is closed—some prefer to place jewelry in a wire strainer before placing under the running water) and pat dry with a soft, lint-free cloth or paper towel.

Ruby and sapphire jewelry, especially pieces containing diamonds, can be immersed in a solution of equal parts of hot water (not boiling—you should be able to put your fingers in it without pain!) and ammonia. This can be especially effective at removing built-up dirt and grime. Let the jewelry soak for a few minutes, brush gently, rinse well, and pat dry with a lint-free cloth. Remember, however, that ammonia should *not* be used on most other gems, and washing with warm, sudsy water is usually sufficient for *all* gemstones.

Use Jewelry Cleaners and Ultrasonic Cleaners with Caution

Commercial jewelry cleaners usually are no more effective than the methods suggested above. They seem to be popular because they are convenient. In any case, *never soak gemstone jewelry in commercial cleaners for more than a few minutes.* Leaving stones such as emerald or amethyst in some commercial cleaners for any length of time can cause etching of the surface, which reduces the stone's luster (shine). For difficult pieces, try the new *ionic* cleaners. These are safe for all gems—even emeralds and opals—and are fast, convenient, and affordable.

I do not recommend ultrasonic cleaning for most gems—the new ionic cleaners are safer and equally effective. Ultrasonic cleaning should be restricted to the cleaning of diamonds or gold jewelry only. Washing in sudsy water or using an ionic cleaner is simple, effective, and safe for all jewelry.

A Selected List of Recognized Laboratories

American Gem Society Laboratories
8917 W. Sahara Ave.
Las Vegas, NV 89117

American Gemological
 Laboratories (AGL)
580 Fifth Ave., Ste. 706
New York, NY 10036

Asian Institute of Gemological
 Sciences (AIGS)
Jewelry Trade Center, 6th Fl.
919/1 Silom Rd.
Bangrak, Bangkok 10500
Thailand

CISGEM-External Service for
 Precious Stones
Viale Achille Papa, 30
20149 Milano, Italy

Gem and Jewelry Institute of
 Thailand (GIT) Gem Testing
 Laboratory (GTL)
Gem Research and Testing Bldg., 5th Fl.
Faculty of Science, Chulalongkorn
 University
Phayathai Rd., Patumwan,
 Bangkok 10330
Thailand

Gemlab Laboratory for Gemstone
 Analysis and Reports
Gewerbestrasse 3, FL-9496 Balzers
Principality of Liechtenstein

Gemological Association of All Japan
8F Daiwa-Ueno Building
5-25-11 Ueno, Taito-ku
Tokyo 110-0005, Japan

Gemological Association of Great
 Britain (Gem-A)
27 Greville St.
London EC1N 8TN
United Kingdom

Gemological Institute of America (GIA)
 Gem Trade Laboratory (GTL)
580 Fifth Ave., Ste. 200
New York, NY 10036
 and
5345 Armada Dr.
Carlsbad, CA 92008

German Gemological Laboratory (DSEF)
Prof.-Schlossmacher-Str. 1
D-55743 Idar-Oberstein, Germany

Gübelin Gem Lab
Maihofstrasse 102
6006 Lucerne, Switzerland

Hoge Raad voor Diamant (HRD)
Hoveniersstraat 22
BE-2018 Antwerp, Belgium

Professional Gem Sciences (PGS)
5 S. Wabash Ave., Ste. 1905
Chicago, IL 60603

Swiss Gemological Institute (SSEF)
Falknerstrasse 9
CH-4001 Basel, Switzerland

Selected Readings

Arem, Joel E. *Color Encyclopedia of Gemstones.* 2nd ed. New York: Van Nostrand Reinhold, 1987. Excellent color photography makes this book interesting for anyone. An invaluable reference for the gemologist.

Downing, Paul B. *Opal Identification and Value.* 2nd ed. Baldwin Park, Calif.: Gem Guides, 2002. For the serious opal lover. Retail price guides.

Gübelin, Eduard J., and J. I. Koivula. *Photoatlas of Inclusions in Gemstones.* Zurich: ABC Editions, 1986. Most comprehensive collection of inclusions ever photographed.

Hughes, Richard W. *Ruby & Sapphire.* Boulder, Colo.: RWH, 1997.

Keverne, Roger, ed. *Jade.* New York: Lorenz Books, 2000. Superb, encyclopedic; 450 lavish photos.

Matlins, Antoinette. *Engagement & Wedding Rings: The Definitive Buying Guide for People in Love.* 3rd ed. Woodstock, Vt.: GemStone Press, 2003. Beautiful photos of rings from fifteenth century to present.

———. *Jewelry & Gems at Auction: The Definitive Guide to Buying & Selling at the Auction House & on Internet Auction Sites.* Woodstock, Vt.: GemStone Press, 2002. As buying and selling at auctions move into the mainstream, this book tells consumers all they need to know to "play the game."

———, and A. C. Bonanno. *Gem Identification Made Easy: A Hands-On Guide to More Confident Buying & Selling.* 4th ed. Woodstock, Vt.: GemStone Press, 2008. A nontechnical book that makes gem identification possible for anyone—even without a science background. A "must" for beginners, and the experienced may pick up a few tips, too. Practical, easy to understand.

———. *Jewelry & Gems: The Buying Guide—How to Buy Diamonds, Pearls, Colored Gemstones, Gold & Jewelry with Confidence and Knowledge.* 7th ed. Woodstock, Vt.: GemStone Press, 2009. Covers every aspect of purchasing and enjoying jewelry and gems.

Nassau, Kurt. *Gemstone Enhancement: History, Science and State of the Art.* Woburn, Mass.: Butterworth-Heinemann, 1994. Comprehensive and understandable.

O'Donoghue, Michael. *Gemstones.* New York: Chapman & Hall, 1988. Excellent photographs and an excellent general reference work.

Schumann, Walter. *Gemstones of the World.* 4th ed. Translated by E. Stern. New York: Sterling, 2009. Superior color plates.

Sinkankas, John. *Emerald and Other Beryls.* Tucson, Ariz.: Geoscience Press/Harbinger House, 1994. A classic work on the beryl family.

Weber, Christianne, and Wilhelm Lindemann. *Reflections in Stone: Bernd Munsteiner.* Stuttgart, Germany: Arnoldsche Art Publishers, 2004. An introduction to the masterful works of this legendary gem carving pioneer. Superb images of his art.

Wise, Richard W. *Secrets of the Gem Trade: The Connoisseur's Guide To Precious Gemstones.* Lenox, Mass.: Brunswick House Press, 2006. Excellent photos; interesting insights into all facets related to bringing gems into the marketplace and judging quality.

Zeitner, June C. *Gem and Lapidary Materials: For Cutters, Collectors, and Jewelers.* Tucson: Geoscience Press, 1996. A beautifully illustrated book about gemstones and how they are fashioned into works of art.

Color Plates and Exhibits

Black-and-White Photographs and Illustrations

All illustrations by Kathleen Robinson.
Page 38: Cabochon emerald ring by Jack Abraham, President of Precious Gem Resources.

Color Photographs

We wish to thank the following persons and companies for the color photographs appearing in this book:

Color Insert 1

Page 1: From the Precious Collection, courtesy of Jack Abraham, President of Precious Gem Resources.

Page 2: Star ruby from International Colored Gemstone Association (ICA) (photo/Bart Curran). Selection of red and pink gemstones and rhodochrosites from Pala International, Inc. (photo/Sky Hall). Red beryl from Rex Harris (photo/Sky Hall).

Page 3: Star sapphire and moonstones from International Colored Gemstone Association (ICA) (photos/Bart Curran). Selection of blue gemstones from Pala International, Inc. (photo/Sky Hall). Chrysocolla from American Gem Trade Association (AGTA), cut by Glenn Lehrer, AGTA Cutting Edge competition winner (photo/Sky Hall). Blue Paraiba tourmaline from Cynthia Renee Co. (photo/Robert Weldon).

Page 4: Selection of yellow and orange gemstones from Pala International, Inc. (photo/Sky Hall). Topaz from American Gem Trade Association (AGTA) (photo/Natural Arts, Inc.). Sunstone from Ponderosa Mine, Inc. (photo/Bart Curran). Sapphire, andalusite, and cat's-eye chrysoberyl from Krementz Gemstones (photo/Sky Hall). Fancy-cut citrine with concave facets from American Gem Trade Association (AGTA), cut by Cutting Edge winner Richard Homer, American Lapidary Artists (photo/Sky Hall). Yellow beryl from AGTA, cut by Cutting Edge winner Karl Egan Wilde (photos/Sky Hall).

Page 5: Selection of green gemstones and tsavorite garnet from Pala International, Inc. (photos/Sky Hall). Emerald-cut emerald from International Colored Gemstone Association (ICA) (photo/Sky Hall). Paraiba tourmaline from Cynthia Renee Co. (photo/Robert Weldon). Laboratory-grown synthetic stones from Chatham Created Gemstones. Period art deco jadeite brooch from Christie's, NY.

Page 6: Andamooka crystal opal, Andamooka matrix opal beads, and two free-form black opals from Western Opal (photos/Sky Hall). Mexican opals from International Colored Gemstone Association (ICA) (photos/Bart Curren). Boulder opal ring by Gaia Pelikan (photo/Gaia Pelikan). Zultanite, courtesy of Zultanite Gems, LLC. Color-change alexandrite, courtesy of ABC Gems, Inc. (photo/Tino Hammid; retouching/Lawton and Associates). Color-change garnet and color-change spinel, courtesy of Pala International (photos/Wimon Manorotkol; www.palagems.com).

Page 7: Briolettes from Rough and Ready Gems (photos/Azad). Trilliant from

David Brackna (photo/Robert Weldon). Oval, round, cushion, and emerald cut from John Parrish Photography. Marquise and pear shape photos by Sky Hall. Princess from Lucent Diamonds™ (photo/Tino Hammid). Cabochons from James Alger (photos/Van Pelt).

Page 8–11: All courtesy of the gemstone cutters, artists, designers, and companies listed.

Page 12: Belt buckles from Elizabeth Rand Studio. Stone cabochons and beads photo by Sky Hall. Sedona Landscape agate from the collection of Rare Earth Mining Co., Trumbull, Connecticut.

Color Insert 2

Page 1: Courtesy Richard Krementz Gemstones.

Page 2: Classic oval, clockwise from top left, from: James Breski; James Breski; James Breski; and a private collection (photo/Tibor Ardai). Emerald cuts, clockwise from top left, from: Antiquorum Auctioneers; Barnett Robinson; Russ Coping, from Geoffrey Kudlick for Jewelers of America; and Barnett Robinson. Cushion cut, from left, from: Barnett Robinson; Richard Krementz Gemstones; and Precious Stones Company. Princess cuts from Chris Correia.

Page 3: All courtesy of the artists, designers, and companies listed. Simon G rings courtesy Simon G Jewelry. Richard Krementz rings courtesy Richard Krementz Gemstones. Classic stone bands courtesy James Breski.

Page 4: All courtesy of the artists, designers, and companies listed. Claude Thibaudeau rings courtesy Claude Thibaudeau Montreal. Nikolai Tsang ring courtesy Jade by Nikolai.

Page 5: All courtesy of the artists, designers, and companies listed. Stefan Hafner collection © Stefan Hafner. Tamara Comolli rings courtesy Tamara Comolli Fine Jewelry Collection.

Page 6–8: All courtesy of the artists, designers, and companies listed.

Page 9: All courtesy of the artists, designers, and companies listed. Original designs by American designer Bellarri for BELLARRI International. Tamara Comolli pieces courtesy Tamara Comolli Fine Jewelry Collection.

Page 10: All courtesy of the artists, designers, and companies listed. De Vroomen pieces courtesy De Vroomen, London. Murphy Designs pendants and earrings © Patrick T. Murphy.

Page 11: All courtesy of the artists, designers, and companies listed. Gumuchian cabochons from the "Lace Collection" by Gumuchian. Richard Krementz ring courtesy Richard Krementz Gemstones.

Page 12: All courtesy of the artists, designers, and companies listed. Tamara Comolli bracelet courtesy Tamara Comolli Fine Jewelry Collection. Nafco images © 2005 Nafco, Ltd. Murphy Designs pendant and earrings © Patrick T. Murphy.

Index

Notes

DIAMONDS, 2ND EDITION
THE ANTOINETTE MATLINS BUYING GUIDE
How to Select, Buy, Care for & Enjoy Diamonds with Confidence and Knowledge
by Antoinette Matlins, P.G.

Practical, comprehensive, and easy to understand, this book includes price guides for old and new cuts and for fancy-color, treated and synthetic diamonds. **Explains in detail** how to read diamond grading reports and offers important advice for after buying a diamond. **The "unofficial bible" for all diamond buyers who want to get the most for their money.**

6 x 9, 228 pp, 12 full-color pages, with over 150 color and b/w photos and illus.; index
Quality Paperback Original, 978-0-943763-46-0 **$18.99**

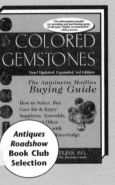

COLORED GEMSTONES, 3RD EDITION
THE ANTOINETTE MATLINS BUYING GUIDE
How to Select, Buy, Care for & Enjoy Sapphires, Emeralds, Rubies and Other Colored Gems with Confidence and Knowledge
by Antoinette Matlins, P.G.

This practical, comprehensive, easy-to-understand guide **provides in depth** all the information you need to buy colored gems with confidence. Includes price guides for popular gems, opals, and synthetic stones. Provides examples of gemstone grading reports and offers important advice for after buying a gemstone. **Shows anyone shopping for colored gemstones how to get the most for their money.**

6 x 9, 232 pp, 24 full-color pages, with over 200 color and b/w photos and illus.; index
Quality Paperback Original, 978-0-943763-72-9 **$18.99**

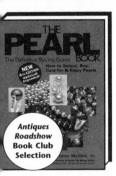

THE PEARL BOOK, 4TH EDITION
THE DEFINITIVE BUYING GUIDE
How to Select, Buy, Care for & Enjoy Pearls
by Antoinette Matlins, P.G.
COMPREHENSIVE • EASY TO READ • PRACTICAL

This comprehensive, authoritative guide tells readers everything they need to know about pearls to fully understand and appreciate them, and avoid any unexpected—and costly—disappointments, now and in future generations.

- A journey into the rich history and romance surrounding pearls.
- The five factors that determine pearl value & judging pearl quality.
- What to look for, what to look out for: How to spot fakes. Treatments.
- Differences between natural, cultured and imitation pearls, and ways to separate them.
- Comparisons of all types of pearls, in every size and color, from every pearl-producing country.

6 x 9, 248 pp, 16 full-color pages, with over 250 color and b/w photos and illus.; index
Quality Paperback, 978-0-943763-54-5 **$19.99**

FOR CREDIT CARD ORDERS CALL 800-962-4544 (8:30AM–5:30PM ET Monday–Friday)
Available from your bookstore or directly from the publisher. **TRY YOUR BOOKSTORE FIRST.**

The "Unofficial Bible" for the Gem & Jewelry Buyer

AWARD WINNER

Antiques Roadshow Book Club Selection

JEWELRY & GEMS
THE BUYING GUIDE, 7TH EDITION

Updated Retail Price Guides

How to Buy Diamonds, Pearls, Colored Gemstones, Gold & Jewelry with Confidence and Knowledge

by Antoinette Matlins, P.G., *and* A. C. Bonanno, F.G.A., A.S.A., M.G.A.

—over 400,000 copies in print—

Learn the tricks of the trade from *insiders:* How to buy diamonds, pearls, precious and other popular colored gems with confidence and knowledge. More than just a buying guide . . . discover what's available and what choices you have, what determines quality as well as cost, what questions to ask before you buy and what to get in writing. Easy to read and understand. Excellent for staff training.

6 x 9, 352 pp, 16 full-color pages, with over 200 color and b/w photos and illus.; index
Quality Paperback, 978-0-943763-71-2 **$19.99**

ENGAGEMENT & WEDDING RINGS, 3RD EDITION

by Antoinette Matlins, P.G., *and* A. C. Bonanno, F.G.A., A.S.A., M.G.A.

COMPREHENSIVE • EASY TO READ • PRACTICAL

Tells **everything you need to know to design, select, buy and enjoy that "perfect" ring** and to truly experience the wonder and excitement that should be part of it.

Updated, expanded, filled with valuable information.

Engagement & Wedding Rings, 3rd Ed., will help you make the *right* choice. You will discover romantic traditions behind engagement and wedding rings, how to select the right style and design for *you,* tricks to get what you want on a budget, ways to add new life to an "heirloom," what to do to protect yourself against fraud, and much more.

6 x 9, 320 pp, 16 full-color pages, with over 400 color and b/w photos and illus.; index
Quality Paperback Original, 978-0-943763-41-5 **$18.95**

JEWELRY & GEMS AT AUCTION
The Definitive Guide to Buying & Selling at the Auction House & on Internet Auction Sites

by Antoinette Matlins, P.G.

with contributions by Jill Newman

As buying and selling at auctions—both traditional auction houses and "virtual" Internet auctions—moves into the mainstream, **consumers need to know how to "play the game."** There are treasures to be had and money to be saved and made, but buying and selling at auction offers unique risks as well as unique opportunities. This book makes available—for the first time—detailed information on how to buy and sell jewelry and gems at auction without making costly mistakes.

6 x 9, 352 pp, 16 full-color pages, with over 150 color and b/w photos and illus.; index
Quality Paperback Original, 978-0-943763-29-3 **$19.95**

Buy Your *"Tools of the Trade"*...
Gem Identification Instruments Directly from *GemStone Press*

Whatever instrument you need, GemStone Press can help.
Use our convenient order form, or contact us directly for assistance.

ITEM / QUANTITY	PRICE EA.*	TOTAL $
Pocket Instrument Sets		
_____ **Premium:** With Bausch & Lomb 10X Loupe • RosGem Dichroscope • Chelsea Filter	$197.95	$ _____
_____ **Deluxe:** With Bausch & Lomb 10X Loupe • EZview Dichroscope • Chelsea Filter	$179.95	_____
Loupes—Professional Jeweler's 10X Triplet Loupes		
_____ Bausch & Lomb 10X Triplet Loupe	$44.00	_____
_____ Standard 10X Triplet Loupe	$29.00	_____
_____ Dark-field Loupe	$58.95	_____
• Spot filled diamonds, identify inclusions in colored gemstones. Operates with Standard Mini Maglite (additional—see below).		
Analyzer		
_____ Gem Analyzer (RosGem)	$299.00	_____
• Combines Dark-field Loupe, Polariscope, and Immersion Cell. Operates with Standard Mini Maglite (additional—see below).		
Calcite Dichroscopes		
_____ Dichroscope (RosGem)	$135.00	_____
_____ Dichroscope (EZview)	$115.00	_____
Color Filters		
_____ Chelsea Filter	$44.95	_____
_____ Synthetic Emerald Filter Set (Hanneman)	$32.00	_____
_____ Tanzanite Filter (Hanneman)	$28.00	_____
_____ Bead Buyer's & Parcel Picker's Filter Set (Hanneman)	$24.00	_____
Diamond Testers and Tweezers		
_____ SSEF Blue Diamond Tester	$695.00	_____
_____ SSEF Diamond-Type Spotter	$150.00	_____
_____ DiamondNite Dual Tester	$269.00	_____
_____ Diamond Tweezers/Locking	$10.65	_____
_____ Diamond Tweezers/Non-Locking	$7.80	_____
Jewelry Cleaners		
_____ Speed Brite Ionic Jewelry Cleaner	$85.00	_____
_____ Ionic Solution—16 oz. bottle	$20.00	_____

Buy Your *"Tools of the Trade..."*

Gem Identification Instruments Directly from *GemStone Press*

Whatever instrument you need, GemStone Press can help.
Use our convenient order form, or contact us directly for assistance.

ITEM / QUANTITY	PRICE EA.*	TOTAL $
Lamps—Ultraviolet & High Intensity		
_____ UV-Blocking Goggles	$24.95	_____
• Recommended for use with all UV lamps.		
_____ Small Longwave/Shortwave (UVP)	$85.00	_____
_____ Large Longwave/Shortwave (UVP)	$237.00	_____
_____ Viewing Cabinet for Large Lamp (UVP)	$195.00	_____
_____ **Purchase Large Lamp & Cabinet together**	$385.95	_____
and save over $45.00		
_____ SSEF High-Intensity Shortwave Illuminator	$499.00	_____
• Operates with SSEF Diamond-Type Spotter (additional—see above).		
Other Light Sources		
_____ Solitaire Maglite	$11.00	_____
_____ Standard Mini Maglite	$15.00	_____
_____ Flex Light	$29.95	_____
Refractometers		
_____ Precision Pocket Refractometer (RosGem RFA 322)	$625.00	_____
• Operates with Solitaire Maglite (additional—see above).		
_____ Refractive Index Liquid 1.81—10 grams	$69.95	_____
Scale		
_____ GemPro50 Carat Scale	$174.95	_____
Spectroscopes		
_____ Spectroscope—Pocket-sized model (OPL)	$98.00	_____
_____ Spectroscope—Desk model w/stand (OPL)	$235.00	_____

Shipping/Insurance per order in the U.S.: **$7.95 first item,**   SHIPPING/INS. $_____
$3.00 each add'l item; $10.95 total for pocket instrument set.

Outside the U.S.: Please specify *insured* shipping method you prefer
and provide a credit card number for payment.   **TOTAL $ _____** **

TOTAL SATISFACTION GUARANTEE
If for any reason you're not completely delighted
with your purchase, return it in resellable condition
within 30 days for a full refund.

*Prices, manufacturing specifications and terms subject to change
without notice. Orders accepted subject to availability.

**All orders must be prepaid by credit card, money order or check
in U.S. funds drawn on a U.S. bank.

CAMEOS OLD & NEW, 4TH EDITION

by Anna M. Miller, G.G., RMV; revised, updated and expanded by Diana Jarrett, G.G., RMV

Newly updated and expanded, *Cameos Old & New*, 4th Ed., is a **concise, easy-to-understand guide** enabling anyone—from beginner to antique dealer—to recognize and evaluate quality and value in cameos, and avoid the pitfalls of purchasing mediocre pieces, fakes and forgeries.

6 x 9, 416 pp, with over 250 photos and illus., 60 in full color; index
Quality Paperback, 978-0-943763-60-6 **$19.99**

ILLUSTRATED GUIDE TO JEWELRY APPRAISING,

3RD EDITION • *Antique, Period, Modern*
by Anna M. Miller, G.G., RMV

This beautifully illustrated guide **provides step-by-step instruction** in jewelry identification and dating, reviews the responsibilities of the appraiser, and describes in detail virtually every style of antique and period jewelry for the hobbyist and serious collector alike.

8½ x 11, 216 pp, with over 150 b/w photos and illus.; index
Hardcover, 978-0-943763-42-2 **$39.99**

GEMS & JEWELRY APPRAISING, 3RD EDITION

Techniques of Professional Practice
by Anna M. Miller, G.G., RMV; revised, updated and expanded by Gail Brett Levine, G.G.

The **premier guide to the standards, procedures and ethics of appraising gems, jewelry and other valuables.** *Gems & Jewelry Appraising* offers all the information that jewelers, gemologists and students will need to establish an appraisal business, handle various kinds of appraisals and provide an accurate, verifiable estimate of value.

8½ x 11, 256 pp, with over 150 b/w photos and illus.; index
Hardcover, 978-0-943763-53-8 **$39.99**

TREASURE HUNTER'S GEM & MINERAL GUIDES TO THE U.S.A.
4TH EDITION

Where & How to Dig, Pan and Mine Your Own Gems & Minerals
—IN 4 REGIONAL VOLUMES—
by Kathy J. Rygle *and* Stephen F. Pedersen • *Preface by* Antoinette Matlins, P.G., *author of* Gem Identification Made Easy

From rubies, opals and gold, to emeralds, aquamarine and diamonds, each guide offers **state-by-state details on more than 250 gems and minerals** and the affordable "fee dig" sites where they can be found. Each guide covers:

- **Equipment & Clothing:** What you need and where to find it.
- **Mining Techniques:** Step-by-step instructions.
- **Gem and Mineral Sites:** Directions & maps, hours, fees and more.
- **Museums and Mine Tours**

All guides: 6 x 9, Quality Paperback Original, illus., maps & photos; indexes.
$14.99 each

Northeast (CT, DC, DE, IL, IN, MA, MD, ME, MI, NH, NJ, NY, OH, PA, RI, VT, WI)
224 pp, 978-0-943763-57-6
Northwest (AK, IA, ID, MN, MT, ND, NE, OR, SD, WA, WY)
192 pp, 978-0-943763-55-2
Southeast (AL, AR, FL, GA, KY, LA, MO, MS, NC, SC, TN, VA, WV)
200 pp, 978-0-943763-58-3
Southwest (AZ, CA, CO, HI, KS, NM, NV, OK, TX, UT)
224 pp, 978-0-943763-56-9

Please send me:

CAMEOS OLD & NEW, 4TH EDITION
_____ copies at $19.99 (Quality Paperback) *plus s/h**

COLORED GEMSTONES, 3RD EDITION: THE ANTOINETTE MATLINS BUYING GUIDE
_____ copies at $18.99 (Quality Paperback) *plus s/h**

DIAMONDS, 2ND EDITION: THE ANTOINETTE MATLINS BUYING GUIDE
_____ copies at $18.99 (Quality Paperback) *plus s/h**

ENGAGEMENT & WEDDING RINGS, 3RD EDITION: THE DEFINITIVE BUYING GUIDE
_____ copies at $18.95 (Quality Paperback) *plus s/h**

GEM IDENTIFICATION MADE EASY, 4TH EDITION:
A HANDS-ON GUIDE TO MORE CONFIDENT BUYING & SELLING
_____ copies at $36.99 (Hardcover) *plus s/h**

GEMS & JEWELRY APPRAISING, 3RD EDITION
_____ copies at $39.99 (Hardcover) *plus s/h**

ILLUSTRATED GUIDE TO JEWELRY APPRAISING, 3RD EDITION
_____ copies at $39.99 (Hardcover) *plus s/h**

JEWELRY & GEMS AT AUCTION: THE DEFINITIVE GUIDE TO BUYING & SELLING
AT THE AUCTION HOUSE & ON INTERNET AUCTION SITES
_____ copies at $19.95 (Quality Paperback) *plus s/h**

JEWELRY & GEMS, 7TH EDITION: THE BUYING GUIDE
_____ copies at $19.99 (Quality Paperback) *plus s/h**

THE PEARL BOOK, 4TH EDITION: THE DEFINITIVE BUYING GUIDE
_____ copies at $19.99 (Quality Paperback) *plus s/h**

THE SPECTROSCOPE AND GEMMOLOGY
_____ copies at $49.95 (Quality Paperback) *plus s/h**

TREASURE HUNTER'S GEM & MINERAL GUIDES TO THE U.S.A., 4TH EDITION:
WHERE & HOW TO DIG, PAN AND MINE YOUR OWN GEMS & MINERALS
IN 4 REGIONAL VOLUMES $14.99 per copy (Quality Paperback) *plus s/h**
_____ copies of NE States _____ copies of SE States _____ copies of NW States _____ copies of SW States

* In U.S.: Shipping/Handling: $3.95 for 1st book, $2.00 each additional book.
  Outside U.S.: Specify shipping method (insured) and provide a credit card number for payment.

Check enclosed for $_____ (Payable to: GEMSTONE Press)

Charge my credit card: ❑ Visa ❑ MasterCard

Name on Card (PRINT) _____ Phone (_____)_____

Cardholder Address: Street _____

City/State/Zip _____ E-mail _____

Credit Card # _____ Exp. Date _____

Signature _____ CID # _____

Please send to: ❑ Same as Above ❑ Address Below

Name (PRINT) _____

Street _____

City/State/Zip _____ Phone (_____)_____

<table>
<tr><td>**TOTAL SATISFACTION GUARANTEE**
If for any reason you're not completely delighted with your purchase, return it in resellable condition within 30 days for a full refund.</td><td>*Phone, mail, fax, or e-mail orders to:*
GEMSTONE PRESS, Sunset Farm Offices,
Rte. 4, P.O. Box 237, Woodstock, VT 05091
Tel: (802) 457-4000 • *Fax:* (802) 457-4004
Credit Card Orders: (800) 962-4544
(8:30AM–5:30PM ET Monday–Friday)
sales@gemstonepress.com • www.gemstonepress.com
Generous Discounts on Quantity Orders</td><td>Prices subject to change</td></tr>
</table>

Try Your Bookstore First